ENERGY FUTURES:

TRADING OPPORTUNITIES

Third Edition

ENERGY FUTURES:

TRADING OPPORTUNITIES

Third Edition

John Treat, Editor

PennWell Corporation
1421 South Sheridan Road
P.O. Box 1260
Tulsa, Oklahoma 74101

Cover design by Brigitte Coffman
Layout design by John Potter

Library of Congress Cataloging-in-Publication Data

Energy futures : trading opportunities / John Treat, editor.-- 3rd ed.
    p. cm.
  Includes bibliographical references and index.
    1. Petroleum industry and trade. 2. Energy Industries. 3. Commodity exchanges.
I. Treat, John Elting.

HG6047.P47 E54 2000
332.64'4228--dc21

                                                                    00-056519

Printed in the United States of America.

TABLE OF CONTENTS

I History and Overview

   John Elting Treat

II Major Markets: Physical and Derivative (Futures/Options)

   John Elting Treat

   Dr. Benjamin Schlesinger

   Dr. Benjamin Schlesinger

III Trading Theories and Strategies

   Rutheford S. Poats, Douglas F. McDonald, Art Holland

   Bruce Kamich

   Maureen Lynch

   Robert Boslego

LIST OF FIGURES

LIST OF TABLES

List of Acronyms

ADP	Alternate Delivery Procedures
AGA	American Gas Association
AP	Associated person
API	American Petroleum Institute
APO	Average price options
ASTM	American Society for Testing and Materials
Bpd	Barrels per day
BSA	Ben Schlesinger Associates
CATO	Cross Alps Traders of Oil
CBOT	Chicago Board of Trade
CCCT	Combined-cycle combustion turbine
CDD	Cooling degree days
CEA	Commodity Exchange Act
Cf	Cubic feet
CFO	Chief Financial Officer
CFTC	Commodity Futures Trading Commission
CME	Chicago Mercantile Exchange
COB	California-Oregon Border
COMEX	Commodity Exchange (NY)
COT	Commitments of Traders
CPO	Commodity Pool Operator
CTA	Cumulative translation adjustment
CTA	Commodity trading advisor
DIM	Deutsche Institut für Normung

DOE/EIA	Department of Energy/Energy Information Administration
EC	European Community
ECAR	East Central Area Reliability Coordination Agreement
EFP	Exchange of futures for physicals
EITF	Emerging Issues Task Force
EFRA	Energy Futures Research Associates
EMA	Exponential moving average
E&P	Exploration and Production
EPACT	Energy Policy Act of 1992
ERC	Electric reliability councils
ERCOT	Electric Reliability Council of Texas
EVA	Economic value added
EWG	Electric wholesale generator
FASB	Financial Accounting Standards Board
FCM	Futures Commission Merchant
FERC	Federal Energy Regulatory Commission
FOB	Free on board
FPC	Federal Power Commission
FSA	Financial Services Authority
FSU	Former Soviet Union
FT	Firm Transportation
GDP	Gross Domestic Product
HDD	Heating degree days
IB	Introducing brokers
IEA	International Energy Agency
IOU	Investor-owned utilities
IPE	International Petroleum Exchange
IPP	Independent power producer

ISO	Independent system operator
ISO-NE	New England independent system operator
IT	Interruptable Technology
KCBT	Kansas City Board of Trade
LDC	Local distribution company
LNG	Liquified natural gas
LOKI	Light Oil Kerosene & Insulation (fictitious name)
M&A	Mergers & Acquisitions
MAAC	Mid-Atlantic Area Council
MAIN	Mid-America Interconnected Network
MAPP	Mid-Continent Area Power Pool
MAS	Monetary Authority of Singapore
MERC	New York Mercantile Exchange
MG	Metallgesellshaft
MIPS	Millions of instructions per second
MBD	Thousand barrels per day
MMBD	Million barrels per day
MMBtu	Million British thermal units
MOMBA	Missouri Oil Marketers & Buyers Association (fictitious name)
MT	Metric ton
MW	Megawatt
MWh	Megawatt hour
NAFTA	North American Free Trade Agreement
NEPOOL	New England Power Pool
NERC	National Electric Reliability Council
NFA	National Futures Association
NGL	Natural gas liquids

NGPA	Natural Gas Policy Act of 1978
NOPR	Notice of Proposed Rulemaking
NPCC	Northeast Power Coordinating Council
NYMEX	New York Mercantile Exchange
NYH	New York Harbor
NYPP	New York Power Pool
OCI	Other comprehensive income
OECD	Organization for Economic Cooperation & Development
OPEC	Organization of Petroleum Exporting Countries
OTC	Over-the-counter
P/C Ratios	Put/call ratios
PAWS	Saladin Petroleum Analysis Workstation
PJM	Pennsylvania-New Jersey-Maryland Power Pool
PUC	Public Utility Commission
PUHCA	Public Utility Holding Company Act of 1935
PURPA	Public Utility Regulatory Policy Act of 1978
RCH	Recognized clearinghouse
RIE	Recognized investment exchange
RMC	Risk management committee
ROCE	Return on capital employed
RPB	Recognized professional bodies
S.B. Blend	Sweet Border Blend
S&C	Supply and crating
SERC	Southeastern Electric Reliability Council
SFA	Securities and Futures Authority
SFAS	Statement of Financial Accounting Standards
SIB	Securities Investment Board
SIMEX	Singapore International Monetary Exchange

SPILL	Standard Petroleum of Illinois (fictitious name)
SPP	Southwest Power Pool
THOR	Trading Heating Oil Resellers (fictitious name)
TOP	To-be-priced
TVA	Tennessee Valley Authority
U.K.	United Kingdom
WEPEX	Western Region Power Exchange
WODEN	Wise Oil Distributors Energy Company (fictitious name)
WSCC	Western Systems Coordinating Council
WTI	West Texas Intermediate

HISTORY AND OVERVIEW

ENERGY FUTURES,
PAST & PRESENT

by John Elting Treat

Energy futures are not nearly as young as you think. In the second half of the 19th century, a "Petroleum Exchange" flourished in New York. Again, in the early 1930s—when market discipline was briefly disrupted by the explosive growth of oil production in Oklahoma and Texas, causing oil prices to fall dramatically—an oil futures market (in West Texas Intermediate) was established in California. It soon collapsed as a formidable alliance of big oil and big government restored discipline to the marketplace. Nearly 40 years of relative price stability ensued, leaving little incentive for the emergence of an oil futures market.

Only with the traumatic price increases accompanying the Arab oil embargo of late 1973 was another attempt made, this time in New York at the Cotton Exchange. The contract called for Rotterdam delivery (to avoid the constraints of U.S. price regulations). That attempt was stillborn, however, doomed by continuing U.S. government price controls and a skeptical oil industry.

In the decade that followed, the commercial realities and—equally important—the perceptions of those realities by the international oil industry had gradually changed to the point where oil futures could fulfill the industry's need for risk management and provide an outlet for the speculative impulses of investors whose interest in oil had been captured by the commodity's new prominence in daily headlines and nightly newscasts.

The emergence of oil futures markets and their remarkable growth were a natural, indeed inevitable, consequences of three concurrent, but only partly interrelated, trends in petroleum, financial, and commodity markets. By far the most important determinant was the structural change in oil markets themselves. The nationalization of production by the Organization of Petroleum Exporting Countries (OPEC) and non-OPEC governments alike, and the subsequent pressures to eliminate large third-party crude resales, resulted in a disintegration of the oil market that had been highly integrated since the days of J. D. Rockefeller. In the 10 years following the 1973 Arab oil embargo, the crude oil available to the major companies fell by nearly 50%, from about 30 million barrels per day (bbl/day) to just more than 15 million bbl/day. Equity oil available to the majors fell even more sharply, by some 75%. The net result was a drop in the major's share of internationally traded oil from 62% to 37%.

In addition to the newly created national oil companies, a host of oil trading firms and independent refineries entered the picture. The links that had traditionally tied upstream and downstream (vertical integration) were weakened to the breaking point. The reduction of horizontal integration (as large third-party crude sales were curtailed, and joint venture production was nationalized) further eroded the ability of the larger oil companies to exercise control over markets. Simply, there were too many actors with divergent commercial and political interests to guarantee market stability. The consequences were not long in coming. After a decade of virtually universal confidence that oil prices would rise, prices began to weaken and fluctuate over an ever-wider range, climaxing in the dramatic events of 1986, when prices fell from nearly $30/bbl to less than $10/bbl in a period of only nine months (Table 1–1). Although many feel stability

1950	$2.51				
1960	2.88	1970	$3.18	1980	$32.27
1961	2.89	1971	3.39	1981	35.10
1962	2.90	1972	3.39	1982	32.11
1963	2.89	1973	3.89	1983	27.73
1964	2.88	1974	6.74	1984	27.44
1965	2.86	1975	7.56	1985	25.83
1966	2.88	1976	12.17	1986	12.52
1967	2.92	1977	13.24	1987	16.69
1968	2.94	1978	13.30	1988	13.27
1969	3.09	1979	20.19	1989	15.50

Table I–I *Crude Oil Price Trends (average annual prices).*

Prices shown for 1950–75 are "U.S. Wellhead." After 1975, series is "FOB Cost of Imports" into the U.S. Prices for 1989 are based on the first quarter. *Source*: U.S. Energy Information Administration, *Monthly Energy Review*, March 1989 (published June 1989)

	Interest Rate[1]	Crude Oil Price/Bbl[2]	Monthly Holding Cost (MT x 1 million)	Oil Company Inventories[3]
1976	6.1%	$13.48	$.07 /bbl	391
1977	6.4	14.53	.08	398
1978	9.2	14.57	.11	432
1979	12.2	21.67	.22	387
1980	14.0	33.39	.39	414
1981	16.7	36.69	.51	431
1982	13.6	33.38	.38	395
1983	9.9	29.19	.24	367
1984	11.3	28.60	.27	333
1985	8.6	26.78	.19	331
1986	6.2	15.01	.08	313

Table I–2 *Effect of Interest Rates and Inventory Holding Costs*

[1] Average annual London Interbank 6 mo. rate [2] Landed price of crude in the U.S. [3] Total Organization for Economic Cooperation and Development crude and product stocks at Jan. 1 of each year. *Source*: Philip Verleger Jr., "The Role and Impact of Commodity Market Institutions in the Determination of Oil Prices," *1988 Annual Review of Energy.*

returned in 1987, it is interesting to note that prices oscillated between $15 and $22/bbl between September and December of that year alone. The fact is that stability has yet to rear its hoary head in current-day oil markets.

Along with the structural change that was reshaping oil markets during the decade, a second important trend was emerging from the financial markets. High interest rates (along with high oil prices) at the beginning of the 1980s were making inventory maintenance very expensive. This caused oil company managements to rethink traditional approaches to inventory and risk management (Table 1–2). Also, hedging of financial risks was increasingly becoming a fact of life in foreign currency and interest rate markets. These trends ensured that oil companies were increasingly receptive to the hedging potential of the fledgling oil future markets.

Finally, the third important factor that set the stage for energy futures' ultimate success was the general growth and diversification of futures contracts in a wide variety of new markets, the growing sophistication with which they were being used, and modification offering an ever-wider range of hedging tools. For almost 100 years, futures markets (then commonly called commodity markets) were largely confined to the traditional agricultural products (especially grains).

In the past two decades, however, there has been an explosion in the variety of products served by these markets. The first waves of expansion brought in new agricultural contracts (especially meats) and precious metals. The second phase, starting in the 1970s, saw the introduction of financial instruments, including currency, interest rate, and stock index contracts. A third phase brought in oil and a number of other industrial products. The fourth stage saw the introduction and rapid acceptance of options on futures contracts. The fifth stage saw an explosion of trading in over-the-counter (OTC) derivatives, often in direct competition with exchange-traded instruments.

The introduction and success of oil futures was a product of the first three trends. The growing volatility and loss of confidence in the future stability of oil prices demanded the emer-

	Physical Cargoes	Forward Cargoes	Cargoes Total
1973	54	0	54
1974	96	0	96
1975	154	0	154
1976	330	0	330
1977	327	0	327
1978	291	0	291
1979	315	0	315
1980	290	0	290
1981	405	0	405
1982	573	122	695
1983	1,014	806	1,820
1984	3,149	2,254	5,403
1985	5,628	3,058	8,142

Table I–3 *Growth of Spot and Forward Crude Oil Markets (survey of physical and forward cargo transactions).*

Where actual delivery of the cargo is taken. *Source:* Philip Verleger Jr., "The Role and Impact of Commodity Market Institutions in the Determination of Oil Prices," *1988 Annual Review of Energy.* Dr. Vereger compiled the data from the Petroleum Argus database, which, while only a partial listing of spot transactions, is the most comprehensive record available.

gence of new market structures and institutions. One obvious sign of the change was the rapid growth of spot markets and the trading companies that thrived on price volatility (Table 1–3).

Prior to 1979, less than 5% of internationally traded crude moved at spot prices, outside of official term supply contract arrangements. By the end of 1985, virtually all crude moved at some sort of market-related pricing, and experts estimated that oil companies were acquiring anywhere from 30 to 50% of their supplies on a spot, noncontract basis. Although the proportion of oil sold on a purely spot basis has subsequently shrunk, the price risks remain, because term contracts today almost universally call for market-related prices.

The trading companies, independent refineries, and increasingly the larger companies developed trading techniques to cope with the growing price volatility of these markets. Their first response was to create informal, "forward markets". At first they were only 30 days, then 60 days, and more recently 90 days out. A second response was an explosive growth in the demand for rapid (often real-time) pricing and other market information. Against this backdrop, futures became inevitable: a time-proven and efficient technique for coping with broad market instability.

Energy futures trading in the 1980s focused on growth of the liquid petroleum markets for crude oil, natural gas liquids (NGL), and the major refined products (gasoline, heating oil, and fuel oil). In the 1990s, the boundaries of the energy complex have expanded to include natural gas (in 1990) and electricity (in 1996).

While the breadth of energy markets has expanded, their fundamental purposes remain the same. Futures markets, basically spot markets for standardized forward contracts, serve three functions:

Price discovery — Giving an instantaneous reading of marginal price movements.

Risk management — Allowing companies to hedge their price risks for limited periods of time. However, the hedging opportunity rarely extends more than six months forward as a result of a lack of market liquidity in the more distant months.

Speculative opportunity — Attracting additional risk capital to the market from outside the oil industry. Low margin requirements—lower than in equity markets—enhance the attraction of futures as a vehicle for speculation.

These are the necessary conditions for a successful contract—but they are often not sufficient. In reality, new futures contracts often fail. The reason is that the criteria for a successful futures contract are simply too stringent, with too few physical markets that can actually meet those criteria.

Criteria for Successful Futures Markets

In assessing the suitability of any commodity/market for futures trading, the following conditions need to be analyzed:

Price volatility. This is perhaps the single most important criterion. It provides the basic economic justification for futures trading, which is to provide protection to the hedger against adverse price fluctuations. If a commodity is characterized by a relatively stable—or at least predictable—price, there would be little associated risk and there would be no need for a futures market. Price volatility is also necessary to attract risk capital from speculators and essential to ensure sufficient liquidity to maintain the market.

Quantitative indicators: Variations of plus or minus 20% per annum are assumed to be the minimum necessary to sustain futures trading. In general, the greater the degree of volatility, the more likely a futures market will survive.

Uncertain supply and demand are generally the causes of price volatility and therefore are generally present when price volatility is found.

Quantitative indicators: In energy markets, which typically display a rather high inelasticity of price demand, variations of plus or minus 10% during a two-year period should be sufficient to sustain futures trading.

Sufficient deliverable supplies are the Catch-22 of futures trading. If there are not sufficient deliverable supplies of the commodity *meeting the quality specifications of the contract,* futures trading will fail. However, there must be some uncertainty about the sufficiency of supplies if the previous conditions are to be met. In the U.S., this dilemma is heightened by the regulatory requirements of the Commodity Futures Trading Commission (CFTC), whose fear of market squeezes at times forces exchanges to overstate deliverable supplies in order to gain government approval.

Quantitative indicators: Storage capacity equal to at least 30 days average demand is highly desirable.

Product homogeneity is another prerequisite. Futures contracts are traded on the premise that product taken on a delivery will meet certain quality specifications. The commodity must therefore have certain key characteristics that are quantifiable, allowing the clear differentiation of the product from other grades. Standardized tests and generally accepted procedures are essential. In oil, for example, the various American Petroleum Institute (API), Deutsche Institut für Normung (DIM), and ASTM standards generally provide the necessary references. In addition, the existence of generally trusted independent inspection agencies or inspectors to administer these tests is an important aspect. A range of different products (*e.g.*, several types of crude oil) may be suitable for delivery, if the price differences between the various grades are relatively stable, and if the technical characteristics of the various deliverable grades are sufficiently close to one another.

This is often a difficult aspect of contract design, since the price variation between various grades of products fluctuates from time to time. For example, it may be desirable to allow several grades to be deliverable, perhaps with price adjustments for quality, in order to ensure sufficient deliverable supplies. However, if buyers are uncertain of what grades they will receive, and if they place different values on the quality differences among the grades, they may be deterred from trading.

Quantitative indicators: The quality of the product must be capable of being described by objective, quantifiable standards.

Product perishability can be a deterrent to trading. In general a product should have a shelf life sufficiently long enough to permit storage and delivery as called for under the contract. In addition, the maintenance of inventories of the commodity will both facilitate deliveries and provide a ready pool of potential hedgers. While perishability is not usually a major concern in oil and natural gas markets, the stability of some oil product blends is an issue. Long storage of gasoline, for example, can result in separation of blended product.

Quantitative indicators: Products should have a minimum shelf or stock life of 6-12 months.

Market concentration is a difficult factor to quantify. A successful futures market is a highly competitive market, marked by a large number of buyers and sellers. No one market participant, or plausible combination of market participants, should possess sufficient market power to exert unilateral control either on the supply or the demand for the commodity, either in the short or medium term. In oil, however, the existence of OPEC has not prevented the emergence of highly successful futures markets. The answer lies in the inability of OPEC to act decisively, and in the availability of alternative sources of supply and stocks that seriously limit OPEC's ability to achieve its stated objectives. However, the concentration of producers and/or consumers can be a serious obstacle in specific regional oil markets. Thus, a U.S. west coast gasoline market would be risky, given the relative concentration of production in the hands of a small number of refiners. Similarly, an east coast residual fuel market might be too much dominated by the demand from a small number of very large utilities to sustain liquid futures trading.

Quantitative indicators: In general, the market share of the top five firms should be less than 50%, and the top 10 firms should have less than 80%.

Readily available price information is critical to market success. It should be noted that the opening of a futures market might stimulate a rapid growth of price information services. However, at the outset, market participants must have a sufficiently broad base of price information to permit evaluation of spot prices and their relationship to futures prices. Convergence between these two prices as the delivery period approaches is essential. A market in which all products are traded on the basis of long- term contracts where prices remain undisclosed would be a very difficult market in which to establish futures trading.

Quantitative indicators: Daily cash market prices should be available from at least two independent sources.

Unique trading opportunity is another key factor. If an existing market for a commodity has reasonable liquidity and is serving its customers well, it is extremely difficult to launch a copycat contract. Inertia, habit, and personal relationships will tend to keep the traders loyal to the preexisting market. In addition, even if there is no active market at present, recent failures of similar contracts can be a substantial (but not fatal) deterrent.

Quantitative indicators: The ideal candidate would be a commodity that is not currently traded on any futures exchange in the world and has not been the subject of a failed attempt in the previous five years. However, special circumstances may override these concerns.

Market timing (and blind luck) are often critical to the success or failure of a contract. However, they are often impossible to forecast. Ideally, contracts should be introduced to coincide with periods of high volatility and high levels of cash market activity. For example, a heating oil or natural gas contract would be best introduced in the fall months when physical trading is at its yearly high. Conversely, a gasoline contract would be best introduced in the spring, prior to an anticipated surge of summer driving.

Quantitative indicators: Contracts should be introduced to coincide with high levels of cash market activity, to the extent these are predictable. Alternatively, one might just as well consult an astrologer.

EXCHANGES AND THEIR CONTRACTS

Two exchanges currently dominate trade energy futures contracts: the New York Mercantile Exchange (NYMEX) and the International Petroleum Exchange (IPE) in London. In addition, several smaller exchanges also offer energy futures contracts: the Singapore International Monetary Exchange (SIMEX) and the Kansas City Board of Trade (KCBT). As discussed in the final chapter, the future of open-outcry trading on exchange floors is increasingly being challenged by the advent of electronic trading. While the exchanges and their floor traders still have the upper hand, the growth of electronic trading and the success of all-electronic marketplaces (such as the Internet) raise serious questions about the long-term future of the exchanges and their trading floors.

New York Mercantile Exchange (NYMEX)

Founded more than 100 years ago, the "Merc," as it is often called, has enjoyed a diverse and colorful history. It evolved from a produce exchange in lower Manhattan whose contracts included butter, eggs, and even apples. NYMEX began to diversify some two decades ago, adding precious metals and, briefly, even stocks to its portfolio. Nevertheless, it ended the 1970s as one of the smallest exchanges in the U.S., outpaced by the growth of the large Chicago markets and by most other New York exchanges as well. After an abortive attempt to start a residual fuel oil contract in 1974, the Merc launched its first successful energy futures contract—New York heating oil—in 1978. Trading grew slowly but steadily while a companion contract for residual fuel was stillborn. With the addition of a leaded gasoline contract for New York delivery in 1981 (later replaced by an unleaded version of the same contract) and

West Texas Intermediate crude oil in 1983, NYMEX achieved international prominence in the 1980s—its energy contracts grew at spectacular rates. The subsequent addition of options on crude oil, heating oil, and gasoline as well as futures contracts on propane, natural gas, and electricity added another dimension and further impetus to the growth of the NYMEX energy complex.

Since its merger with the Chicago Mercantile Exchange (CME) in the mid 1990s, NYMEX has been known as the NYMEX Division of the merged exchange. Today, the NYMEX Division is the leading energy futures exchange and the third largest futures exchange in the world, following only the Chicago Board of Trade (CBoT) and the CME. While contracts for platinum and palladium still survive on the Merc's trading floor, energy contracts regularly account for more than 90% of its turnover.

NYMEX is controlled by a board of directors dominated by members from its own trading floor—a fact that has sometimes created tensions with other market users (and with the Exchange staff). However, the Merc's spirit of innovation, the luck of its timing, and its strong marketing efforts have paid off handsomely. It is difficult to conceive of any other exchange soon overtaking the Merc's leading role in energy futures. NYMEX has 816 seats, which currently sell for more than $700,000. Approximately 54 companies are members of the Exchange's clearinghouse, which guarantees all transactions. In addition to meeting certain financial requirements, all clearinghouse members must hold a minimum of two seats on the Exchange. NYMEX also maintains an electronic exchange for after hours trading known as ACCESS.

In May 2000, NYMEX received permission to convert itself to a for-profit corporation. It also announced the creation of eNYMEX, to trade over the counter (OTC) commodities electronically. While eNYMEX plans to focus initially on energy products, they may eventually expand into other areas such as bandwidth, weather, and/or emissions.

International Petroleum Exchange (IPE)

An independent outgrowth of London's loosely linked futures markets, IPE was created in 1981 by a diverse coalition of oil traders and commodity brokerage firms who saw the emerging success of the NYMEX heating oil contract in New York, and were determined to build an energy futures market on the other shore of the Atlantic. Early success with a gas oil contract was followed by a series of unsuccessful attempts to trade crude oil. Finally, in 1988, the right set of circumstances and contract terms allowed IPE to launch a Brent crude oil market that has established good liquidity and a substantial following.

The IPE board is more balanced than NYMEX's board, having much less representation from the floor. This broader mix has not, however, assured success. While IPE occupies second place among the world's energy exchanges, the gap between IPE and NYMEX is very large, with London's turnover averaging well under half of New York's volume.

Traditionally, the IPE had 35 floor memberships, who elected two-thirds of the board of the Exchange. Floor memberships sold until recently in the vicinity of £75,000. There were, however, three other classes of membership—local, general associate, and trade associate—that permit additional individuals or companies to participate under various restrictions.

In February 2000, the IPE members voted to transform the Exchange into a for-profit corporation.

Singapore International Monetary Exchange (SIMEX)

SIMEX was created in 1983 as a restructuring of the former Gold Exchange of Singapore (founded in 1978) with the strong support of the Chicago Mercantile Exchange (CME). CME and SIMEX operate an innovative mutual offset agreement, whereby positions on one exchange can be offset against positions on the other.

Initially, the Exchange concentrated on financial futures. But in February 1989, SIMEX launched a high-sulfur residual fuel oil contract that provided about 20% of total trading volume that first year. It includes the far larger contract for Eurodollars and a number of other financial futures contracts. In 1990, the exchange added a second energy contract, on Dubai crude oil.

Heavily supported by the government through its Monetary Authority of Singapore (MAS), SIMEX was merged with the Stock Exchange of Singapore to form the new Singapore Exchange, which has been "demutualized"—*i.e.,* transformed into a for-profit corporation.

Other exchanges

From time to time, other futures exchanges—most recently Kansas City—have launched energy futures contracts. However, none of these have succeeded in building the liquidity needed to attract significant trading.

FUTURES PRESENT

Since 1974, there have been some 50 attempts to launch energy futures markets. The success rate has averaged about 20%—typical of the experience in other commodity markets. In spite of thorough research by the exchanges, often excruciating governmental reviews (particularly in the U.S.), and extensive marketing campaigns, roughly 80% of all future markets opened fail to reach the critical mass needed for takeoff (commonly defined as reaching an average open interest of 5,000 contracts).

Today—after the smoke has settled from various attempts by exchanges in New York, Chicago, London and Singapore—there are seven well-established futures contracts (crude, heating oil, unleaded gasoline, natural gas, and electricity in New York; plus crude and gasoil in London) [(Table 1–4)]. In addition, options contracts have been successful as extensions of those future markets.

When first introduced in late 1978, heating oil futures attracted smaller, independent marketers and refiners who turned to the Merc as an alternative source of supply. Physical deliveries were initially quite high, as these smaller firms sought alternatives in a marketplace dominated by the larger companies. These initial participants were quickly joined by the spot oil traders and by a growing number of pure speculators on and off the trading floor, drawn from other financial and commodity markets. This phase lasted until well into 1983. Then, with the introduction of crude oil futures and the increasing instability of prices, the larger refiners and integrated companies reluctantly entered the market.

By 1984, more than 80% of the 50 largest companies were using futures. Larger end-users, such as airlines and other major energy consumers, also appeared. In addition, a far wider range of speculators entered the scene, as trading volume and open interest rose high enough to meet the minimum liquidity requirement of the commodity funds.

Finally, another phase, dating from 1986, brought in almost all the remaining holdouts among the larger U.S. companies, more foreign participation, and a new group of traders—the Wall Street Refiners. These were companies such as Morgan Stanley and Bear Stearns, which were attracted by the rising volatility of oil prices and the speculative opportunities presented by that price instability, particularly relative to other markets.

As one Bear Stearns trader put it, "Plywood was dead, so we looked around for some better action and found it in oil." The low internal cost of capital for margin maintenance and a built-in trading infrastructure made these new entrants formidable competitors for the older oil trading and supply companies.

However, even today, participation by independent producers and smaller end-users remains limited. The former's participation is limited by the lack of liquidity in the more distant months; the latter by ignorance of how the markets operate, the high management cost of setting up a futures trading department, and for a number of domestic as well as international companies, a very real basis-risk problem.

	Commodity	Delivery	Point	Exchange Status
1974	Crude Oil	Rotterdam	NYCE	Failed
	Residual Fuel	Rotterdam	NYMEX	Failed
1978	Heating Oil	New York	NYMEX	Active
	Residual Fuel	New York	NYMEX	Failed
1981	Gas Oil	Rotterdam	IPE	Active
	Heating Oil	Gulf Coast	NYMEX	Failed
	Leaded Gasoline	New York	NYMEX	Replaced
	Leaded Gasoline	Gulf Coast	NYMEX	Failed
	Unleaded Gasoline	Gulf Coast	CBOT	Failed
	Unleaded Gasoline	Gulf Coast	NYMEX	Unopened
	Propane	Texas	NYCE	Failed
1983	WTI Crude Oil	Cushing	NYMEX	Active
	LLS Crude Oil	St. James	CBOT	Failed
	Brent Crude Oil	Rotterdam	IPE	Failed
	Heating Oil	Gulf Coast	CBOT	Failed
1984	Unleaded Gasoline	New York	NYMEX	Active
	Leaded Gasoline	Gulf Coast	CME	Failed
	Unleaded Gasoline	Gulf Coast	CME	Unopened
1985	Brent Crude Oil	North Sea	IPE	Failed
1986	WTI Crude Oil Options	Cushing	NYMEX	Active
1987	Heating Oil Options	New York	NYMEX	Active
	Brent Crude Oil Options	Rotterdam	EOE	Failed
1988	Brent Crude Oil	Cash Settlement	IPE	Active
	Propane	Texas	NYMEX	Active
1989	High Sulfur Oil	Singapore	SIMEX	Failed
	Unleaded Gasoline Options	New York	NYMEX	Active
	Brent Crude Oil Options	Cash Settlement	IPE	Active
	Gasoil Options	Rotterdam	IPE	Active
	Brent Crude Oil	Rotterdam	ROEFEX	Failed

Table I–4 *Energy Futures Markets, Authorized, Opened, or Proposed, 1974–2000*
(dated by year first traded or, if never opened, year first authorized).

	Commodity	Delivery	Point	Exchange Status
1989	Gasoil	Rotterdam	ROEFEX	Failed
	Residual Fuel Oil	Rotterdam	ROEFEX	Failed
	Residual Fuel Oil	Cash Settlement	IPE	Lightly Traded
	Residual Fuel Oil	Gulf Coast	NYMEX	Failed
1990	Natural Gas	Henry Hub, LA	NYMEX	Active
	Dubai Crude Oil	Cash Settlement	SIMEX	Failed
	Dubai Crude Oil	Cash Settlement	IPE	Failed
1991	Gasoil	Singapore	SIMEX	Failed
1992	Sour Crude	Gulf Coast	NYMEX	Failed
	Gulf Coast	Gulf Coast	NYMEX	Failed
	Natural Gas Options	Henry Hub, LA	NYMEX	Active
1994	NY Gasoline/Crude Crack Spread	New York	NYMEX	Active
	NYH Heating Oil/Crude Crack Spread	New York	NYMEX	Active
1995	Brent Crude Oil	Cash Settlement	SIMEX[1]	Active
1996	COB Electricity	CA-OR Border	NYMEX	Active
	Palo Verde Electricity	Palo Verde	NYMEX	Active
	COB Electricity Options	CA-OR Border	NYMEX	Active
	Palo Verde Options Electricity	Palo Verde	NYMEX	Active
	Permian Basin Natural Gas	Permian Basin	NYMEX	Failed
	Alberta Natural Gas	Alberta	NYMEX	Active
1998	Cinergy Electricity	Ohio	NYMEX	Active
	Cinergy Electricity Options	Ohio	NYMEX	Active
	Entergy Electricity	Arkansas	NYMEX	Active
	Entergy Electricity Options	Arkansas	NYMEX	Active
	PJM Electricity	NJ	NYMEX	Active
1999	Coal	Ohio	NYMEX	Pending
2000	Middle East Sour Crude	Cash Setlement	NYMEX	Active
	Electricity	UK	IPE	Planned

Futures trading has thus survived adolescence and entered a period of youthful maturity. Growth in the coming years will have to come from an expansion of futures trading opportunities in the form of new contracts rather than from bringing in new participants. In other words, to continue to grow, the exchanges will have to offer a bigger and more diverse menu, not just put more seats around the table. The recent success of options would seem to confirm this point of view.

TRADING FUTURES: A PRIMER

Many readers of this book will be thoroughly familiar with the basic mechanisms and concepts of futures trading. This section is not for them. However, for those who are new to any type of futures trading, it is important to understand a few fundamentals about futures markets. Futures markets offer both *hedgers* or *commercials* (*i.e.*, those who use a particular commodity in their business) and speculators the opportunity to buy or sell standardized contracts for a given commodity. In many cases, the same exchanges also offer options contracts on those same commodities. Options contracts as presently traded are options on the futures contract for the same commodity, which is often called the *underlying* futures.

Contract identification

Both futures and options contracts are identified not only by the particular type of commodity being traded (*e.g.*, heating oil, unleaded gasoline, Brent crude oil), but also by the delivery month called for in the contract. In practice, traders often abbreviate the names of months, so that one should not be surprised to hear references to "Feb Brent" or "Jan gas."

Options contracts are further identified by their strike prices and whether they are options to buy (call) or sell (put). Thus an options trader will talk about "Jan gas 55 puts," meaning options to sell January unleaded gasoline futures contracts at 55¢/gal. A buyer of a commodity contract is said to be *long* while he holds that contract. A seller is said to be *short*. The contracts traded are highly standardized with respect to volume, quality, and delivery terms. The terms of selected contracts are printed for reference in the appendices to this book. Exchanges do, however, change the terms of these contracts from time to time, to keep pace with changes in the physical market. The samples included should therefore not be assumed to be up to-date. Please check with the appropriate exchange to obtain a copy of the latest contract terms.

Placing orders

Except in the case of exchange members operating on their own account, all transactions must be conducted through a member of the exchange, who must also be registered to accept customer orders by the Commodity Futures Trading Commission (CFTC) in the U.S. or its counterparts in other countries. Orders can be placed any time a broker is willing to answer the telephone, but exchange trading hours tend to fall between 9:00 A.M. and 5:00 P.M., with the New York exchanges closing earlier and the London exchanges closing later. A buyer normally places an order by telephone to the broker, who may be located anywhere in the world. The broker in turn executes this order by telephone through exchange members on the floor of the appropriate exchange. Buyers can place various conditions on their orders, including price limits or time limits, and they may also simultaneously request a broker to close out the position if losses exceed a certain amount. While brokers will generally accept such conditions on orders, they usually offer no guarantees they can execute the order as given. Only a *market order*, in which the buyer (or seller) agrees to accept the prevailing market price, is virtually guaranteed for execution. Brokers will most often execute orders through the employees of their own firm on the floor. In order to camouflage larger orders, execution will sometimes be shared with independent floor brokers, who execute orders on behalf of others.

On the exchange floor, all trading must be by *open outcry*, giving all present—at least in theory—an equal opportunity to take the other side of the trade. Assuming a willing seller is found to meet the buyer's order, the trade is posted with the exchange. In practice, exchanges publish price quotations over the various electronic information services to provide an up-to-date record of pricing trends even before the official record of the transaction is entered. The actual trade is usually entered into the exchange's computer within a few minutes of the transaction.

The buyer and seller, however, are not matched permanently. At the end of the day, each broker is assigned an appropriate long or short position with the exchange's clearinghouse. Thus, while there must be an equal number of buyers and sellers each day, their respective positions are maintained totally independently. Thus each buyer and seller is free to close his or her position at any time. To do so, the buyer will simply sell his or her contract back into the market, effectively clearing the position from the exchange's books.

Spreads

In addition to straightforward orders to buy or sell a single commodity for a single month, many traders take *spread* positions, which are positions in several different contracts to profit from the relative price movements between those contracts. For example, spreads can be placed between contracts for different delivery months for a single commodity—they can cover different commodities for delivery in the same month—they can cover different commodities and different months. One popular type of spread position in the energy contracts is the *crack spread,* in which a position in crude oil is balanced against positions in both gasoline and heating oil, to approximate the refining process (in which crude oil is transformed by catalytic cracking into refined products). NYMEX has offered option contracts of such spreads since 1994. A newer type of spread trading is the "spark spread" that pairs positions in natural gas with those in electricity to approximate the gross margin of power generation using natural gas.

Margins and clearinghouses

Exchanges collect margins (or deposits, as they are called in England) from each broker on behalf of his or her customer (and in most cases, the broker in turn collects similar funds from his or her customer). These margins, which are usually in the range of 5 to 10% of the contract's total face value, are normally designed to be equal to the average daily fluctuation in value of the contract being traded. Exchanges will therefore tend to lower margins in times of low price volatility and raise them in times of high price volatility. Every night, based on the final closing or settlement price, the exchange calculates the effect of that price on each position, and either requests additional margin or pays excess margin to each broker.

If prices go up from one day to the next, a buyer's margin is credited with a gain and a seller's margin is debited. The rules of "margin maintenance" between customers and brokers vary considerably from country to country.

The exchange and its clearinghouse are therefore always in a very strong position to guarantee all outstanding positions. Moreover, the clearinghouse holds its member-brokers—not the ultimate customer—responsible for performing under the contracts. In the unlikely event that a broker is unable to perform as called for under the contract, all the members of the clearinghouse are called upon to guarantee performance. Futures markets therefore offer several levels of financial performance guarantees.

Prices on an exchange are freely determined by the interplay of buyers and sellers. However, exchanges do place certain limits on both the minimum and maximum amounts of fluctuation that can occur in a given time period. The minimum price is referred to as a *tick*, and in the oil contracts is typically equal to 1.00¢/bbl, 25.00¢/metric ton (MT), or 0.01¢/gal in New York. In all cases, there are no limits on the *spot contract*, which is the contract that is next scheduled to go to delivery. All other contracts face limits. In New York, these are typically $1/bbl, $15/MT, or 2.00¢/gal. In a given day, no trades may take place outside these ranges. However, if a limit is reached on one day, the limits are expanded by 50% for the next day's trading, and so on, up to a maximum of $2/bbl or 4.00¢/gal. In London, the limits don't apply for a full day, but rather trigger cooling off periods before trading is resumed.

Delivery

These markets should always be thought of primarily as financial markets, being used in parallel to physical movement of oil and natural gas. Nevertheless, delivery does take place and serves to ensure that the prices on futures markets remain closely linked to the real world.

The standardization of contracts and their delivery terms are often unnecessarily rigid for the commercial participants, who prefer greater flexibility in their day-to-day operations. As a consequence, delivery typically occurs in only about 2% or less of all futures contracts. In simplest form, all those holding positions in a given contract at the closing bell on the last day of trading for a given contract are automatically required to take or make delivery of the specified commodity. The timing and methods of delivery are clearly spelled out in each contract and in the exchange's rules. The exchanges' staffs match buyers and sellers, and the matched companies are then obligated to meet their respective obligations.

Exchanges have found it useful, however, to permit several variations of this simple process. Prior to the exchange matching process (typically the day after the end of trading), any two market participants may agree to an exchange for physicals (EFP) and transfer title to oil (or natural gas) by mutual agreement in lieu of closing out their position on the exchange. EFPs can also be used to establish future positions by mutual agreement. In fact, in the U.S. crude markets, this mechanism is widely used as a routine means of buying and selling crude, since it has the attraction of the exchange's financial performance guarantees.

Once trading in a given contract has ended and participants are matched, the two matched companies may elect to
use an alternative delivery procedure (ADP), which also allows
the two to make alternative arrangements. In the case of both
EFPs and ADPs, the exchanges are relieved of any responsibility for guaranteeing performance. See chapter 7 for a more
complete discussion of delivery choices and issues.

Regulation

Exchanges are self-regulating, not-for-profit corporations
owned by their members. The degree of governmental oversight and regulation has traditionally been most extensive in
the U.S. and least intrusive in the United Kingdom. However,
the widespread publicity over the U.S. government's investiga-
tion of trading practices in 1989 seems certain to increase government regulations everywhere.

The exchanges maintain active compliance and market
surveillance programs to enforce trading rules and to detect
any evidence of market manipulation. Traders caught violating
rules are typically fined and, in relatively infrequent instances,
barred from trading. If evidence of market manipulation is
uncovered, exchanges possess a wide range of powers to reme-
dy the situation. These powers include the right to order a given
participant to reduce or even eliminate his or her position, to
substitute alternative delivery points or additional supplies (*i.e.*,
by broadening quality specifications), or even to impose a cash
settlement in place of physical delivery (assuming the contract
calls for such delivery). These powers are not often used, but
their very existence serves as a powerful disincentive to
would-be market manipulators.

Perhaps the most controversial aspect of futures trading
(particularly in the U.S.) is the permitting of dual trading; *i.e.*,
allowing the same individuals to trade for their own account
while simultaneously executing orders for customers as a floor
broker. Many critics have argued that this practice provides
opportunities for floor brokers to jump ahead of large customer

orders, profiting from the market movements that those large orders are likely to provoke. While such actions are a clear violation of exchange rules, detection is not always easy. Exchanges counter with the argument that dual trading promotes liquidity and that exchange enforcement activities are sufficient to prevent serious abuses.

As the widespread arrests and prosecutions in both Chicago and New York showed, there will always be temptations. Clearly, exchanges can improve their rules and surveillance. At a minimum, exchanges that want to allow dual trading have an obligation to create clear audit trails so that violations are easier to detect. It seems likely, however, that dual trading will be prohibited in futures trading as it is in securities trading. The exchanges and their floor communities can be expected to resist this development until the bitter end. Chapter 11 discusses the regulatory and legal issues more thoroughly.

That makes it all sound quite simple. All you have to do is figure out whether to go long or short. The following chapters are designed to help you make that decision. If it all seems too simple, just turn to the options chapter and figure out how to do straddles, strangles, fences, and butterfly spreads.

MAJOR MARKETS:
PHYSICAL AND DERIVATIVE
(FUTURES/OPTIONS)

OIL TRADING AND FUTURES MARKETS

by John Elting Treat

The history of the oil industry is a long and fascinating story—too long and complex to be retold here— already brilliantly documented in two landmark and high readable histories: Dan Yergin's *The Prize* and Anthony Sampson's *The Seven Sisters*. However, it is useful to summarize here a few of the more recent events that have transformed the oil industry over the last three decades of the 20th century, which set the stage for the oil industry of the twenty first.

INTRODUCTION AND BACKGROUND

As the 1960s ended, world oil markets remained firmly controlled by the world's major integrated oil companies. They dominated the flow of oil from wellhead to gasoline pump. Trading was a rare event—primarily to rebalance the majors' integrated supply systems. The turbulent events of 1973 changed the industry in a profound and sudden way. Producing governments seized control over pricing and subsequently over production itself through an unprecedented rash of nationalizations and the development of new distribution channels for their oil. In response to the rapid price increases and the perceived uncertainty of supply, the governments of oil-importing countries reacted by imposing a series of price control and allocation regulations that, combined with the actions of the producing governments, created massive imbalances in oil supply and demand. While the overall restriction of oil supply was modest and short-lived (only about six months), local imbalances were often greater.

This situation was the crucible in which the basic structure of today's oil trading markets was born. Trading grew slowly at first, but by the early 1980s traders were enjoying a golden age. Small and large trading companies grew up overnight and made fortunes—or went bankrupt. Some traders succumbed to temptation and went to jail for violating the myriad of regulations imposed around the world.

In the early 1980s, consumer governments began to remove the various regulatory measures (especially price controls) they had hastily erected in the aftermath of 1973's price shocks. The impact on oil trading was immediate.

Oil price volatility exposed oil producers, refiners, marketers, and consumers to unprecedented commercial risk. In the face of that risk, financial markets responded by creating instruments for risk management. At first the instruments were simple—forward contracts at known prices—but gradually they became more complex. Futures trading began with heating oil in 1978 and gradually expanded to gasoline, fuel oil, and finally, crude oil itself in the early 1980s. Following the development of futures, off-exchange instruments began to proliferate. They were first called swaps—later, derivatives—and constituted a multitude of tailored financial instruments designed to transfer or share risk between parties.

Today's oil industry is a mature commodity industry. In fact, with nearly $1 trillion in revenues annually, it is the largest commodity industry in the world—a close rival of the automotive industry.

OIL SPOT AND TERM MARKETS

The oil trading market today can be segmented by major product and by geography. In crude oil, there are three great world markets:

- The large and vibrant North American crude market, in which the futures market almost exclusively sets prices for West Texas Intermediate (WTI) delivered in Cushing, Oklahoma. Most of the western hemisphere's crudes are now priced off this market. Futures and derivatives are widely used in this market.

- The equally large North Sea crude market with prices set by Brent futures. The influence of this market is felt throughout Europe, the Mediterranean, and West Africa. Futures and derivatives are commonly used in North Europe but less used in the Mediterranean and African trade.

- The Asian market remains less well developed. It uses a variety of pricing conventions—some related to Brent, others to Middle Eastern crudes, and still others to various pricing indexes. Futures and derivatives play a relatively minor role in this market.

The world's products markets are somewhat more regional in their structure, but follow similar patterns. The difference is there are more markets, since there are more products and more regions. In general, there are two major markets for products in the Americas—East and West. Europe is split between Rotterdam and the Mediterranean. In Asia, Singapore remains the primary market for most products. As in the case of crude oil, the use of futures and derivatives is most extensive in North America (primarily in the East) and in North Europe. In Asia, futures use remains light, but there are liquid derivative markets for certain products (especially jet fuel).

Each of these markets trades according to a variety of conventions too numerous to document here. However, there are certain characteristics common to all markets. They all tend to have a trading cycle—determined by physical scheduling constraints. For example, trading of crude or products delivered by pipelines will reflect the nomination windows by the major pipeline companies, while crudes delivered from production platforms will follow the scheduling requirements for tanker loadings. These requirements generally have the effect of creating an unavoidable price exposure since the day of trading is certain to lead the day of delivery by a week or more.

THE OIL TRADING COMMUNITY

While smaller trading companies and "Wall Street Refiners" were the poster children of the 1980s, the supply and trading groups of the major companies staged a major comeback in the 1990s. Trading off large internal volumes and with superior insight into and control over logistics, the major companies today dominate oil trading. They are joined in the paper markets by major hedge funds and commodity funds that trade markets on technical factors (technical analysis is covered in chapter 6).

Based on various studies conducted by Booz-Allen & Hamilton over the past decade, we believe that major oil companies today:

- sell roughly 2/3 of their crude production to third parties and retain only 1/3 for use by their own refineries

- buy 3/4 of their refinery feedstocks from other companies or governments

- sell 1/2 of their refinery output to third parties

This activity reflects an industry that is increasingly vertically *de-integrated*—each segment (production, refining, marketing) operates as a separate profit center. If you look at the degrees of dependency implied in the figures quoted above, you would conclude that the link between production and refining is the weakest, while there remains a somewhat closer link between refining and marketing.

OIL FUTURES TRADING

Oil futures trading today is focused on six major futures contracts and options on those contracts (Table 2–1):

- NYMEX WTI crude oil (future): the largest and most active contract, averaging 153 million barrels/day (153,000 contracts/day) in 1999

- IPE Brent futures: the second most active contract, trading 66 million barrels/day in 1999

- NYMEX heating oil futures: traded 38 million barrels/day in 1999

- NYMEX unleaded gasoline futures: traded 34 million barrels/day in 1999

- NYMEX WTI options: traded 32 million barrels/day in 1999

- IPE gasoil futures: traded 26 million barrels/day in 1999

Detailed specifications on each of these contracts and other contracts can be found on the appropriate exchange web sites: www.nymex.com, www.ipe.com, and www.singaporeexchange.com.

Contract	Exchange	1982	1983	1984	1985	1986	1987	1988	1989	1990	1991	1992	1993	1994	1995	1996	1997	1998	1999
Crude Oil																			
WTI	NYMEX	–	1.7	7.4	15.9	33.3	57.9	74.8	81.8	94.4	83.0	83.8	99.5	106.8	94.4	93.6	98.3	121.1	153.4
Brent	IPE	–	0.0	0.0	0.0	0.0	0.0	2.2	6.6	16.2	20.8	24.5	35.1	40.0	38.8	42.4	40.9	53.6	66.5
Brent	SIMEX	–	–	–	–	–	–	–	–	–	–	–	–	–	0.5	0.2	0.1	0.1	0.1
Products																			
Heating Oil	NYMEX	6.9	7.4	8.4	8.8	13.1	17.0	19.6	22.9	25.4	26.4	31.8	34.5	35.8	33.1	33.2	33.2	35.3	37.8
Gasoil	IPE	2.5	2.4	2.1	2.0	3.7	4.4	6.2	7.8	10.3	11.3	13.7	14.3	15.0	17.8	17.3	16.0	19.5	25.5
Unleaded Gas	NYMEX	–	–	–	0.5	1.8	8.2	13.1	17.9	20.7	21.8	26.5	29.6	29.8	28.3	25.1	29.7	31.9	34.5
Resid	SIMEX	–	–	–	–	–	–	–	4.6	0.8	0.7	1.1	1.2	0.7	0.0	0.0	–	–	–
Propane	NYMEX	–	–	–	–	–	0.2	0.1	0.1	0.2	0.2	0.2	0.2	0.2	0.2	0.2	0.2	0.2	0.2
Natural Gas	NYMEX	–	–	–	–	–	–	–	–	0.5	1.7	7.6	18.7	25.3	32.3	35.1	47.3	63.3	54.5
Natural Gas	IPE	–	–	–	–	–	–	–	–	–	–	–	–	–	–	–	0.3	1.3	1.1
Electricity																			
Palo Verde	NYMEX	–	–	–	–	–	–	–	–	–	–	–	–	–	–	0.1	0.6	0.6	0.2
COB	NYMEX	–	–	–	–	–	–	–	–	–	–	–	–	–	–	0.3	0.5	0.6	0.3
Cinergy	NYMEX	–	–	–	–	–	–	–	–	–	–	–	–	–	–	–	–	0.4	0.1
Entergy	NYMEX	–	–	–	–	–	–	–	–	–	–	–	–	–	–	–	–	0.4	0.1

Table 2–1a Growth in Energy Futures Trading
(daily average volume of contracts traded in thousands)

Contract	Exchange	1982	1983	1984	1985	1986	1987	1988	1989	1990	1991	1992	1993	1994	1995	1996	1997	1998	1999
WTI	NYMEX	–	–	–	–	4.5	12.4	21.7	22.7	20.9	19.6	26.0	28.6	22.6	15.9	21.0	23.0	28.9	32.5
Brent	IPE	–	–	–	–	–	–	–	0.2	0.6	0.9	3.1	4.2	2.1	2.3	1.5	1.0	11.8	9.3
Heating Oil	NYMEX	–	–	–	–	–	1.1	0.5	1.2	1.6	3.4	5.0	3.2	2.8	2.8	4.4	4.8	2.6	2.9
Gasoil	IPE	–	–	–	–	–	0.0	0.1	0.1	0.4	0.4	0.8	0.9	0.5	0.5	0.4	0.3	7.4	3.5
Gasoline	NYMEX	–	–	–	–	–	–	–	1.3	1.7	2.3	3.4	2.6	2.3	3.1	2.6	4.1	3	2.6
Natural Gas	NYMEX	–	–	–	–	–	–	–	–	–	–	0.3	1.4	2.0	3.7	4.9	8.3	10.3	15.5
Gasoline Crude Oil spread	NYMEX	–	–	–	–	–	–	–	–	–	–	–	–	0.2	0.3	0.1	0.2	0.1	0.1
Heating Oil Crude Oil spread	NYMEX	–	–	–	–	–	–	–	–	–	–	–	–	0.2	0.3	0.2	0.1	0.1	0.2
Palo Verde	NYMEX	–	–	–	–	–	–	–	–	–	–	–	–	–	–	0.1	0.1	0.1	0
COB	NYMEX	–	–	–	–	–	–	–	–	–	–	–	–	–	–	0.3	0.1	0	0
Cinergy	NYMEX	–	–	–	–	–	–	–	–	–	–	–	–	–	–	–	–	–	–
Entergy	NYMEX	–	–	–	–	–	–	–	–	–	–	–	–	–	–	–	–	–	–

Table 2–1b Growth in Energy Options Trading
(daily average volume of contracts traded in thousands)

FUTURE DIRECTIONS

The world oil market is relatively mature, but will continue to evolve as the supply/demand balances shift. On the supply side, this implies an increasing dependence on the Middle East and the Caspian Area, creating pressures for the evolution on new marker crudes to replace the gradually diminishing supplies of WTI and Brent.

On the products side, the inevitable growth of demand in the developing world will also challenge the traditional role of the U.S. Gulf and Rotterdam as the pricing reference points. This may in turn increase the importance of Singapore, and eventually lead to a more favorable market for the evolution of futures and options in that city.

Price volatility seems unlikely to retreat, so we are confident that the need for risk management instruments—on and off exchanges—will remain a constant in these markets for decades to come.

SUMMARY

The oil markets led the way for the entire futures complex. This was no accident. As the largest and most global energy source, oil is the natural leader. In addition, government regulations were first removed from oil before deregulation hit the natural gas and power markets. While the natural gas and power markets have distinct characteristics, there is no doubt that the experience of oil markets in deregulation provide an important indicator of future directions for all energy markets.

However, by the end of the 1990s, the rapid growth of e-commerce in natural gas and power propelled those markets into a period of rapid growth, temporarily leaving oil the laggard (see chapter 15 for more details).

NATURAL GAS TRADING AND FUTURES MARKETS

by Dr. Benjamin Schlesinger

INTRODUCTION

A look at natural gas commerce in North America at the dawn of the 21st century reveals an extraordinarily competitive, robust business, one that has become the commercial model for gas industries throughout the world. Gas supplies are traded in spot markets alongside long-term contracts, and capacity in pipelines and storage caverns is likewise traded on a commodity basis. Electronic markets (screen trading) and price risk management tools are widely used. All this is taking place in a climate of ample supplies and growing demand.

It was not always this way. Until the mid 1980s, natural gas was a rather invisible, staid, utility-like business operating under heavy-handed economic regulation. This chapter traces the growth of open trading (commoditization) of natural gas in North America, which led to one of the most successful new futures contracts in the history of commodity markets. It then characterizes the way gas markets worked as of the turn of the century, including spot and long-term contracting, gas futures and derivatives, and trading of transportation and storage capacity. A final section then projects where key trading and futures developments appear to be leading the North American gas industry.

BACKGROUND

Natural gas is distributed to 56 million households and businesses in the U.S. and Canada and has, for the past three decades, provided about one out of four units of energy consumed. Once delivered into any major gas pipeline system, natural gas is a completely fungible commodity composed chiefly of methane, with trace amounts of propane, carbon dioxide, and other gases. Natural gas in pipelines is virtually free of sulfur and is odorless; that common odor of natural gas is actually mercaptan—a substance injected for identification (safety) purposes.

Gas is produced in 25 states and six provinces of the U.S. and Canada, respectively, including onshore and offshore producing fields. Most gas used in North America (75%) is produced from gas wells—the remainder is produced in association with oil. The continent is largely self-sufficient in natural gas, with relatively small amounts of liquefied natural gas (LNG) imported into the U.S. East Coast, approximately offset by amounts of LNG exported from Alaska to Japan. Most North American gas is produced on and off the Texas-Louisiana Gulf Coast and the mid-continent regions, with major rising production in Alberta, British Columbia and the U.S. Rocky Mountain states. Substantial gas production takes place in Mexico as well. To a lesser extent, gas is also produced in Appalachia, Mobile Bay, California, and offshore eastern Canada.

In 1982—following 35 years of commodity price regulation—the U.S. gas industry began to completely change the way it bought and sold gas. From the Phillips decision in 1954 through the initial gas shortages in the 1970s, price controls on interstate gas seemed to succeed in ensuring adequate supplies of low-priced gas to customers and maintaining the pre-existing commercial structure of the business. That is: gas was sold by producers under long-term contracts primarily to regulated pipeline companies and then to regulated local utilities for distribution to final consumers.

However, massive shortages of interstate natural gas in the 1970s—culminating in the temporary unemployment of more than one million people in the winter of 1977—resulted in passage of the Natural Gas Policy Act of 1978 (NGPA). The NGPA raised gas prices and set them on a gradual course toward deregulation. Indeed, natural gas was never actually in short supply in the U.S., but price-controlled gas was!

From the enactment of the NGPA through 1982, the gas industry resumed its long-term contracting practices in a period of intense exploration and development efforts, buoyed by high and seemingly ever-rising oil prices. The decline in proven gas reserves that had worried so many policy makers in the 1970s was immediately arrested.

After 1982, however, oil prices slipped amid a sluggish economy, and competitive forces became irresistible. The Federal Energy Regulatory Commission (FERC) promulgated a set of rules that turned gas pipelines primarily into transporters of gas on behalf of shippers. Highlights included:

- In 1983, Orders 319/234B allowed self-implementing transportation for gas users. The importance of this step cannot be overstated: The parties could henceforth conduct short-term buy-sell transactions and essentially have the gas transported on a basis that was, at least temporarily, unregulated.

- In the following year, 1984, the FERC's Order 380 invalidated minimum commodity bills in pipelines' existing sales contracts with local distribution companies (LDCs). As a result, most of the pipelines' gas customers were suddenly freed from the requirement to buy any gas at all from their traditional pipeline suppliers.

- Orders 436/500/528, promulgated during 1985-1989, following successive U.S. Appeals Court rulings, instigated and perpetuated a system of non-discriminatory gas transportation. For interstate pipelines, participation in FERC's open transportation program became an absolute requirement, even though defined officially as voluntary. The FERC essentially gave pipelines an offer they couldn't refuse by holding pipelines hostage through inaction on needed rate cases and/or capacity expansion approvals.

- Order 636 became effective in 1993. Under this ruling, pipelines were fully and finally divested of their merchant role, and capacity release became possible through electronic bulletin boards. Under Order 636, interstate pipelines must and will transport gas for others on a nondiscriminatory basis. Indeed, space on pipelines is a commodity that may often be worth as much as natural gas itself—it can be bought, traded, and sold.

A burgeoning spot market evolved in the 1980s, bringing thousands of gas buyers and sellers into direct contact through the free trade in gas as a physical commodity. For many gas pipelines and distribution companies, however, severe contract problems ensued, creating a new market complexity: Each cubic foot of gas transported in the open market displaced gas that regulated buyers had otherwise contracted to take, but now could not. Only the passage of time, diligent contract negotiations, renegotiations, reforms, and finally, the FERC's Order 636, alleviated this problem by the 1990s.

Meanwhile, in Canada, gas decontrol became effective through the Western Accord in 1986, which allowed TransCanada Pipe Line to transport gas for shippers using a series of "buy-sell" arrangements effectuating a spot market. Take-or-pay problems faced by Canadian pipelines were dealt with in the "Topgas" agreement through which major financial institutions in Canada participated in a structure aimed at resolving the issue in a more organized way than the contract difficulties being experienced at the time in the U.S. Beginning in 1987, therefore, Canadian gas markets became integrated with those in the U.S. to form a continent-wide North American gas market from a commercial perspective. Passage of the North American Free Trade Agreement (NAFTA) in 1994 further solidified the unified nature of the Canadian-U.S. gas market.

Since the early 1990s, therefore, North American gas pipelines have largely been gas transporters, involved in a set of predictable market mechanisms including physical and financial trading of gas and capacity. The system is characterized by monthly nominations for spot gas supplies and pipeline space and LDC transportation services; ongoing price bidding and resolution; and geographical posting and price reporting—all facilitated by nearly 300 active gas marketing companies (Fig. 3–1). In this manner, daily, monthly, multi-month, and multi-year term contract markets proceed in tandem, within an essentially unregulated environment.

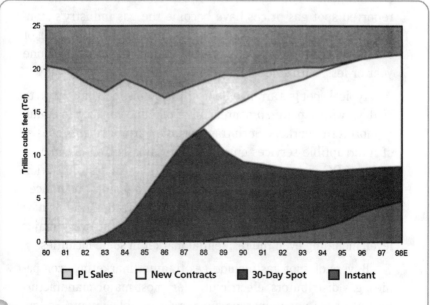

Figure 3–1   *Evolution to Direct Gas Marketing in the U.S.*

Complementing the competitive commercial environment is the fact that long-standing antitrust laws forbid price collusion among producers, and regulations generally no longer prohibit any party from selling or buying gas to or from any other third party.

Gas Spot and Term Markets

North American gas markets are segmented into immediate-term, spot, medium-, and long-term contracts. For convenience, these may be thought of as spot and term markets, the former consisting of arrangements of one month or less in duration, and the latter consisting of arrangements of all longer terms (*e.g.*, three months, one year, or up to 15 years).

Spot markets—where unimpeded by government—exist to reconcile immediate imbalances in supply and demand for a commodity. Spot gas markets evolved in the U.S. and Canada throughout the 1980s and 1990s in increasingly fluid trading environments. Throughout the North American gas industry, reported spot gas prices have become the gas industry's standard reference for gauging fair market value. By 1998, four of every five units of natural gas were traded in contracts of one year or less, with some 40% of one month or less.

Typical spot gas arrangements involve flows of a day or two to 30 days, with separate procurement of pipeline capacity in equally short-term markets. Such transportation arrangements consist of interruptible services on a best efforts basis from a pipeline and/or LDC, released capacity, short-term firm transportation arrangements directly with pipelines, or pipeline "no-notice" transportation arrangements. Gas and transportation trading now commonly takes place throughout the industry at every major level, including even the residential market in some localities.

Buyers of spot gas include gas trading (marketing) companies, gas distributors, electric utilities, most major manufacturing industries, and numerous commercial establishments. Sellers include gas marketing companies, most major and independent gas producers, processors, and utilities.

As comfort with gas spot trading increased during the 1980s, the spot market provided a foundation for resurgence of long-term gas contracts (often referred to as "term" contracts). Typically, industrial users, electric utilities, and gas utilities enter into term contracts to purchase gas for a season, a year, and two to three years. Term contracts rely on spot markets in several ways. For example, they draw their price signals from the spot market through their use of price indexation, they presume the spot market will be there when the parties terminate, and they may often use the spot market as an alternative channel. In particular, pricing provisions in term contracts are written with reference to prices reflective of gas spot markets (*e.g.,* Henry Hub NYMEX futures or spot gas plus or minus a locational basis—explained below—as well as averages of indices reported in trade press, spot price reports at several pipeline inlets, and more).

Where customers must borrow or spend substantial sums on gas-consuming equipment, still longer-term gas contracts are often an essential, and sometimes a required, commercial mechanism (*e.g.,* to support debt financing of independent power projects).

THE GAS MARKETING SERVICES INDUSTRY

A new, fourth segment of the gas industry has emerged and is here to stay—the gas marketers. The role of these players is to lend flexibility and fluidity to gas marketing transactions at all levels. More than 300 independent and affiliated natural gas marketing companies evolved in the 1980s to conduct gas trading, including buying and selling gas, trading pipeline capacity, arranging transportation through gas distributors, and otherwise facilitating markets. By 2000, the numbers had not changed greatly but the composition changed, with more marketers involved in a wide variety of additional trading activities, including electricity, power generating capacity, financial risk management and local residential and commercial gas services. Overall, marketing natural gas has by itself grown into a multi-billion dollar business including earnings.

Early on, traditional players in the gas business (*i.e.,* in the three preexisting segments of the industry—producers, pipelines, and LDCs) formed gas marketing subsidiaries to capture newly recognized profit opportunities and often simply to facilitate gas transportation. The FERC responded by issuing rules and otherwise acting to prevent pipeline-affiliated gas marketers to secure market advantages. With the advent of gas futures trading in 1990, the gas marketing industry grew intensely competitive, with many financial services companies becoming involved in gas marketing. By the late 1990s, as understanding of the benefits of this industry grew, more firms from different industries entered the business, including independent power generators, fuel oil distributors, merchandising and retail firms, and more.

TRANSPORTATION CAPACITY TRADING AND "BASIS"

Trading of pipeline and storage capacity takes place in primary and secondary markets, although the two mechanisms are economically intertwined and often indistinguishable.

Primary capacity markets consist of a set of contracts, typically either firm or interruptible, between the physical pipeline and storage asset owners and gas shippers. Secondary markets consist of arrangements among shippers for "parcels" of firm transportation, including short- and long-term releases.

As the gas spot trade grew in the 1980s and early 1990s, pipeline capacity arrangements for shipping spot and other direct market gas were made entirely in primary markets, *i.e.,* firm and interruptible transportation contracts directly to shippers. By the late 1990s, secondary capacity markets had grown in importance to at least equal primary markets, with capacity release as the major trading instrument. Indeed, primary and secondary transportation markets have melded into a fairly competitive commodity trade in pipeline capacity, whose currency (*i.e.*, the price variable) is referred to as "basis."

Basis competition dominates markets for gas pipeline capacity. The basis differential (or simply basis) is defined as the difference in the value of gas, the commodity, at one location vs. another location. As competitive pipeline capacity markets gained in trading activity, competitive basis differentials emerged among dozens of market centers, or hubs, throughout North America. Basis need not equate to cost-of-service transportation rates on pipelines. Instead, basis is determined by supply-demand balances in different markets and, as a consequence, constitutes a valid measure of the value that markets place on pipeline capacity at any point in time.[1] If points A and B both represent active gas hubs, then the basis difference is the most (or the least) that markets will pay for pipeline transportation between A and B on a spot basis.

For example, if the cost of spot gas at A and at B is $2.00/Mcf and $2.15/Mcf, respectively, then the basis differential is $.15/Mcf. Thus, pursuing this example, if we assume that the pipeline's maximum transportation rate to haul gas from A to B equals $.25/Mcf, then basis in secondary markets works as follows:

> *If basis is less than maximum rates,* then releasing shippers typically discount to meet basis:[2] Apart from long-term contract arrangements that may be in force, no releasing shipper can reasonably expect to receive on a short-term basis more than today's basis for shipping gas from A to B today, regardless of its lawful maximum tariff rates. In short-term capacity markets, an attempt to collect maximum rates would at least encounter basis competition: a shipper in our example would sell off the gas at A for

$2.00/Mcf, and repurchase gas at B for $2.15/Mcf, calling the loss of $.15/Mcf the cost of "transportation" from A to B. Thus, basis limits the rates releasing shippers can charge over a period of time.

If basis exceeds maximum rates, then releasing shippers are limited to charging below market rates for transportation services: Likewise, if basis reaches $.40/Mcf in our example, marketers will "receive" the full $.40 to "transport" gas from A to B, even while the pipeline collects only its maximum rate of $.25/Mcf under current regulation. A marketer's price of gas at B would reflect the basis difference, with any mark-up included in the gas commodity cost as a bundled add-on.[3] Note that markets at A and B are assumed to be competitive, *i.e.,* they are reflective of the instant supply-demand balance at each point. Thus, it may be said that the market is capping at $.40/Mcf, the transportation "rate" that a shipper would need to pay for capacity from A to B, in this example.

It is clear from the foregoing that, at any given time, competitive basis relationships may have little to do with pipeline's cost-of-service rates, but instead, they relate more directly to the nexus of supply and demand at each hub or market center.

Market Mechanisms

The North American gas business has evolved and solidified a monthly spot market bidding system that has become a normal, institutionalized part of the industry's commerce. The mechanisms described below are intended only as an approximate guide to the basic flows of information and will differ from marketer to marketer, customer to customer, pipeline to pipeline, jurisdiction to jurisdiction. In summary, the process regularly works as follows for thousands of gas market participants:

- Toward the end of each month (bid week), gas marketers and others complete commercial arrangements for gas supplies in the next month. Such arrangements are not limited to bid week, and may take place throughout the month via phone, fax, the Internet, and/or pipeline-based and other electronic bulletin boards.

- Within approximately a week before the end of each month, those planning to physically transport gas on pipelines (known as shippers) make or confirm their transportation arrangements either directly from pipelines' transportation departments or in secondary markets by bidding for and obtaining released pipeline capacity.

- As required by their capacity arrangements, shippers then submit nominations for daily transportation capacity to pipelines over the next month, identifying expected daily gas volumes, receipt and delivery points, and other key information.

- Over the next hours or day, pipeline capacity reconciliation staff review nominations and provide feedback to shippers as to capacity limitations, bottlenecks, and/or similar issues.

- Financial risk management steps are taken at this time, including completion of hedge arrangements, EFPs and other transactions (see below). As required, credit and related information is provided among parties to transactions, both commodity and transportation.

As the month ends, the business enters a clean up phase, in which the final deals are completed for the new month and final transportation arrangements are made—hurriedly at times. At this point, any final changes to transportation pricing are also agreed upon to the extent warranted by capacity and competition.

Throughout the month, trade publications report gas prices at some three-dozen geographical points on a daily and weekly basis. Increasingly, the business is also relying on the Internet, pipeline-based and other electronic bulletin boards, instant price reports, and the like.

As information systems improve, the above process will continue to streamline in several respects, including shorter capacity bidding periods, faster cycling of customer demand information (*e.g.*, for power generation and industrial uses), and improved price reporting and averaging (*e.g.*, on-screen changes throughout the day).

GAS FUTURES TRADING

Following six years of steadily maturing gas spot markets during the 1980s, natural gas futures trading commenced on NYMEX on April 3, 1990. The NYMEX gas contract emerged as one of the Exchange's biggest successes, with open interest nearly two thirds of NYMEX crude oil as of the late 1990s—impressive because natural gas is a North American market, while crude oil is worldwide.

In general, futures markets seek to provide three essential functions—price discovery, risk management, and investment opportunity, as follows:

Price discovery. First, well-developed futures markets tend to become preeminent price discovery tools, promoting increased competition in markets. Futures prices are widely disseminated and available to all regardless of whether or not they are involved in futures market trading per se. In particular, NYMEX gas futures prices are carried by The New York Times, The Wall Street Journal, more than a dozen gas trade press reports, and most Internet-based commodities reporting services. Since trades in the gas futures market are based on cash commitments, convergence between gas spot and NYMEX Henry Hub futures prices has been excellent (r-squared coefficient of 98.95% in 1997). With this high degree of price exposure and confidence, it is not surprising that Henry Hub gas has become the standard price index for the North American continent, and NYMEX and/or Henry Hub cash prices are commonly found in long-term contracts as the parties' agreed upon index. Price referencing to NYMEX extends to term contracts written for Canada and Mexico as well, each enabled by confidence in continuing market volumes of trade, liquidity, and price transparency of the futures market.

Risk management. Trading of commodity futures provides a mechanism to cope with fluctuating prices through the process of hedging, *i.e.,* exchanging uncertain cash flows in physical market transactions with certain cash flows in futures market transactions. Gas marketers are especially prone to hedge on the NYMEX Henry Hub futures market because they experience price risk on both sides of their transactions, *i.e.,* buying and selling gas in physical markets. By taking positions in commodity markets, they effectively lock in prices at known levels, rather than await future price fluctuations. There are two classic types of hedges—the short hedge and the long hedge.

An example: In the short hedge, Short Company (ShortCo) owns a volume of natural gas reserves, but fears its value may drop in the future. Therefore, ShortCo decides to protect the value of its reserves by selling a futures contract. For example, suppose that in January, the futures price of natural gas for May delivery is trading at $2.00 per million British thermal units (MMBtu). However, ShortCo believes that by the time May arrives, gas prices will turn out lower than $2.00 per MMBtu. By selling into the futures market, ShortCo has locked in a price of $2.00 per MMBtu. When the end of April arrives, if gas prices have indeed fallen to $1.50 per MMBtu as feared, ShortCo will buy back its futures contract at the market price of $1.50 per MMBtu. It will thus realize a $.50 per MMBtu profit in futures that will offset the decline in the value of its hedged reserves. On the other hand, if May cash prices increased to $2.50/MMBtu, ShortCo will surely lose $.50 per MMBtu in gas futures, but that loss will be offset by the $.50 per MMBtu gain in the value of its gas reserves. The point is that, in either case (whether prices rose or fell), ShortCo accomplished its goal of hedging (or offsetting, or locking in) the value or price of its gas reserves.

Note that, to the hedger, it becomes immaterial whether May gas prices turn out to be higher or lower than expected, at least insofar as the hedged volumes were concerned. The hedger's goal was to shed risk, as opposed to the goal of the speculator, who is discussed further below. The example of the long hedge works in a parallel but opposite way: LongCo, a manufacturer, has promised to deliver the goods it produces at a fixed price, despite the risk of considerable increases in its production costs with potentially rising gas prices. To protect against the feared increase in gas prices, LongCo buys a gas futures contract and thereby locks in the current price of gas for later delivery. If prices actually rise, LongCo's increase in production costs will be offset by the profit made in selling the gas futures contract back at a higher price than the price for which it was originally bought. Thus, the short and long hedges are simply mirror images of one another, in a financial sense.

Investment opportunity. As the hedger passes on the price risk, someone must be willing to incur it, which brings up the third major function of a futures market—investment opportunity and the role of the speculator. The principal attraction of futures markets to the speculator is the high leverage and accompanying profit potential produced by low margin requirements. Speculators are attracted to volatile markets, where prices fluctuate frequently. Natural gas is no exception. However, unlike the 300 gas marketing companies that physically trade natural gas and hedge to manage price risk, speculators do not generally have a cash market commitment to back their trades; they simply take a position, hoping that the price will move in their favor, leaving them with a profit. The private funds that flow to commodity trading provide the necessary liquidity and a fresh source of risk capital to the natural gas industry.

NYMEX GAS FUTURES CONTRACT

As approved by the Commodity Futures Trading Commission (CFTC) in 1990 and modified throughout the 1990s, the NYMEX Henry Hub gas futures contract contains the following major elements:

- A volume of 10,000 MMBtu delivered ratably over a period of one month in even daily deliveries of approximately 320,000 cubic feet per day

- Physical deliveries available in Erath, Louisiana, at Texaco Pipeline's Henry Hub, which is the most active spot gas trading point in the U.S. linking most major U.S. gas pipelines in the Texas-Louisiana Gulf Coast region with direct or indirect service to every gas market in North America

- Natural gas meeting standard pipeline quality specifications, thus acceptable for transportation on any major pipeline

- Arrangements for exchanges of futures for physicals (EFP), alternative delivery procedures (ADP), and other options

- Trading cessation three business days before the end of the month to allow time to complete pipeline transportation arrangements consistent with existing gas pipeline nomination deadlines

- Trading available through three years (36 months)

Options trading of the Henry Hub natural gas futures contract commenced on October 2, 1992.

Each gas futures contract calls for delivery, in the month specified, of 10,000 MMBtu (or about 974,000 cf) of pipeline quality gas at the Henry Hub in Louisiana. This rather modest contract size is necessary to ensure successful support by the commodity industry, which prefers relatively small units with reasonable margin requirements. In dollar terms, the natural gas contract (assuming $2.00/MMBtu) is worth $20,000, which is of similar order of magnitude as the NYMEX crude oil contract (assuming $20/bbl). As pointed out earlier, speculative interest is essential in futures trading because speculators take on price risk passed along by hedgers. Hedgers, on the other hand, can be expected to carry multiple contracts positions, often in groups of 100 or even 1,000 contracts.

A key element to the successful operation of any futures market is the assurance of a viable delivery mechanism. Henry Hub was selected as the delivery location for gas based on two overall criteria—existence of a competitive spot market characterized by substantial liquidity, and consistency with industry practice—as follows:

- Activity in gas spot markets (liquidity)—number of pipelines with immediate access, number of transacting parties and transactions, delivery capacity, including receipts and transit, volume of gas moved

- Competitiveness of markets in general, including acceptance by the trading industry, frequency of price quotes, demonstrated reliance on physical deliveries, and psychological comfort level

The foregoing do not necessarily ensure a successful futures market. Several other gas futures contracts have been introduced since 1990—two others by NYMEX (Permian on May 31, 1996 and Alberta on September 27, 1996)[4] and one by the Kansas City Board of Trade (Waha, Texas, starting in August 1, 1995)—but these were experiencing comparatively small trading volumes or nearly none at all by the late 1990s. Even though they generally met the above criteria, their low trading volumes are attributable primarily to the snowballing success of the NYMEX Henry Hub contract.

A final point that must be emphasized is that successful futures contracts are generally used as financial planning tools and rarely result in physical delivery of the product traded. In fact, less than 1% of the natural gas contracts traded on the Exchange are actually delivered.

In summary, gas futures trading has fit the gas business and its participants quite well, given the extensive degree of gas spot trading, widespread availability of open non-discriminatory transportation services, and continuing—indeed, rising—price volatility in gas markets in the 1980s and 1990s. The most active users of gas futures have been gas marketing companies, as originally predicted. Regulated gas utilities have been constrained in their ability to use futures because of the nature of the regulatory oversight they experience and their hard-to-measure, often indirect or oblique price risks. As gas utilities gradually relinquish their merchant function to gas marketing companies under state-guided deregulation programs, their need to become involved in gas futures will dissipate even further.

OVERALL DIRECTION FOR THE TWENTY-FIRST CENTURY

Gas demand in the U.S. and Canada is continuing to grow. Overall North American sales bottomed out in the early mid 1980s and increased strongly in the 1990s. Gas has recaptured the initiative in the home heating market, with installation of gas furnaces currently outpacing electric heat pumps by more than two to one. More importantly, the North American electric power industry has rediscovered natural gas, which is now the preferred fuel for electricity generation because of its abundant supply in fluid markets, economic advantages, financeability, and environmental and safety benefits vs. the alternatives—oil, coal, and nuclear power. Some three-quarters of new North American power generation capacity was being installed with natural gas as the primary fuel, as of the turn of the century.

Overall gas supplies have remained adequate for market needs, and it is clear that both ample supplies and physical system capacity will continue to exist for the foreseeable future in North America for several reasons:

- First, the sum of proved reserves plus gas resources is large enough to suggest a strong outlook for U.S. gas supplies, one that will outlast any equipment currently being installed to use gas. In 1995, U.S. Geological Survey (in Circular 1118) concluded that 1,106 trillion cubic feet of gas supplies remain to be produced in the U.S. Earlier studies have shown that the majority of this gas is likely to be recovered at competitive prices.

- Canadian and Mexican natural gas resources together nearly equal those of the U.S. Expansions of TransCanada Pipeline, the Alliance Pipeline, and other major new gas transmission systems were in planning and under construction as of 1999 to transport western Canadian gas to markets throughout the U.S. Growing gas markets in Mexico, particularly for power generation, have attracted suppliers from the U.S. southwest and as far away as Alberta, with the Samalayucca Project in Ciudad Juarez and the Rosarita project in Endenada representing the first in a chain of Mexican power plants fed by natural gas from north of the Rio Grande.

- As of 1999, a number of major overseas gas suppliers were actively arranging or seeking markets in the U.S. that can be served by importation of LNG at the nation's four existing receiving terminals—Everett, MA; Cove Point, MD; Elba Island, GA; and Lake Charles, LA.

With the FERC having nearly completed its own agenda for opening U.S. gas markets, the focus of attention and policy debate pertaining to natural gas markets has substantially turned toward the states and to what kinds of regulatory policies they are promulgating with regard to transportation by gas utilities. Industrial and large commercial gas users have participated in open gas trading and markets since the late 1980s. Residential and small commercial customers appeared to be on the threshold of participating in competitive gas markets as of the turn of the century. Through this process of broadening customer awareness at the retail level, many gas marketers and state regulators are optimistic that retail gas deregulation is at hand.

Finally, the need to reduce air emissions contributing to the greenhouse effect of global warming is gaining increasing acceptance among policy-makers and fuel consumers. Moreover, U.S. oil imports may well resurface as a national priority, as oil imports continued to rise throughout the 1990s to more than half the nation's consumption of oil and petroleum products. Because of the significant amount of inter-fuel substitution capability in the U.S., expanded sales of natural gas, including Canadian gas, will result from any such policy.

SUMMARY

The foregoing chapter may be summarized as follows:

- Long-term, price-regulated contracts between pipelines and producers broke down in the 1980s and disappeared altogether in the 1990s. Most gas is traded by gas marketing companies, and in contracts of one year or less. Gas spot markets currently serve about 40% of U.S. natural gas requirements.

- Having nearly completed its regulatory reform of gas markets, congressional, state, and FERC emphasis currently lies with reform of electricity markets. As power generation moves toward the independent sector and power markets are deregulated, commercial mechanisms in the electricity industry will rationalize and natural gas demand will increase as a result.

- Expertise in the commerce of the natural gas business resides within the gas marketing service companies, many of which are affiliated with gas producers, power producers, pipelines, distributors, and even oil traders.

- Gas futures trading, along with various derivative over-the-counter instruments, has become a crucial mechanism in the gas business. The major gas price identifier in North America is Henry Hub (NYMEX or cash markets) plus or minus locational basis, the latter of which is only incidentally related to cost of service on pipelines, or their tariffs.

- After the turn of the century, therefore, despite routine transportation and exchange bottlenecks that will occur on a regional basis (*e.g.,* during winter peak-load seasons), the North American pipeline system will continue to accommodate the gas market successfully, and expand where needed.

Competition among marketers, producers, shippers, and fuels has created an aggressive climate in the North American gas business, with economically attractive pricing. Power markets in the U.S. and natural gas markets in Great Britain, South America, and other places have begun to emulate the unique North American experience, and some elements of the European and Asian markets are likely to follow. Nonetheless, we fully expect the course to continue to evolve in the U.S. and Canada, as new trading and market technologies rise to enable an even more efficient and market responsive gas industry.

NOTES

1. Basis is also commonly used to describe non-geographical market differentials, *e.g.,* physical spot to futures markets, gas to oil markets, etc.

2. In the U.S., the ensuing example applies to pipelines as well, since U.S. pipelines may discount interruptable transportation (IT) and firm transportation (FT) in order to meet basis competition, subject to "undue discrimination" requirements.

3. In Canada, secondary capacity transactions are not capped at maximum pipeline rates; in the U.S., the FERC has issued a Notice of Proposed Rulemaking (NOPR) seeking to accomplish the same end. Note that, in the NOPR, the FERC has included primary IT and short-term FT markets within secondary market transactions for purposes of the proposed rulemaking.

4. The NYMEX Permian and Alberta gas futures contracts are for delivery, respectively, into the Keystone facilities of El Paso Natural Gas in west Texas and into the Alberta Energy Company AECo-C hub in eastern Alberta, Canada. The KCBT Western Natural Gas futures contract is for delivery into the Valero Transmission Co.'s Permian/ Waha Hub in west Texas. Each of these has terms and conditions that are similar to the NYMEX Henry Hub gas futures contract.

ELECTRICITY TRADING AND FUTURES MARKETS

by Dr. Benjamin Schlesinger

INTRODUCTION AND BACKGROUND

Electricity as a commodity has a relatively recent history in the U.S. Until the 1980s, integrated power generation and transmission companies produced, transported, and delivered electricity to retail consumers in the household, commercial, and industrial sectors. The industry was dominated by investor-owned utilities (IOU) whose franchised retail service regions formed autonomous control areas, with trading of electricity across borders generally limited to emergency power supply arrangements between neighboring utilities.

Close regulatory oversight governed the electric power industry at each level of government—federal, state, and often municipal as well. Wholesale transmission of electricity was regulated by the Federal Power Commission (FPC) under the Federal Power Act of 1937 and then by the FERC, as the successor to the FPC. State public utility commissions (PUC) regulated retail distribution and sales of the electricity by some 243 IOUs. A number of other entities operated in the electricity industry, including more than 2,000 publicly owned utilities—approximately 960 rural electric cooperatives of varying sizes, and five federal power authorities (such as the Tennessee Valley Authority, Bonneville Power Authority, and others).

Moreover, the Public Utility Holding Company Act of 1935 (PUHCA), which limited the IOUs' ability to diversify into non-regulated businesses involving electric power, also exerted an important part of economic regulation of IOUs.

Between the 1940s and 1960s, the system functioned satisfactorily. Following a major service disruption in the northeast in 1965, the National Electric Reliability Council (NERC) was formed in 1968, along with nine regional electric reliability councils (ERC), as shown in Table 4–1. Distribution of electricity within each ERC continues to be facilitated by a set of agreements and interchange facilities aimed at preventing another widespread blackout. No service disruption of the kind that took place in 1965 has recurred.

ECAR	East Central Area Reliability
NPCC	Northeast Power Coordinating Council
ERCOT	Electric Reliability Council of Texas
SERC	Southeastern Electric Reliability Council
MAAC	Mid-Atlantic Area Council
SPP	Southwest Power Pool
MAIN	Mid-America Interconnected Network
WSCC	Western Systems Coordinating Council
MAPP	Mid-Continent Area Power Pool

Table 4–I *Electric Reliability Councils*
Source: North American Electric Reliability Council

FOUR FORCES FOR CHANGE

From the mid 1980s through the beginning of the 21st century, the electricity industry changed in fundamental ways, inspired by the four major forces—natural gas, technology, regulation, and "infection".

Natural gas

Gas markets effectuated change in the electricity industry in many ways, although none proved to be more important than the abundance of gas supplies in North America. Large volumes of gas have been available from the mid 1980s onward at reasonable prices. This development shattered one of the most important fuel planning precepts of the electricity industry—namely, that the continent had insufficient reserves of oil and gas and so conversion to coal, nuclear power, and "alternative" energy sources such as solar energy was necessary and inevitable. Since the mid 1980s, most new electric power plants have been gas-fired for strong economic and environmental reasons.

Technology

Advances in jet aircraft engineering made available to the electricity industry relatively low-cost, reliable combustion turbines that readily were adaptable to stationary use for power generation. Since the mid 1980s, combined-cycle combustion turbine (CCCT) plants have enabled waste heat produced by combustion turbines to be channeled into steam turbines, enabling steam sales and/or greatly boosting power plant output and efficiency. Further advances—*e.g.*, ceramic turbine blades—further enabled new high-efficiency gas-powered CCCT plants with heat rates below 6,000 Btu/kwh.

Regulation

Legislation in the late 1970s through the early 1990s opened the electricity industry to a host of competitors and broadened competition among generators. The most important laws were the Public Utility Regulatory Policy Act of 1978 (PURPA) and the Energy Policy Act of 1992 (EPACT).

PURPA required IOUs to purchase power generated from biomass, renewables, and cogeneration plants, thereby creating the opportunity for third parties to generate electric power for sale to IOUs and other electric utilities. EPACT broadened independent generation categories created under PURPA essentially to any independent non-utility electric wholesale generator (EWG) on its economic merits, and required IOUs to "wheel" (*i.e.,* to transport) electricity to wholesale customers. EPACT left the question of retail competition to the states.[1]

"Infection"

The gas industry's massive structural, commercial, and regulatory changes in the 1980s and 1990s spilled over to the electricity industry because they demonstrated that energy commoditization could succeed despite energy's great importance to every day life and economic growth. By the late 1990s, gas marketers and independent power generators were forcing fundamental change in the electricity industry as well as the gas industry.

Throughout the 1980s, independent power developers built more than 200 large-scale cogeneration plants throughout the U.S. These electricity generation facilities principally used natural gas and were economically attractive, competitive, and highly efficient. Some, however, were constructed with contracts for sales of power to utilities at relatively high prices. Such contracts came to be treated as "stranded costs" as the industry transitioned to market mechanisms, as described below.

Much as take-or-pay afflicted the gas industry in its shift toward spot trading, stranded costs plagued the electricity industry throughout the 1990s, slowing the pace of change as IOUs struggled with ways to deal with the high-cost generation assets on their books. Such assets typically included aging nuclear power plants burdened by great outlays for meeting public safety requirements. States seeking to introduce retail electricity competition first had to resolve the question of paying IOUs for disposal of stranded assets that were prudently acquired in an earlier market and regulatory context.

The process of unbundling generation assets (*i.e.,* power plants) from transmission and distribution assets (*i.e.,* the "grid") was well underway at the beginning of the 21st century. Major IOUs involved in selling their non-nuclear power plants to independent, unregulated owner-operators included, for example, Pacific Gas & Electric Company and New England Electric, both in 1998. While these and other IOUs have retained the role of regulated transmission and distribution utility, electric power per se (*i.e.,* the commodity) is transacted among buyers and sellers in a marketplace environment, as described below.

MAJOR MARKET ATTRIBUTES

Unlike most fuels, costs associated with storing electricity for future use greatly exceeds costs of producing and moving electricity. Indeed, battery storage, pump storage, and other technologies for storing electricity are still under development as far as very large-scale power supplies are concerned, and had not yet evolved at the turn of the century to an economical extent. Likewise, economical technologies for long-distance transmission of electricity were continuing to be developed (*e.g.,* cryogenics). Consequently, markets for electricity are sharply segmented along both regional and diurnal lines, as follows.

First, relatively short economic transmission distances, together with constrained low inter-ERC transmission capacities, have combined to foster strongly regional markets for electricity. As of the late 1990s, markets and trading remained most fluid within the ERCs rather than among them, and movement of electric power is often confined to one or two IOU control areas. Unlike natural gas, however, electricity is produced and consumed in even measure within control areas because historically each IOU sought to meet its own needs, planning on little export or import traffic. As a consequence of this segmentation, electricity in one region ordinarily cannot substitute for electricity in another far-off region.

Second, diurnal peak period electricity is essentially a different commodity from off-peak electricity. These commodities typically come from wholly different suppliers, at wholly different prices, and serve different markets as well. For example, peak afternoon and evening power demands are typically met by peaking units—generating plants constructed to operate for only a few weekday hours per day, perhaps 500 to 1,000 hours annually out of a total of 8,760 hours, and designed for throttling characteristics. Since these facilities sit idle for most of the day, power generation companies are far more concerned with minimizing their initial capital cost than their operating costs—so many "peakers" are low-efficiency oil or gas-fired power plants that can be rapidly started-up and shut-down.

Off-peak generating plants, conversely, consist of intermediate and base load units that operate all day or around the clock, respectively, for most days of the year. Base load power plants meet demands that rarely change, such as air circulation and filtering, communications networks, maintenance and hospital lighting, some industrial processes, and the like.

Intermediate load plants meet such demands as office lighting, industrial processes, transit, etc. Power generation companies are less concerned with initial capital costs of such facilities than they are with operating costs, since capital costs may be recovered over far more hours of the year but operating costs must be minimized. Base- and intermediate load units typically include nuclear power plants, coal-fired generators, run-of-the-river hydro, and increasingly, high-efficiency gas-fired CCCTs.

Understandably, the marginal price of electricity varies greatly in the diurnal markets, with peak period power prices exceeding off-peak prices by factors of five or six in some areas. Pricing also varies from one region to another, although to a lesser extent, because fuels are transported far more readily than electric power itself, thus fuel prices tend to differ less from region to region.

EMERGENCE OF COMMODITY TRADING

Commodity trading of electricity began on an open, competitive basis with the encouragement of regulators and within a climate of recognition of the need to address corollary issues—stranded costs, third party access to the grid, and the need to operate the overall system reliably and safely. As a consequence, electricity trading encountered little of the kind of business resistance among IOUs and other market participants that early gas trading encountered.

Moreover, electricity trading benefited from the presence (some might say, the onslaught) of natural gas marketing companies in search of new opportunities. More then half of all active electricity marketers are also gas marketers, or are at least affiliated with gas marketers. These firms and personnel were savvy in the ways of identifying and marketing customers, managing price risk, providing billing and administrative services, and arranging transportation and deliveries from grid operators who were often unaccustomed to dealing with marketers and their needs.

As shown in Figure 4–1, volumes of electricity traded increased dramatically through the mid- and late-1990s, and the number of transactions increased as well. Power marketers operate in an increasingly competitive environment, with more participants entering the field in an active way each year. In 1995, only 5–10 marketing companies actually moved electricity to customers. In 1996, more than 50 power marketers were active, although the top five companies occupied 75% of the market. In 1997, more than 90 power marketers were active, and the top 10 served 75% of the market. In the first three months of 1998, the top 10 served only 59% of the market.[2] Thus, competition increased throughout the late 1990s. Information is widely available on electricity markets, with at

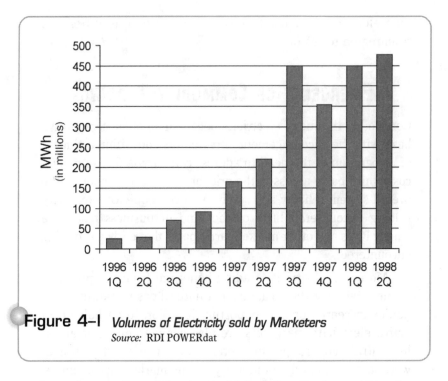

Figure 4–1   *Volumes of Electricity sold by Marketers*
Source: RDI POWERdat

least four trade publications widely subscribed to within the trading community.

The power marketing community received its first significant upset during summer 1998, when the demand for electricity spiked suddenly beyond the ability of many traders to meet commitments to their customers. In the brief but difficult period that ensued, electricity prices rose more than ten-fold in spot markets in the Midwest and at least three business defaults took place.[3] This event taught power marketers that supplies are not infinite, prices can be volatile, and more prudent risk management practices were required. In particular, it brought home the need to make use of price risk management tools already available to the industry more carefully, *e.g.*, hedging price risk on the growing NYMEX electricity futures markets (see below). Price shocks of mid-2000 in several regions also rocked the industry, with especially severe price spikes in New England and Southern California.

POWER POOLS AND INDEPENDENT SYSTEM OPERATORS

Trading electricity as a commodity would not be possible without access to customers through the grid in a predictable, reliable, and economical way. Key among the early efforts, California (Western Power Exchange, or WEPEX) and the Northeast (New England Power Pool [NEPOOL] and Pennsylvania-New Jersey-Maryland [PJM]) each organized power trading exchanges involving deployment of a single firm to act as the independent system operator (ISO).

The power market concept, as variously applied in California and the Northeast,[4] basically involves establishment of a centralized market entity (the ISO) to dispatch all electricity requirements needed each day to meet all of the region's power demands. The ISO receives bids from all generators due by a date and time certain, and accepts bids in the order of the offered price—*i.e.*, dispatching the lowest bid, next to lowest, and so forth until the ISO has dispatched a sufficient amount of electricity to meet all the region's estimated power demands. Payment is made to all generators accepted by the ISO at the marginal bid price, *i.e.*, the price of the highest bidding unit dispatched.[5] In this manner, enough electricity is produced and delivered into the pool to meet power demands in the pool region, and each user pays the marginal bid price of power. The process is an open one—*i.e.*, public disclosure is made of all accepted bids following completion of the auction. Participation in the power pool is open to generators whom the ISO has pre-qualified, based on reliability criteria, grid access, and other conditions.

Apart from the power pools, bilateral transactions also take place, much as in the natural gas, fuel oil, coal, and other commodities trades within and beyond the energy industry. Bilateral transactions involve a willing buyer and seller agreeing to the purchase and sale of electricity under a contract of any length, whose terms spell out pricing, deliveries, and other required conditions. As of the beginning of the 21st century, it is not yet clear which system will predominate in electricity markets—organized power pools, bilateral contracts, or a system enabling both, such as the Northeast power pool.

Electricity Futures

As it became clear that spot trading of electricity would soon emerge, the NYMEX undertook to develop an electricity futures contract. Unlike its earlier successes introducing oil and natural gas contracts, NYMEX had little existing physical trading experience on which to rely. Instead, NYMEX and its advisors acted on their understanding, some foresight, and luck as well, to develop a set of workable electricity contracts that the industry could trade.

Trading of the first two electricity futures contracts on NYMEX began in 1996 for delivery at the California-Oregon border (COB) and the Palo Verde power plant switchyard in Arizona (March 1996 and April 1996 introductions, respectively). Volumes traded of each contract have increased significantly.

In addition—as shown in Figure 4–2—NYMEX introduced two Eastern electricity contracts in 1998—one for delivery into the Cinergy system in the Ohio River Valley and the other for delivery into the Entergy system in Louisiana. NYMEX anticipates opening a third Eastern electricity contract—for delivery into the Pennsylvania-New Jersey-Maryland (PJM) pool—in the early part of 2000.

Specifications of the four NYMEX electricity contracts, in general, are as follows:[6]

- *Contract unit:* 736 MWh of firm electric energy in the delivery month

- *Delivery rate:* 2 MW throughout every hour of the delivery period

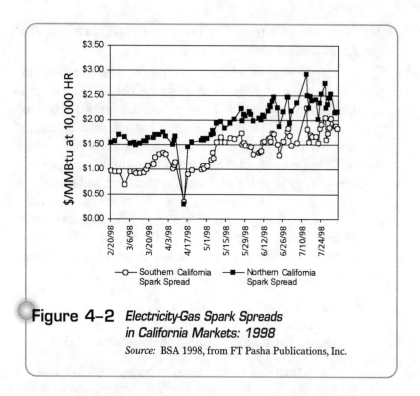

Figure 4–2 *Electricity-Gas Spark Spreads in California Markets: 1998*

Source: BSA 1998, from FT Pasha Publications, Inc.

- *Delivery period:* Contract unit based on 23 on-peak days of the delivery month, 16 on-peak hours per day

- *Delivery unit:* Based on number of on-peak days in the delivery month:

If the number of on-peak days in the delivery month equals:	Then the delivery unit equals:
23	736
22	704
21	672
20	640
19	608

The Eastern contracts are "5x16 markets," meaning that deliveries are scheduled Monday through Friday for 16 hours per day. The Western contracts are 6x16 markets—*i.e.*, Saturdays are included.[7]

By introducing electricity futures contracts before the physical trade had fully established, NYMEX reversed the usual direction and provided a degree of definition to the electricity spot trade. The physical trade has adapted its market mechanisms to a degree. One interesting respect in which NYMEX's efforts shaped the cash trade was in the area of spark spreads—*i.e.*, differentials between natural gas and electricity. This form of trade involves hedging the risk that electricity prices will temporarily disassociate from gas prices. As Figure 4–2 demonstrates, spark spreads in California markets have remained relatively stable, and appear to be less volatile than fuel prices in different geographic markets, as follows:

- Gas prices in northern California (Malin, OR) and in southern California (Topock, AZ) correlate reasonably with one another, with an R^2 coefficient of 79.5%.

- Power markets in the same two regions (COB and Palo Verde near-month futures) also correlate reasonably with one another, with an R^2 coefficient of 77.3%.

- The spark spreads in northern California (COB electricity vs. Malin gas) appear to correlate well with spark spreads in southern California (Palo Verde electricity vs. Topock gas), however, with an R^2 coefficient of 85.4%.

The foregoing demonstrates the relative consistency of power-gas prices between the two regions despite differences in geography, the derivation of gas supplies and the composition of electric power supplies. In effect, NYMEX introduced a new variable—spark spread—into the business of energy planning and analysis, one that may prove to be of value in risk management as the markets mature and expand into other regions.

This form of risk management is of value, for example, to marketers involved in trading of both gas and electricity ("tolling" arrangements) who must bear risks on four sides of their transactions—gas purchases and sales and electricity purchases and sales. Examples of tolling arrangements include:

- Leasing of capacity in two interconnected power plants, each on separate gas grids, so gas pipeline capacity constraints leading to one power plant may be by-passed by switching generation to the other power plant

- Operating electric compression on a pipeline system, so arbitrage may be realized on the value of moving natural gas along the line on one hand, vs. the value of producing added electricity on the other hand

Finally, several additional electricity futures markets were beginning as of 1998 that were worth watching, including NYMEX options markets on each of the four electricity futures contracts, and two Chicago Board of Trade (CBoT) electricity futures markets, one each for delivery into the Commonwealth Edison system and into the TVA system.

DIRECTIONS

Because most electric power (63% in 1997) is consumed in residential and commercial establishments, the future direction of electricity trading is inevitably toward the retail markets. As of 1999, most states were establishing the means by which small residential and commercial customers could select suppliers, and thereby participate in deregulated electricity markets. Stranded costs were largely being treated seriously, with funding to address the problem drawn from surcharges to power transmission and distribution system rates. Most analysts believed that stranded cost surcharges would largely succeed in compensating IOUs and other asset holders for stranded assets within a few years after the turn of the century.

Following the example set in allied industries (particularly natural gas), the number of active power marketers was destined to rise significantly as of 2000, pushed by the emergence of retail electricity marketing. Recurrent, brief—but intense—market upsets are likely to continue and, as volatility becomes apparent, power traders are likely to make greatly increasing use of hedging instruments to manage price risk.

By 2000, electricity futures trading had slowed nearly to a halt, reflecting the stabilization of power trading generally, insufficient liquidity, and the industry's sharp regionalization. Increasing electricity price volatility in the early 21st century, however, portended a resumption in electricity futures markets.

Finally, the use of natural gas for power generation is projected to increase from 10% of U.S. power generation fuels in 1995 to 30% by 2015, potentially straining the continent's gas supplies. Moreover, 108 nuclear power plant retirements are scheduled to take place during the next three decades, further adding to potential gas demand (Fig. 4–3). In all, therefore, electricity generation is expected to become the single largest market for natural gas in the U.S.

NOTES

1. Implemented by the FERC in Order 888 *et seq.*

2. Note that 344 independent and 94 affiliated power-marketing companies had registered as such with the FERC by August 1998, although fewer than 100 firms were actually marketing electricity as of then.

3. Federal Energy Sales, Power Company of America, and the City of Springfield (Missouri) Water, Light & Power.

4. As well as in Great Britain, Colombia and other locations.

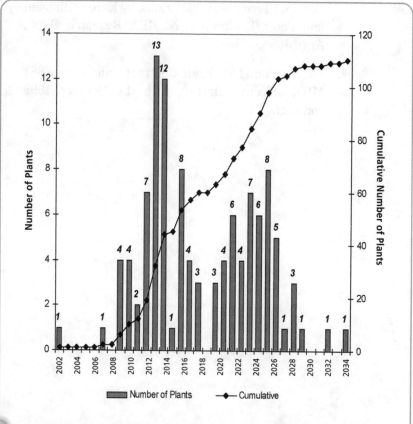

Figure 4-3 *U.S. Nuclear Plant Licenses Expiring: 2002-2035*
Source: BSA 1998, from DOE/EIA Electric Power Monthly

5. Note that prices bid by generators determine the
    ISO's dispatch sequence, rather than marginal oper-
    ating costs. Indeed, the bid price reflects a strategic
    decision on the part of a generator, and may bear no
    resemblance at all to the marginal cost of operating
    any particular power plant at any time.

6. Contract specifications and other factual informa-
    tion in this subsection taken from NYMEX Eastern
    Electricity Futures and Options: Development and

Contract Terms and Conditions, by Karen Klitzman and Peter T. Skywark, NYMEX Research Dept., April 1998.

7. The COB and Palo Verde Contract Unit became 864 MWh effective starting with the October 1999 contract.

TRADING THEORIES AND STRATEGIES

FUNDAMENTAL ANALYSIS OF ENERGY COMMODITIES 5

by *Rutheford S. Poats,*
Douglas F. McDonald,
Art Holland

INTRODUCTION

The 21st century promises to be the springboard for a booming energy commodities market. Not only will trading volumes continue to rise but there will be innovations in trading strategies, information technology, and business applications that significantly alter the market landscape.

Several years ago "commoditization" and globalization characterized the evolution of the energy markets. More recently, the buzzword has been the "convergence" between energy commodities via energy conversion infrastructure—namely, power plants and other end-users or intermediate re-processors of energy. With power plants and smaller generators converting MMBtus to newly "commoditized" kilowatt-hours, the value of energy production and processing assets increasingly will be determined by the ability to capitalize on price difference between fuels and power.

In addition, fuel-intensive manufactured products, emission credits, and even weather derivative values are key determinants of the "convergence value" of energy through their impact on fuel and power consumption, hence price. Convergence, along with continued energy market deregulation around the globe, raises the importance and complexity of fundamental analysis in understanding market price movements and their interrelationships. Further growth in and convergence among the "big three" NYMEX-listed energy commodities (petroleum, gas, and electricity) will mark the first decade of the new millennium. Other markets poised for substantial growth include coal, for which NYMEX has received CFTC approval to launch futures trading; current "fringe" commodities such as emission credits (SO_2, NO_X, and CO_2); weather derivatives, and cross-commodity hedge products. Such cross-hedge applications as "bark" spreads, "spark" spreads, and "arc" spreads will continue to fuel the cross-industry growth and diversification of the energy commodity trade.[1] Thus, fundamental analysis is not only for the outright commodity, but is increasingly relevant to related (energy intensive) commodity applications, specialty products, and environmental applications.

This chapter presents a layman's guide to market fundamentals underlying the three major energy commodity groups currently traded on regulated futures and option exchanges, and on off-exchange (over-the-counter) markets, namely:

- Petroleum (encompassing a range of crude oils and refined products)

- Natural gas

- Electricity

The goal is to provide the reader with a basic framework for applying fundamental analysis and with an appreciation for the multiple factors and interrelationships affecting energy price movements over a range of time horizons.

FUNDAMENTAL ANALYSIS ISSUES

Fundamental vs. technical analysis

Fundamental analysis refers to the study of observable physical and financial forces that ultimately determine the market price of a commodity or equity. More narrowly defined, fundamentals are observable developments affecting price through their impact on the supply and demand balance of a commodity (Table 5-1). Fundamentals are typically distinguished from technical market analysis, which focuses exclusively on the "internal" information contained in the trading market, including its volume, open interest, range and direction of price movement, and volatility levels and trends.

The fundamental analyst believes that market prices eventually reflect the net balance of fundamental forces, so that advanced or more effective analysis is assumed to lead to a more informed price outlook than is currently reflected in market values. The technical analyst's view is that the market price already reflects the best available information, so that the key to forecasting or "reading the tea leaves" is to observe the nature of the market's internal "technical" information. Skeptics of fundamental analysis also point to the fact that the variables influencing price are too numerous, unsettled, or late in being revealed to provide more than minimal informational value. While this observation is occasionally true, at other times one or several fundamental developments may be so pronounced as to clearly dominate or redirect the market's internal technical character.

Fundamental analysis may be useful in characterizing the general expected trend and high-low range in a commodity price series over time, but technical analysis often provides more detailed guidance about expected trends and ranges, including directional change rules and buy-sell signals within the price range established. Technical market analysis tools are typically

	Petroleum	Gas	Power
Demand	Two-thirds for transportation; relatively flat trend.	Broad-based; moderate growth trend; power market is key source of incremental demand.	Broad-based, rapidly growing in recent years.
Supply	Over 50 percent imported; significant variability in product specifications that impact value.	Only 12-15 percent imported, mostly from Canada; low degree of product variability.	Generating costs vary widely with fuel; active investment in new generating capacity to relieve regional supply constraints.
Storage	Low-cost storage throughout distribution chain.	More expensive & less flexible than for oil, but plays key role in market dynamics.	Very limited.
Transport	Flexible, cost-effective transport on global to local scale by various modes.	Limited to pipeline in dry form.	Feasible over moderately long distances, subject to capacity bottlenecks and transmission losses.
Availability of Substitutes	Limited.	Industrials and power generators may have dual fuel capability.	Limited.
Regulatory Environment	Prices deregulated; products subject to environmental specifications.	Wellhead prices deregulated; open inter-state pipeline access; retail prices regulated.	Wholesale market deregulated, retail market.

Table 5–1 *Comparison of U.S. Energy Commodity Fundamentals*

more specific as to the price series and threshold conditions contained in a price forecast. This is because technical analysis normally selects a given trading month as its reference point and identifies relatively "mechanistic" and clear rules of interpretation as to whether prices are expected to rise or fall. Similarly, technical tools can be used to develop very specific measures of price volatility and expected price ranges.

Consequently, fundamentalists often become market technicians, or at least incorporate some technical methods, in an attempt to fine-tune their analytical approach. For instance, the Commodity Futures Trading Commission's (CFTC) "Position of Traders" report indicates the percentage of a total futures market's reportable positions among commercial and non-commercial participants. An increase in the percent of total market share comprised of commercial participants holding "long" (buy) positions during a period of rising prices may be associated with increased commercial buying pressure, suggesting further potential upward movement. By contrast, an increase in commercial short positions during a period of rising prices may signal that the commercials are selling—hence, prices may soon peak. Another example of how fundamentals and technicals converge is the quantitative application of forward price information from the futures market to determine the incentive to purchase or sell the commodity, whether for storage, production, or conversion purposes.

This chapter focuses primarily on the tools and resources of the fundamental analysis of energy commodity market behavior. However, their measurement may often be best structured in a quantitative manner, similar to technical market analysis, thus achieving a greater degree of precision and definitive interpretation. This "convergence" of technical and fundamental methods is becoming increasingly common, as external market events (*i.e.,* fundamentals) and the market's digestion of these events through their internal behavior (*i.e.,* technicals) become more closely linked.

Fundamental factors

In general, fundamental analysis incorporates two classes of information and, therefore, two approaches to the process. The first class is the foreseeable and routinely reported information carried in the trade press and other government or industry reports. These data are most conducive to pure quantitative analysis and modeling, but typically in a longer-term, predictive framework. The key fundamental variables in this category are:

- Reported production, consumption, inventory, imports, exports, related stocks, and flow data

- Price-cost or microeconomic relationships within the energy sub-sector, such as refining margins (*i.e.,* crack spreads), power plant margins over fuel costs (*i.e.,* spark spreads), or reserve replacement costs

- GDP and sector-specific growth rates for major consuming nations, together with energy intensity trends (*e.g.,* energy consumption per unit GDP)

- Seasonal weather variations, particularly temperature (heating degree days)

- Changes in the price of substitute energy forms (*e.g.,* coal vs. gas, oil vs. gas, etc.)

- Broader macroeconomic trade, tax, and regulatory developments, including price controls, duties, and tariff policy

The second class of fundamental variables includes irregular events that are not clearly foreseeable, and whose impact is not immediately determinable by quantitative analysis alone, but may have a pronounced impact on price. Such fundamental "surprises" include:

- Political and military developments that may influence supply security and availability (*e.g.,* OPEC quotas, wars, strategic reserves, etc.)

- Extreme weather events or natural disasters that disrupt production and delivery logistics

- Sudden shifts in regulatory or tax policy (*e.g.,* user taxes, import fees, and fuel quality specifications)

- Major inventions or technological developments that radically alter prevailing trends in energy consumption or production

Fundamental analysis is the process of observing, often quantifying, and then attempting to predict the impact of these observable variables on the price of the underlying commodity. The approach might be as simple as a "tick list" of key indicators (*e.g.,* production, inventory, apparent demand, economic growth rates, etc.), or as sophisticated as a detailed multivariable econometric model. Importantly, fundamentalists must always be aware of the timing of expected price impacts and trends. Shorter-term influences such as weather, weekly inventory reports, political and economic news, must be distinguished from longer-term developments, such as infrastructure investments, sectoral growth trends, regulatory reform, and technological change.

Fundamental analysis challenges

In analyzing a particular energy market's fundamentals, the challenge is to properly measure and weigh the myriad of factors affecting market prices. No model or set of indicators can account for the full array of variables potentially affecting price. Once relevant fundamental variables are identified, it is necessary to isolate their individual impacts and quantify how they interact to produce observed price changes under various market conditions. Beyond that formidable challenge, there are several potential pitfalls that must be avoided in order to successfully utilize fundamental methods:

It's a matter of time. In addition to the direction and degree of expected price movement, one must also identify the timing. The nature of the commodity game is that it is not good enough to eventually be correct, particularly for traders without deep pockets. Even if a given prediction is ultimately vindicated, losses may accumulate to such an extent during the interim that the trade position must be prematurely liquidated to avoid significant loss. Thus, even with fundamentals, it is critical to have an expectation of the degree of resulting price movement, a time frame defining the "window of opportunity," and the equivalent of a "stop-loss" order consistent with this market view. Identification of the time horizon and price range parameters around any fundamental forecast is critical for the successful application of fundamental analysis.

The target keeps moving. The successful trader's kit of fundamental analysis tools must be regularly updated to reflect the evolution of markets. It is not sufficient to have a model that provides a reasonable good fit of past price behavior because variables affecting future price behavior are changing significantly. Models and indicators can be made obsolete quite rapidly by fundamental changes in the marketplace.[2] For example, the introduction of additional supply from a pending pipeline project, or from a plant coming out of shutdown, can rapidly change the character of a market.

Old news vs. new technicals. The market price response to fundamental developments must be monitored and interpreted on a continual basis to determine whether prices may have already over- or under-reacted to any new information. It is often difficult to distinguish whether or not an expected price reaction has already occurred, and whether the market's price response can be attributed to a particular set of fundamental market relationships or other factors, including the markets internal technical features themselves. The latter may sustain "counter-fundamental" price movements for unexplainable long periods and degrees or price movement.

Expecting market expectations. Distinguishing current and projected fundamental levels from the market's expectations of these levels may introduce significant errors of interpretation. For example, if a "normal" level of inventories for a particular petroleum product is not being achieved, the typical expected price reaction would be bullish (rising prices expected). However, if inventories are low because refinery demand has been soft, or perhaps that refiners/producers are planning to boost output, the typical price reaction from a tight inventory report may not be forthcoming. Indeed, the lack of follow-through on an expected fundamental relationship may itself provide evidence that the market's expectation differs from its "normal" standard, or that other factors may be affecting price to a greater degree than anticipated.

Ultimately, fundamental and technical market analysis must pass the test of market foresight to prove useful over time. The market foresight test involves comparing the forecast generated by a predictive system, stated in quantitative terms on a real-time basis, with actual price results (*e.g.*, contract settle price) and the extreme low and high points of profitability (*i.e.*, maximum gain and loss) during the forecast period to determine the system's usefulness. Such a test requires that the user clearly identify:

- the relevant price series forecasted

- the forward time horizon allowed for

- the range of acceptable price movement and resulting "stop-loss" simulated (or actual) trading results experienced

The third condition reflects the fact that while a price forecast may ultimately be correct, the market may go the other way for a period of time, exposing the trader to unacceptable financial risk. The fundamental forecaster should be held to an acceptable range of conforming price levels. If this range is violated, the underlying assumptions of the forecast should be reexamined in order to demonstrate that the forecast is utilizing an appropriate set of fundamental indicators.

Comparative energy commodity fundamentals

Any analysis of market dynamics and fundamental price "drivers," whether for energy or other commodities, must start with the underlying physical and contractual features of supply, transport, storage, and consumption. The key distinguishing fundamental and contractual features among energy commodities are ultimately related to their physical composition and financial exposures associated with supply contracts. Table 5–1 summarizes some of the key characteristics relevant to energy commodities.

A commodity's physical features establish its cost and ease of production, transportation, storage, and consumption. The contractual features of a commodity are related to its alternatives available in the marketplace, which in turn are based on its physical attributes. Where substitute sources of energy are readily available, contracting tends to be less secure (*i.e.*, carrying lower penalties), and price volatility is less pronounced. For example, the availability of separate storage and commodity services for natural gas reflects the need for seasonal supply and physical balancing, while the capacity and energy pricing components of power reflect the difficulty of storing electric energy.

Another way to highlight the difference between power, gas, and petroleum fundamentals is to consider the cost of a complete interruption in their supply. In the case of natural gas, most large industrial and power generation end-users have backup fuel systems, so the cost of an interruption in gas deliveries is equal to the incremental cost of burning the backup fuel, including recovery of the capital cost of the backup supply system. For residential and commercial users, alternatives to gas heat and power may not be available, but typically these users fall under the mandatory service requirements of a regulated utility. Complete interruption is very unlikely in response to market events, albeit technical *force majeure* interruptions may occur.

In the case of petroleum products, interruption may occur as a result of global shortage (as in 1973-74), or as a result of a temporary local problem (*e.g.*, a pipeline break or depot fire), but long-lasting interruptions are not common. The major impact is on gasoline availability, which can be rationed or conserved fairly effectively with the aid of higher prices and waiting lines. Petroleum is an easily stored commodity, with readily accessible inventories normally ranging from several days to as much as several months worth of supply, depending on its location in the distribution chain.

Natural gas is a storable commodity, but at a higher marginal cost than petroleum, owing to the cost of storage caverns and the need to apply pressure to inject and withdraw stored gas. As a result, gas storage and firm transport services are priced at a higher marginal seasonal rate than petroleum, but with prices limited by the ability to switch from gas to liquid fuels. Gas suppliers also use transportation balancing services to meet incremental swings in demand, thereby reducing the need for storage.

By contrast, electricity is not yet a storable commodity on any significant scale. Modest amounts of electricity can be stored via limited reservoir capacity and pumped storage reserves backing hydropower, and from a limited level of immediately accessible spinning reserves, required by power systems as a mandatory ancillary service among power systems. However, these reserves are limited in capacity and normally used to buffer typical short-term outage exposures and seasonal swings in power supply availability and demand. Therefore, the price pattern of electricity tends to be quite volatile during seasons when peak demand stresses available productive capacity. Temporary imbalances in supply and demand lead to price volatility via the price-clearing mechanism, not by storage withdrawal and additions.

PETROLEUM MARKET FUNDAMENTALS

Background

Crude oil is produced throughout the world, in a variety of grades, and is easily transported, stored, and processed. It is refined into petroleum products, including motor gasoline, heating and diesel fuels, residual fuels, kerosene, and a variety of lesser products, such as liquefied petroleum gases (notably propane), naphtha, petroleum coke, lube oils, and other specialty products. The diversity of crude oil sources, petroleum end-uses, and the ease of transporting, storing, and distributing oil are key enabling conditions for the development of a successful underlying trade. It is not surprising that today's widespread energy commodity trading "complex" was launched with contracts on refined petroleum products and crude oil.

Oil market structure and price determination

Figure 5–1 schematically illustrates how underlying determinants of petroleum supply and demand interact to establish market-clearing prices for crude oil and refined products. Given levels of crude supply and product demand, incentives to buy crude oil and sell refined products are determined by refining economics. As reflected by its central placement in the diagram, our view is that such margin-induced pressures to buy or sell the commodity should be a key focus of any comprehensive fundamental system. By tracking these market drivers and relationships, utilizing either simple indicators or more elaborate quantitative methods, a useful set of analytic tools can be organized to gain insight into the direction, magnitude, and timing of price movement.

As a widely traded international commodity, crude oil fundamentals must be viewed from a global perspective. Table 5–2 provides a regional breakdown of worldwide crude oil reserves

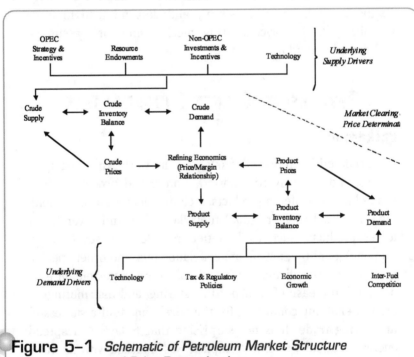

Figure 5–1 *Schematic of Petroleum Market Structure and Price Determination*

and production, petroleum product consumption, and refining capacity. Technology and resource endowments determine the feasible range of crude oil supply, but realized output within that range reflects complex political, economic, and strategic factors—most notably OPEC's internal decision making concerning member production levels.[2]

Crude oil demand is essentially a derived demand for refined petroleum products. The demand for petroleum products is in turn influenced by macro and sector-specific economic conditions, inter-fuel competition, taxation, and product quality requirements. The worldwide demand for petroleum products is largely concentrated in the developed world (*e.g.*, Organization for Economic Cooperation & Development [OECD] countries), but is not dominated by a single region to the extent that the Middle East dominates crude oil supply. Therefore, the number of variables that influence global demand, and the lack of focus on a single entity or factor such

	Crude Oil Reserves	Crude Oil Production[1]	Petroleum Product Consumption	Refinery Capacity
	(Billion bbls)	(Thousand Bbls Per Day)		
United States	30.5	7,995	17,810	16,155
Canada & Mexico	54.6	6,170	3,595	3,245
South & Central America	89.5	6,730	4,635	6,465
Europe	20.7	6,885	16,065	16,305
Former Soviet Union	65.4	7,360	3,700	10,010
Middle East	673.7	22,795	4,230	5,935
Africa	75.4	7,525	2,370	2,935
Asia Pacific	43.1	7,645	19,125	19,390
Total World	1,052.9	73,105	71,530	80,440

Table 5–2 *1998 Global Distribution of Reserves, Production, Consumption, and Refinery Capacity*

[1] Production includes crude oil, shale oil, oil sands, and natural gas liquids (NGL).

Source: BP Amoco Statistical Review of World Energy, 1999.

as OPEC, makes demand analysis a possibly more complex undertaking than OPEC supply-watching.

The U.S. remains the leading world consumer of crude oil and refined products, representing nearly 25% of global petroleum demand in 1998. While U.S. petroleum consumption will continue growing at a moderate rate, the U.S. share of global demand is expected to decline slightly over time. This reflects the likelihood of more rapid demand growth in the Asia-Pacific Rim, led by China, as well as in Central and South America, and Africa, as a function of the continued modernization of these regional economies.

Table 5–3 details historical and projected patterns in U.S. primary petroleum supply.[5] The gap between end-use

	1980	1990	1998	2010
Domestic Crude Production[1]	8,597	7,355	6,243	5,590
Alaska	1,617	1,773	1,175	780
Lower 48	6,980	5,582	5,068	4,810
Net Crude Imports	4,976	5,785	8,440	10,970
Total Crude Supply	13,573	13,140	14,683	16,560
Natural Gas Plant Liquids	1,573	1,559	1,753	2,150
Blending Components and Refinery Processing Gain	680	1,390	1,910	1,210
Net Product Imports	1,388	1,375	1,011	2,730
Total U.S. Primary Supply	17,214	17,464	19,357	22,650

Table 5–3 *Historical and Projected U.S. Primary Petroleum Supply*
(Thousand Barrels Per Day)

[1] To reconcile 1998 domestic crude production in this table with the reported value in Table 5–2, add natural gas plant liquids.

Source: U.S. Energy Information Administration. Projected levels for 2010 are the Reference Case forecast reported in the *Annual Energy Outlook 1999*.

petroleum consumption and domestic supply is bridged by imports of crude oil and, to a much lesser extent, refined products. While crude imports are a large and growing share of U.S. supply, net petroleum product imports represented just 5.1% of total domestic demand in 1998.[5] Figure 5–2 shows the composition of U.S. petroleum consumption by product type. Transportation fuels, including gasoline, jet fuel, and the diesel component of the distillate group, account for approximately two-thirds of U.S. refined product consumption.

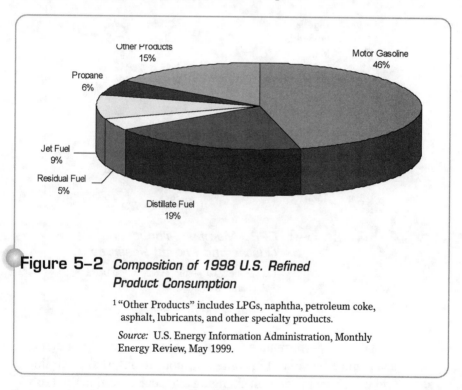

Figure 5–2 *Composition of 1998 U.S. Refined Product Consumption*

[1] "Other Products" includes LPGs, naphtha, petroleum coke, asphalt, lubricants, and other specialty products.

Source: U.S. Energy Information Administration, Monthly Energy Review, May 1999.

Role of OPEC

The single most important determinant of crude oil and petroleum product price levels is the degree of discipline exercised by OPEC in determining appropriate production levels in light of prevailing world demand levels and trends, and adhering to a reasonable set of member quotas. OPEC is comprised of the 11 major oil exporters listed in Table 5–4, who together represent roughly 40% of world oil supply and 77% of proven world reserves ownership.[6] OPEC is dominated by Saudi Arabia, which accounts for nearly one-third of both OPEC production and OPEC-member proved reserves.

	July 1998 Quota (MBD)	Proved Reserves (Billion Bbls.)
Algeria	788	9.2
Indonesia	1,280	5.0
Iran	3,318	89.7
Iraq	NA[1]	112.5
Kuwait	1,980	96.5
Libya	1,323	29.5
Nigeria	2,033	22.5
Qatar	640	3.7
Saudi Arabia	8,023	261.5
United Arab Emirates	2,157[2]	97.8
Venezuela	2,845	72.6
Total	24,387[3]	800.5

Table 5–4 *OPEC Member Production Quotas and Proved Reserves*

[1] Nominally 2,500   [2] Applies only to Abu Dhabi
[3] Excluding Iraq

OPEC's performance in maintaining effective production levels must be viewed in context of both its internal discipline and its ability to adapt to changing external conditions, notably the global forces of supply and demand. OPEC's ability to accurately anticipate world oil demand trends and competing supply sources is a core challenge to exercising influence over market price and member production behavior. Rising demand not met by non-OPEC supply sources will prompt price pressure and encourage marginal production violations to meet the additional market requirements.

OPEC's varied membership and diverse fiscal and political objectives create a number of motives for certain members to be less cooperative in the context of a tight production quota. The evaluation of OPEC behavior requires an understanding of each economy's fiscal and trade balance pressures, and the likelihood of incremental production to be absorbed in context of the market's seasonal and cyclical growth trend. OPEC's lesser members, under political and economic pressure to maximize export revenues, are more likely to engage in excess production than Saudi Arabia. However, the Saudis are also subject to financial pressures to maintain production at levels that allow it to meet fiscal and capital expenditure objectives. For this reason, primary focus on the discipline of the major producers (*i.e.*, Saudi Arabia, Iran, and Venezuela) to defend the quota allocations should be contrasted with the marginal production decisions of OPEC's smaller members, who are more likely to initiate a breakdown of quota discipline.

The 1997-99 period provides a useful framework for observing the range of OPEC and market price behavior. In early 1997, the world economy was cresting prior to the full onslaught of the Asian flu, and crude oil prices were approaching their peak levels in the 1990s. As the Asian flu took hold in the second half of 1997, OPEC lacked not only foresight, but also a concerted plan to reduce output parallel with the decline in global oil demand. Meanwhile, non-OPEC supplies had increased in response to stronger price levels earlier in the year. The combined result was a significant overhang of global oil supply by late 1997 and a corresponding collapse of price levels over the next year.

Reacting to depressed market conditions, OPEC has voted three times since March 1998 to reduce output by a total of 4.3 MMBD.[7] By the spring of 1999, oil demand growth began to recover and OPEC was able to simultaneously establish achievable production constraints at its March 1999 meeting. The result has been a near doubling of oil prices from just more than $10/barrel to nearly $20/barrel by the summer of 1999. The future direction of market fundamental and price direction depends on whether demand growth into the winter of

1999/2000 will exceed the marginal propensity for new supply from both OPEC (extra-quota production) and non-OPEC supplies, prompted by the recent price strength.

Non-OPEC production relative to overall demand growth serves as an excellent barometer of longer-term cyclical price pressure. With the notable exception of the U.S., non-OPEC production has continued to expand despite the recent low-price environment due to innovations in exploration and drilling technologies and investment-friendly government policies. While expected price increases will promote further expansion of non-OPEC production, it is anticipated that the relative share of non-OPEC output will fall due to the strong growth in OPEC output. Highlights of the non-OPEC supply picture include: U.S. crude oil output—which has been declining since 1985 due to a combination of lower prices and rising production costs—will continue falling at a rate of about 1% annually. The impact of sharply lower Alaskan oil output, which has historically represented about 25% of total U.S. crude oil production, is tempered somewhat by technological innovations that improve success rates and lower costs for deep water exploration and production in the Gulf of Mexico.[8]

Optimism remains high concerning the long-term resource potential of the former Soviet Union (FSU) region, but production growth will be slow until after 2005 due to delays in start-up of many Caspian Basin projects as well as a generally pessimistic outlook for investment in Russia.

North Sea production, the largest supply component in OECD Europe, is expected to grow for the next several years before peaking and entering a decline phase.

Refining margins and the "crack spread"

Crude oil demand is translated into product supply by the refining sector. Refiners configure their processing capacity and adjust crude oil and unfinished product feedstocks in an effort to produce a yield of refined products that optimize net refining margins. For example, Figure 5–2 shows that motor gasoline is the primary product consumed in the U.S., and the major contributor to overall refining margins. Therefore, U.S. refiners maximize profit by continually adjusting their physical process design and feedstock flows to maximize gasoline yields. By contrast, diesel and heating fuels are the leading consumption products in the rest of the world, so process configurations overseas will tend to maximize distillate yields.

Table 5–5 lists the typical refined product yields realized by U.S. refineries and documents that NYMEX contracts for gasoline, distillate fuel, and propane allow direct trading on more

	Average Refining Yield	Futures Contract Traded	Prospective Cross-Hedge Contracts
Liquid Petroleum Gases	4.2%	Propane at Mt. Belvieu	
Motor Gasoline	46.7%	Unleaded at New York Harbor (NYH)	
Jet Fuel	9.4%		No. 2 Heating Oil, Light Sweet Crude
Straight-Run Kerosene	0.4%		No. 2 Heating Oil, Light Sweet Crude
Distillate Fuel Oil	20.5%	No. 2 Heating Oil (NYH)	
Residual Fuel Oil	4.3%		No. 2 Heating Oil, Light Sweet Crude
Naphthas & Special Naphthas	1.7%		Unleaded Gasoline, Light Sweet Crude
Petroleum Coke	4.2%		Light Sweet Crude
Asphalt	2.9%		Light Sweet Crude
Still Gas	4.0%		Light Sweet Crude
Other (e.g., Lubes, Misc.)	0.3%		Light Sweet Crude

Table 5–5   *U.S. Refined Product Yield Traded on Futures Markets*

than 70% of the product yield from each barrel. The contract specifications for these products do not exactly match all the grades within each product class, but closely correlate to the primary "traded" grade's specification. Where a direct futures contract is not traded, a number of cross-hedge opportunities utilizing other NYMEX contracts may be available. In addition, the availability of forward cash (up to a year ahead) and over-the-counter markets for these "off-exchange" products enables commercial users to create a wide variety of direct and cross-hedge instruments. For example, naphtha, residual fuel oil, and kerosene do not trade on regulated futures exchanges, but enjoy a relatively active spot cash market and forward market in both physical and financial ("over-the-counter") contract instruments.

Since crude oil prices constitute the largest component of the variable cost of producing refined petroleum products, the price of refined products relative to crude oil is relatively consistent over the long run, but may be subject to pronounced short-run volatility. This difference between the price of a refined product and the cost of the crude oil barrel used to produce a barrel of refined product is referred to as the crack spread.[9] The term stems from the fact that the catalytic cracker is the primary refining process for separating light oils from their heavier fractions.

Figure 5–3 illustrates the relationship between price levels and crack spreads. The top panel plots the absolute price of the nearby futures contract price for WTI crude oil, No. 2 heating oil, and regular unleaded gasoline over the period 1996-1998, while the respective heating oil and gasoline 1:1 crack spreads are shown in the lower panel. The level of the prompt crack spread provides a gross representation of the immediate profitability of refining crude oil into its various petroleum product components.

The simultaneous forward purchase of crude oil and selling of forward product is referred to as taking the crack spread. This spread provides a surrogate for the approximate strength of refining margins, and trades on both a prompt-month and for-

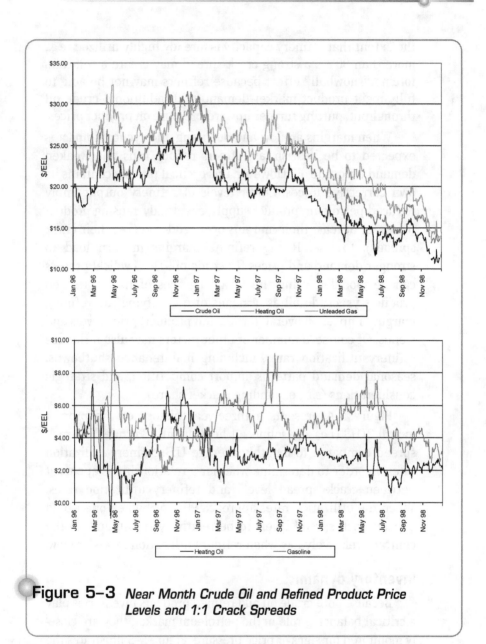

Figure 5-3 *Near Month Crude Oil and Refined Product Price Levels and 1:1 Crack Spreads*

ward basis. A strong or rising crack spread creates an incentive for additional crude oil purchases by refiners in order to capture the strong operating margins, thereby increasing refinery capacity utilization and sustaining upward price momentum. To the extent that refinery capacity is already highly utilized (*e.g.,* more than 90%), a strong crack spread may create a self-rein-forcing "snowball" effect because refiners may not be able to fully meet product market demand with additional crude oil throughput, putting further upward pressure on product prices.

When margins are low and declining, the cyclical impact is expected to be bearish, as refiners reduce runs and weaken demand for crude oil. However, this cyclical process contains its own corrective forces. Lower levels of refinery output imply reduced petroleum product supply, eventually causing product prices, or at least their margins over crude oil (*i.e.,* their crack spreads), to rise. Rising refining margins in turn lead to stronger demand and prices for crude oil. This cyclical process can be modeled using the forward prices of traded refined products vs. crude oil as a means of quantifying the refining margin's impact on overall (crude and product) price levels and trends. Of course, a number of other factors may also influence refinery utilization rates, including maintenance shutdowns, seasonal demand patterns, import competition, and strategic considerations (*e.g.,* expanding market share).

Figure 5–4 presents a three-year history of the prompt month 2/1/3 (*i.e.,* 2 gasoline + 1 heating oil – 3 crude oil) crack spread compared to monthly average U.S. refinery utilization rates, in order to determine whether a relationship is apparent between crack spread levels and refinery utilization rates. When the utilization rates approach 90% or higher, one would expect crack spread levels to be relatively strong and, to the contrary, relatively low when refinery utilization levels are low.

Inventory dynamics

Because both crude oil and refined products inventories play a critical balancing role in the petroleum market, they are close-ly monitored for signs of price pressure. Figure 5–5 illustrates the relationship between inventories and consumption for crude oil, motor gasoline, and distillate fuel. Stocks are typically accumu-lated in the quarter prior to peak consumption periods, thereby smoothing the impact of demand swings on refinery operations.

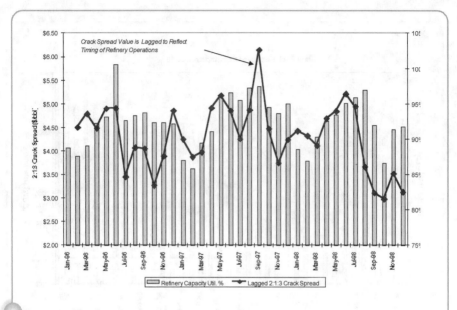

Figure 5-4 *Crack Spread as Leading Indicator of Refining Throughput*

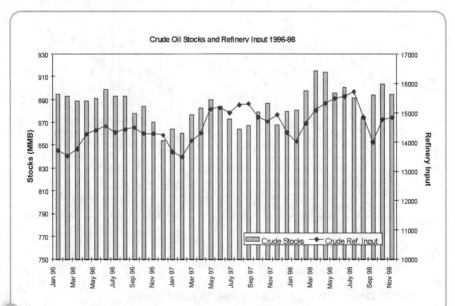

Figure 5-5 *Inventory/Consumption Relationship by Petroleum Type*

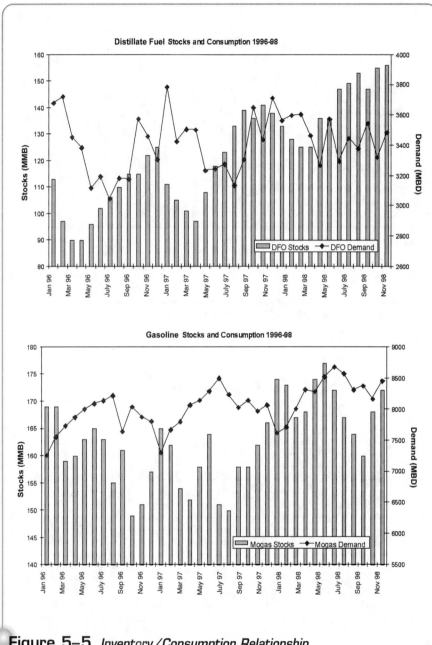

Figure 5-5 *Inventory/Consumption Relationship by Petroleum Type, cont'd*

Overall, the supply curve for crude oil has become less seasonal over the last decade, as increased use of transport fuels (motor gasoline, diesel, and kero-jet fuel) with summer peak usage has offset the traditional winter peak associated with heating fuel consumption (primarily distillates and residual fuel oils).

Note that product inventories are highly seasonal and, therefore, subject to greater price variation, as the gross margins (*i.e.*, crack spreads) of refined product prices over crude oil prices are quite volatile (see Fig. 5–3).

Low inventory levels, evaluated on a seasonal basis relative to current and projected demand, indicate that consumption may be out-pacing supply and *vice versa*. The adequacy of stocks relative to current demand can be measured in terms of the following "days supply" calculation:

$$Days\ Supply\ =\ \frac{Primary\ Inventory}{Daily\ Consumption}$$

Inventory levels measured in days supply are plotted for the three major petroleum categories in Figure 5–6.[10] A useful benchmark for evaluating the relative tightness of inventories, as measured by their days supply, is the use of normal days supply or "norm-day" concept. The idea is to estimate "typical" inventory levels based on recent historical experience for use as a reference in evaluating current inventory levels. For example, the norm-day inventory level for January 2000 might be estimated as the average of ending January stocks for the previous five years, possibly throwing out the high and low readings. Alternatively, a smoothed average of prior years could be utilized, with the smoothing weights applied to more distant years successively reduced. A more simplistic approach would be to just take a moving average for a specified number of months or years, not focusing exclusively on a particular calendar month.[11]

Once selected, the difference between the current month's days supply and the corresponding "normal days supply" can be

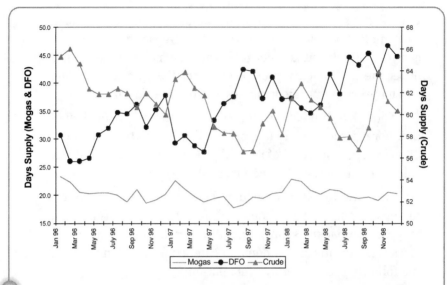

Figure 5–6 *Crude Oil, Motor Gasoline (MoGas), and Diesel Fuel Oil (DFO) Stocks Measured in Days' Supply Monthly, 1996–1998*

used to identify the apparent fundamental strength or weakness of the market. In order to reflect the overall degree of variability in stock levels and make it easier to determine the significance of volumetric deviations, this difference is then divided by its standard deviation. The resulting standardized norm-day indicator is:

$$Indicator = \frac{(Current\ Days\ Supply - Norm\text{-}Day\ Supply)}{Std.\ Deviation\ of\ Days\ Supply}$$

A positive indicator value is bearish because it signals that inventories relative to demand are high relative to comparable historical periods, and *vice versa*. Figure 5–7 plots the standardized norm-day indicator for distillate fuel against distillate fuel prices, generally verifying that negative indicator values tend to be associated with high or rising prices, while positive indicator values imply low or declining prices. Although monthly data are used for this illustration, in practice the indicator would be tracked on a weekly basis to generate timely

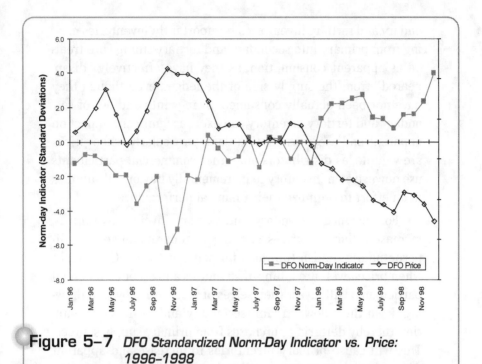

Figure 5-7 *DFO Standardized Norm-Day Indicator vs. Price: 1996-1998*

trading signals. In addition, some threshold indicator value (*e.g.*, ± 2 standard deviations) must be established to filter out market noise and distinguish significant inventory fluctuations.

Crude oil and petroleum product inventories are reported on a weekly basis in the U.S. by the American Petroleum Institute (API) in its *Weekly Statistical Bulletin* and by the U.S. Department of Energy's Energy Information Administration (DOE/EIA). Internationally, the International Energy Agency (IEA), affiliated with the Organization for Economic Cooperation and Development (OECD), reports member country and global inventories on a monthly basis. This information is widely anticipated by the trading community and frequently has an immediate impact on prices.

Reported stocks are confined to primary inventory levels, usually including inventories held at refineries, in pipelines, and at major trans-shipment terminals, but excluding secondary and tertiary inventories.[12] Importantly, inventories moving from primary into secondary and tertiary storage are treated as apparent consumption, as they have effectively "disappeared" from the supply side of the ledger, even though they have not been actually consumed. Swings into and out of secondary and tertiary inventory can exert a significant impact on apparent end-use consumption data, particularly when prices are volatile, as distributors and other commercial participants use downstream inventory to incrementally buy or sell supplies in an effort to optimize their financial performance.

For instance, secondary and tertiary inventories tend to increase with rising prices, creating an apparent and often self-perpetuating bullish (upward) influence on price. Conversely, when price levels are falling, distributors and other commercial participants will divest themselves of inventories by first drawing down their downstream (secondary and tertiary) inventories, thereby deferring purchases from primary supply sources. This will cause primary inventories to increase and apparent demand levels to appear smaller than actual demand, creating a self-perpetuating bearish (downward) price effect.

Another note of caution regarding crude oil inventory data is that reported on-land levels will generally understate the true volume of storage since substantial quantities can be effectively stored on the water via slow-steaming or kept in trans-shipment terminals at the country of origin or offshore of the U.S. This can be a significant number relative to landed U.S. crude oil inventories, as roughly half of U.S. refinery consumption is imported.

Price "basis" relationships reflecting fundamental variables

Other key fundamental variables that exert a critical influence on petroleum price levels include those factors that commonly create price "basis" differentials. Price basis refers to the difference between two price series, whether futures or cash market prices, as a function of the quality, location, timing, or payment conditions of supply. In the case of quality differentials, price spreads between various grades of petroleum products reflect associated production costs and value in the market. For example, within the distillate product class, the move in the U.S. to low sulfur diesel fuel (at 0.05% sulfur) vs. the off-highway standard specification for heating oil of 0.20% sulfur has created an occasional premium for low sulfur diesel. This premium is notably strong in the summer months, when on-road distillate demand peaks. In the case of motor gasoline, efforts to limit vapor pollution have created a positive winter differential for oxygenated gasoline, while reformulated gasoline has emerged as a premium summer motor fuel because of its relative stability in warm temperatures.

Price spreads reflecting supply location are ultimately a reflection of the value of transportation between two market areas. In the long run, location-based price spreads should reflect the cost of transportation between two areas. However, immediate demand pressure and supply or transport capacity constraints can create significant transitory price dislocations. Pipeline prorationing and other measures eventually alleviate such supply and demand imbalances, but the short-term price impact can be substantial. Key shipping costs affecting location differentials include international shipping rates for major trans-Atlantic and Caribbean routes, pipeline tariffs, notably for the major lines running from U.S. Gulf Coast refining centers up to the U.S. East Coast Mid-Continent, and domestic waterborne shipping, rail, and truck rates between primary supply and demand centers.

Timing and payment differentials reflect the value of petroleum today as compared to some future date. This price difference is referred to as the *time spread* and reflects the future value of product relative to its current value. A rising time spread (*i.e.*, forward month more expensive than near month price) is called a *contango* market, while a declining time spread (*i.e.*, forward month price less than near month price) is referred to as a market in *backwardation*. Normally, given that inventory-carrying costs are positive, one would expect the market to more often follow a contango pricing structure. However, because inventories are maintained at relatively low levels in order to control costs, there is a propensity for petroleum markets to trade in a backwardation structure, whereby future prices are lower than current or spot prices.

Surplus of crude oil and refining capacity also contributes to the petroleum market's tendency to discount forward price levels. Seasonal supply and demand factors also have a significant impact on the price spread or "time basis" of a given product. Heating fuels would be expected to be priced in a backwardation structure during the winter and in a contango structure during the fall. Conversely, motor gasoline prices normally trade in contango during the winter and spring and in backwardation during the late summer and early autumn.

NATURAL GAS MARKET FUNDAMENTALS

Background

The natural gas market now has a 10 year track record in the U.S. in a true commodity environment, with trade in the highly successful NYMEX Henry Hub contract growing dramatically since its introduction in the spring of 1990. Along with the Henry Hub futures and option contracts, both NYMEX and the Kansas City Board of Trade have listed contracts for West Texas/Permian Basin gas and NYMEX has introduced an Alberta, Canada-based contract.

Internationally, the U.K.'s International Petroleum Exchange opened a natural gas futures market in late 1997 on the heels of gas sector restructuring and, more recently, the opening of the Interconnector between the U.K. and mainland Europe. Eventually, with gradual deregulation in Western Europe and supply pressure from former Soviet States Russia, Turkmenistan, Azerbaijan, and Kazakhstan, an active European gas commodity market is expected to develop. Rapid progress in the "commoditization" of natural gas is also emerging in Latin America, notably in the Southern Cone, along with

Australia and select African markets, as resource development needs are increasingly supported by a more transparent transport and pricing regime.

Continued competition and deregulation even to the retail distribution level in the U.S. and Canada ensure the long-term role of gas as a vibrant energy commodity well into the 21st century. The emergence of a competitive, commodity-styled power market will further position gas as a key input to this massive and highly regionalized commodity market throughout North America, including Canada and Mexico in the next decade. Its role as the key marginal fuel for new merchant and semi-merchant generating capacity will create a very interesting price dynamic as gas pricing becomes increasingly linked to power prices in significant incremental gas-fired generation markets. Of course, competition between gas and fuel oil will continue, though primarily on a peaking basis, and gas will also compete with coal when gas prices are soft.

The substantial growth in imported gas pipeline capacity from Canada into the U.S. over the next several years, along with the opening of pipeline routes between the U.S. and Mexico, will create a truly unified North American market. Market developments as far south as the equator, and as far north as the Arctic Circle, will ripple through the complex logistic and price-clearing functions of gas, power, liquid and solid fuel commodity, and transportation traders and schedulers.

Gas market structure and price determination

Figure 5–8 schematically illustrates the key drivers and components of gas supply and demand, highlighting the role of the transmission and storage infrastructure as a bridge between them. The Henry Hub market dominates natural gas pricing in the U.S., with most pricing formulas referencing the Henry Hub price of some downstream index (pipeline delivery area) pricing point, which carries a relatively transparent, reliable location, and seasonal pricing basis to the Henry Hub market. Downstream price reference points are based on major

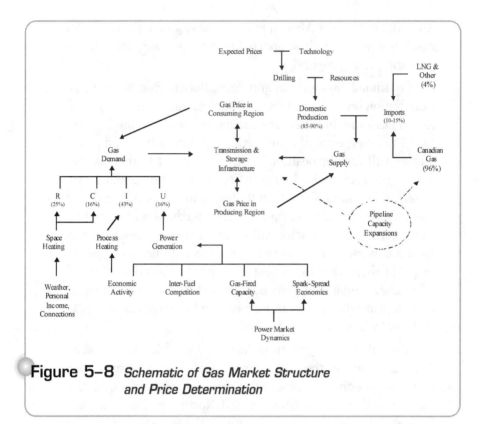

Figure 5–8 *Schematic of Gas Market Structure and Price Determination*

pipeline and consuming area delivery areas, including the U.S. mid-Atlantic and Northeast (*e.g.,* TransCo Zone 6, TetcoM3), the upper mid-West into Chicago, the Southern California (Socal) and Pacific Northwest markets (*e.g.,* Sumas, Washington).[13]

Unlike petroleum products, which are literally "liquid" and therefore quite flexible in their market transportation and storage features, natural gas is largely moved by pipeline. Economic storage is most likely found in natural cavern formations, incremental in pipeline compression, and only sparsely in liquefied form.[14] As a result, the market price for natural gas is largely determined by the availability of inventory, relative to seasonal demand and pipeline capacity. When inventories are adequate and pipeline space is available, the price of natural gas is not likely to be volatile to the upside. However, given the substantial seasonality of gas demand, a balanced market can quickly turn if weather or other cyclical factors combine to stretch the delivery system's storage and transit capacity.

Figure 5–9 presents natural gas monthly demand trends by major sector over the period 1990–98. All four sectors exhibit a substantial degree of seasonality in their demand profiles, led by the weather-sensitive residential sector, and with significant seasonal swings within the electric utility and commercial/transport sectors. Industrial gas demand exhibits the least degree of seasonality, but has shown the greatest cyclical growth over the past 10 years. Importantly, the seasonal pattern of utility gas consumption, with its summer peak reflecting air conditioning power loads, is the mirror-image of other sectors. As the share of gas-fired generating capacity expands, the seasonal profile of gas consumption and prices will tend to flatten.

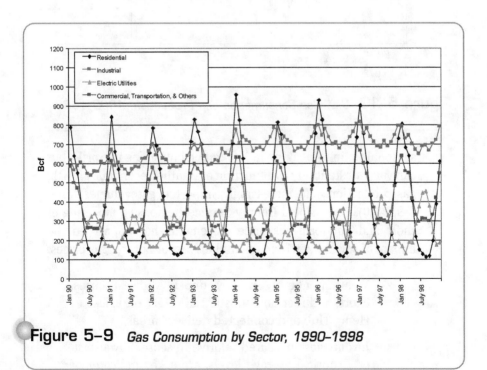

Figure 5–9 *Gas Consumption by Sector, 1990–1998*

Given the relatively stable level of gas production documented in Figure 5–10, the sharp seasonal fluctuations in gas
demand must be absorbed by significant inventory withdrawals
and additions. These inventory swings are quite reliable in their

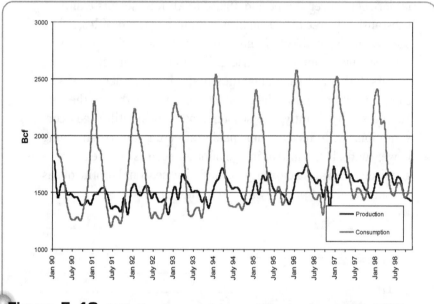

Figure 5–10 *U.S. Gas Consumption and Production: 1900–1988*

seasonal timing—peaking in November, bottoming in April—but
can vary substantially as a function of weather, economic growth,
gas production, and increasingly, imported gas volumes (Figs.
5–9, 5–10). Pace Global Energy Services' extensive modeling of
short and mid-term gas price movements has quantified the
impact of several key fundamental drivers of natural gas prices:

- Weather, notably in key upper Midwest cities,
  exerts a direct and substantial effect on prices at
  Henry Hub and connected delivery areas.

- Inventories, measured relative to seasonally-adjust-
  ed historical average levels, are a key indicator of
  supply availability.

- Economic growth variables, such as disposable personal income and the industrial production index, explain a significant degree of cyclical demand growth.

- The lagged real price of gas exhibits a significant downward impact on current gas prices, as consumer behavior and prices adjust to a long-term norm, motivated in part by changed purchasing patterns, but also by the rapid adjustment of price to supply and demand imbalances.

- Lagged consumption exerts an upward influence on prices over time, as gas demand growth one year earlier results in tighter inventories, and stronger prices the following year, since production levels are relatively stable.

Short-term gas fundamentals

Among these price determinants, the most powerful near-term influence is temperature, which in turn flows through demand to the adequacy of gas inventory levels relative to "norm" levels. As previously documented for petroleum markets, the level of days supply provides a useful "stress test" for the adequacy of gas inventories and is an important indicator of the relative strength of the fundamental market environment. When inventories are drawn down in excess of "normal" seasonal levels, or not accumulated at typical seasonal rates, the reason is often colder than normal temperature patterns—strong heating degree days—or, increasingly, to warmer than normal temperatures in the summer—strong cooling degree days.[15] Cyclical strength in demand growth, like that experienced in the U.S. during the late 1990s (notably for industrial demand in the second half of 1997) also can exert a self-sustaining effect on inventory balances and the resulting directional trend and magnitude of price movements.

When inventory levels are relatively tight, prices tend to strengthen, moving in three to six month trends. When inventory levels are shown to be adequate, relative to their moving average levels, prices tend to soften. The major driver of inventory levels is the degree of seasonality in consumption, prompted largely by colder-than-normal temperatures, and increasingly by warmer-than-normal temperatures, since natural gas-fired generation capacity now represents a significant share of incremental power capacity to meet peak (cooling degree day-driven) summer loads. Figure 5–11 illustrates the relationship between inventories and pricing by plotting monthly storage levels, measured in days supply, against the Henry Hub spot price.[16]

The American Gas Association's (AGA) *Report of Estimated U.S. Working Gas Levels in Underground Storage* is released weekly on Wednesday evenings, and is closely watched by traders to

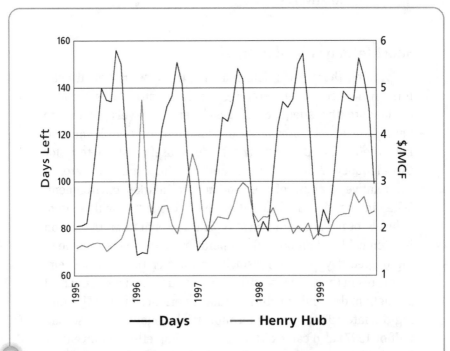

Figure 5–11   *Henry Hub Gas Price vs. Days Supply in Storage*

determine whether apparent demand levels are exceeding or lagging expected levels, after adjusting for recorded temperature levels. The AGA inventory report provides total inventories for the U.S. and regional inventories for a producing area and two consuming areas—East and West. The production region includes the major producing states, notably Texas, Louisiana, and Oklahoma, where gas is stored before moving downstream via interstate pipelines to consuming areas. Consumer region inventories tend to be more sensitive to the seasonal buying patterns of major utilities—local distribution companies—that maintain firm service obligations to their highly seasonal residential and commercial customer base. Producer region inventories tend to be less variable, and therefore often more reliable as an indication of actual demand trends.

Figure 5–12 provides a monthly average comparison of Chicago minimum temperatures (right scale) and Henry Hub spot prices of natural gas (left scale). As shown in the graph, when

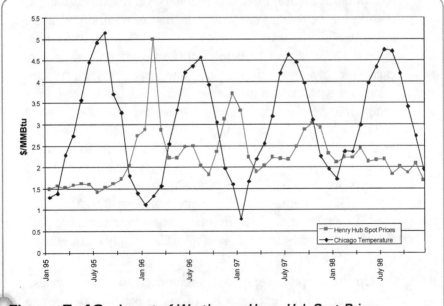

Figure 5–12   *Impact of Weather on Henry Hub Spot Prices, 1995–1998*

average minimum temperatures fall below 20°F, a corresponding increase in average price levels above their seasonal norms can be expected, with the extent of the price increase linked to the adequacy of inventory levels. This occurred in a very pronounced manner in the winter of 1996, and in similar but more subdued fashion in January 1997. Over winters 1998 and 1999, the peak price level has been steadily reduced as a function of warmer temperatures and adequate inventory levels. Increasingly, one should look for greater gas price sensitivity to cooling degree days, especially in markets with a significant amount of gas-fired generation capacity, notably Texas, California, and the mid-Atlantic power regions.

Long-term gas fundamentals

While weather exerts a major short-term influence on natural gas demand—hence price pressures—the analyst evaluating longer-term gas price trends (e.g., beyond three months) must look at other cyclical price determinants. On the supply side, as seen in Figure 5–10, domestic production of natural gas, while rising steadily since 1990, does not display substantial variation. Prior to the winter of 1999, most of the variation in gas supply came from inventory adjustments. However, as projects currently underway to expand pipeline deliverability from Canada are completed, the capacity for the U.S. to receive Canadian imports will rise considerably, creating a more dynamic North American market, with a significant potential contribution from swing Canadian supplies.[17] In addition, two gas production and import projects in the East—the Sabine Pipeline and the Portland Natural Gas System—will provide direct incremental supply into the U.S. northeast markets. In total, Canadian imports are positioned to rise from around 10% of total U.S. supply requirements in 1997 to nearly 20% by 2002.

On the supply side, it is also important to observe investment trends in oil and gas exploration in order to determine whether future indigenous supply levels are likely to follow historical trends. One common indicator followed by the industry is the reported number of gas drilling rigs in service, as shown in Figure 5–13. The active rig count tends to increase as a lagged function of average gas price levels. Greater drilling activity, adjusted for the success rate of rigs in service, will influence domestic production levels. This trend in newly developed supplies must be adjusted for declining productivity from existing fields. In the U.S., on-shore fields have been in a more rapid state of decline, as production technology and scales are too small to keep pace with more sophisticated offshore production technology. In addition to rig counts, a variety of public data are available on drilling activity, finding success rates, productivity per well, upstream investments by the industry, and other indices of future production levels.

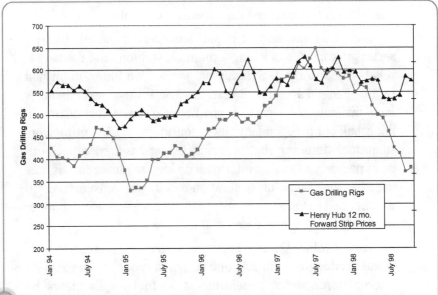

Figure 5–13 *Relationship Between Gas Drilling and Henry Hub 12-Month Forward Prices, 1994–1998*

To identify the magnitude and direction of price pressure, the outlook for supply must be balanced against likely consumption trends. Among the major gas consuming sectors, residential and commercial sector demand growth tends to be relatively tied to disposable personal income trends, as reported by the Department of Commerce. In addition, it is useful to observe the number of new gas service hook-ups reported by such organizations as the AGA and DOE/EIA to check if the growth in service connections is exceeding historical norms. Such data should be examined to determine whether connections are rising more or less rapidly than the macro economic growth indicators indicative of residential and commercial sector consumption. To dial in the influence of weather, most modelers use normal temperature data as the base case, but it is important to modify this assumption to evaluate the impact of seasonably colder and warmer temperature assumptions. Longer-term forecast information is then used to determine which cases are assigned the greatest probability.

Industrial and electric power demands are the other major sectors to consider in a long-term forecast. Industrial demand is reliably tied to the U.S. industrial production index, published by the Federal Reserve Board. Electric utility gas demand is more difficult to forecast, in part because reported statistics do not break out independent power consumption from utility consumption. Moreover, the increasing use of gas-fired capacity to meet peaking, as well as intermediate load requirements, is raising the sensitivity of generation-based gas consumption to weather and to the availability of alternative generating sources, including hydro, nuclear, and coal units.

Pace Global Energy Services utilizes a rigorous utility-grade production planning and dispatch model to develop its internal forecasts of generation-based fuel requirements by major power region. Since such tools are not available to the layperson, however, a simple surrogate must often suffice when attempting to forecast gas demand from power generation facilities. A good starting point is to utilize DOE/EIA data for purposes of relating overall power generation to fuel consumption by region, and then to update one's generation database with data on the fuel supply behind available capacity in each region. As this percentage swings to natural gas, the amount of gas required by gas-fired power generation can be extrapolated from historical trends.

Inter-fuel and gas vs. power "spark" spreads

The price of competitive substitute fuels, notably petroleum, must also be factored into any projection of short, medium, or longer-term price levels. In the short run, the price of competing fuel may be overwhelmed by the impact of weather on gas demand. This is because not all gas use is substitutable by oil. Substitution is greatest in the utility and industrial sectors, but at a cost. Back-up fuel storage and delivery infrastructure is costly, as is the conversion process for certain industrial processes. Longer term, the forward price of petroleum products does tend to place a cap on natural gas prices, as conversion and delivery system decisions can be made with greater foresight, rather than in response to short-term weather extremes.

Figure 5–14 demonstrates the "capping" effect played by oil relative to gas prices in the mid- to longer-term by plotting three-month forward prices of crude oil—converted at 6.0 MMBtu/Bbl—against three-month forward prices for natural gas. Forward gas prices only exceed forward oil prices for brief periods and by small amounts. The extent of this price penetration, hence value of fuel-switching, is directly tied to the magnitude of heating degree days in context to the inventory cushion available at the time of year that extreme cold temperatures occur. When cold spells occur early in the winter, the price reaction tends to be greater, as concerns about future cold spells further stressing gas inventory supplies become paramount and prompt substantial defensive buying pressure.

Given the increasing convergence between power and gas markets, the level of power prices will exert an increasing influence on gas prices in markets with substantial gas-fired generation capacity. Although the annual correlation coefficient between gas and power prices is relatively low, even in signifi-

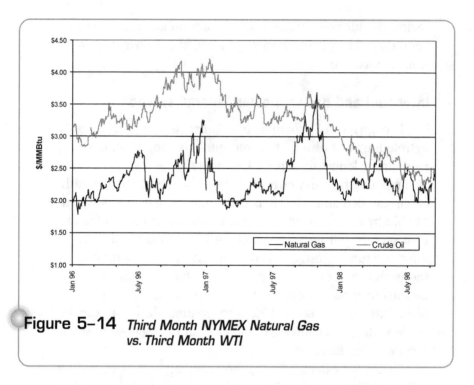

Figure 5-14 *Third Month NYMEX Natural Gas vs. Third Month WTI*

cant marginal gas-fired generation markets, the linkage during peak summer and winter seasons is likely to increase as power generating assets become increasingly sensitive to market forces, including relative fuel prices.

An example of the relatively low correlation of gas and power prices is provided in Figure 5-15, which plots the daily spark spread in the PJM (Pennsylvania-New Jersey-Maryland) power region for 1998, along with its individual component gas and power prices (in $/MWh).[18] High variability in the spark spread indicates a fairly low correlation between gas and power prices. However, even if gas prices do not move in lock-step with power prices, the impact of extreme power price movements will put pressure on fuel prices, whether caused by extreme temperatures or relatively low availability for alternative generating sources. As energy market convergence progresses, gas prices are likely to become more highly correlated with (*i.e.*, sensitive to) power prices.

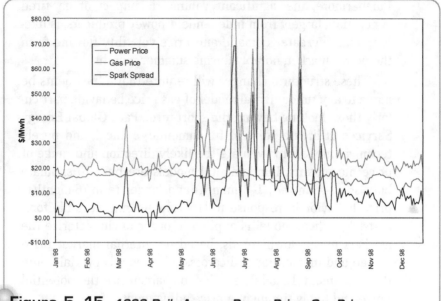

Figure 5–15 *1998 Daily Average Power Price, Gas Price, and Spark Spread in PJM Region*

Gas Summary

In order to evaluate the combination of factors influencing natural gas prices, a fairly sophisticated set of analytical tools may be required, particularly given the volatility of gas price movements in the short term. Natural gas is a highly cyclical short- and mid-term market, but the precise timing and magnitude of cyclical swings are unpredictable. However, temperature forecasts and cumulative degree days relative to inventory levels are a good starting point to anticipate the degree of seasonal influence that gas fundamentals are likely to exert on prices. In addition, when characterizing the market's fundamental drivers, one must take into account an increasingly diverse set of supply sources into the U.S., including increased Canadian imports, Mexican trade, and LNG. Structural change must also be accounted for. For example, as natural gas distribution continues to move towards retail competition, the traditional seasonal storage patterns are also likely to be affected.

Furthermore, the significant volumetric impact of gas-fired generation, largely from independent power producers, is likely to create greater demand and price volatility flowing from the power market, notably during summer months.

These structural changes will require that adjustments be made to any fundamental model of gas price behavior, particularly those looking beyond the short-term. Pace Global Energy Services utilizes a suite of fundamental, cyclical, and purely technical models to evaluate the likely direction and range of price movements. Fundamental models are built to simulate both short-term (*i.e.*, 1–3 month) and longer term (6-month+) price behavior in response to key fundamental variable forecasts. A cyclical model is applied in order to characterize the markets up or down trends, based on internal market price spread and momentum indicators. This model is overlaid onto the fundamental model in order to characterize the potential range and likely timing of a price adjustment.

Finally, owing to the market's extreme volatility, shorter-term technical indicators are utilized in order to characterize the potential threshold price levels and ranges likely to characterize a significant movement of prices. Extracting volatility estimates from option premiums is also helpful in characterizing shorter-term price ranges around the cyclical range of prices established through other modeling techniques. As power price volatility gets transmitted to gas markets, gas and power price relationships will become increasingly important, albeit on a highly seasonal basis.

POWER MARKET FUNDAMENTALS

Background

Electric power generation represents the final frontier in the U.S. energy sector's transition from regulation to competition. While the actual trading of electricity as a commodity is relatively recent, competitive U.S. power markets have been under development for more than 20 years. The Public Utilities Regulatory Policies Act of 1978 (PURPA) provided utilities and independent power producers (IPP) opportunities to experiment with competitive bidding for generating capacity, and established the IPP market. The Energy Policy Act of 1992 created a new type of unregulated power producer, the Exempt Wholesale Generator (EWG). FERC Orders 888 and 889, issued in 1996, facilitated competitive power trading at the wholesale level by mandating open access to the transmission grid. Currently, various legislative and regulatory initiatives at the state level are further shaping the market framework necessary for competition to flourish.

Prior to the emergence of competitive pricing for generation and retail services, regulators determined the prices charged by monopoly utilities operating in franchise service territories. Expected total costs for generation, transmission, distribution, and ancillary services were allocated to classes of customers, then divided by expected total class sales to compute a tariff structure. Cost-of-service regulation provided reliable power at generally reasonable prices for more than 60 years. However, legislative initiatives, technological innovations, and pressure from industrial consumers have resulted in a move from price regulation to competition. The appearance of short-lived price spikes over the last two summers, sometimes reaching thousands of dollars per megawatt hour (MWh), with generally lower prices over the balance of the year, dramatically illustrates that a new era of power pricing has indeed arrived. Competition is emerging in both the wholesale power generation and retail delivery stages of production. Most regions of the U.S. now have some measure of wholesale competition, allowing utilities and other load serving entities that provide power to end-use consumers to procure power on a competitive basis through marketers, or directly from other utility or IPP suppliers. A fully competitive wholesale market will provide the necessary framework to support retail competition, under which end-use consumers themselves can choose the load serving entities that will deliver their power. Interest in retail competition varies by region and is particularly strong in areas where retail prices are significantly higher than the national average (*e.g.*, California and New England). Retail competition is usually accompanied by new market structures to prevent anti-competitive practices.[19]

Power market structure

Figure 5–16 illustrates the key components of a competitive power market, organized by the three primary stages of production and delivery:

- generation

- transmission and trade

- distribution

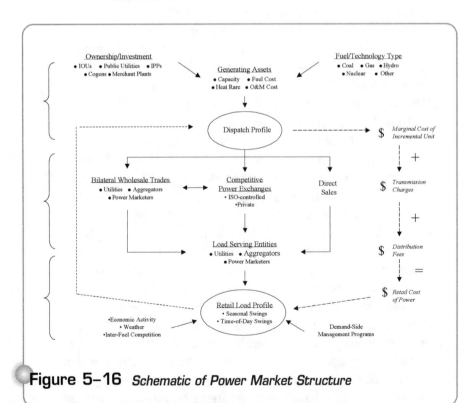

Figure 5–16 *Schematic of Power Market Structure*

The wholesale segment of the market covers sales of electricity to resellers—who in turn sell to retail or other wholesale customers—in-kind exchanges of electricity, and transmission and ancillary services needed to maintain system reliability and power quality. The retail market is where electricity is sold directly to residential, commercial, and industrial end-use customers. While the generation stage is generally considered the initial stage of the three primary stages of production and delivery, it is the transmission and trade stage that defines the regional nature of the U.S. power market structure.

Transmission and trade

An extensive system of high-voltage transmission lines is operated by the nation's larger utilities, serving as the backbone of electrical operations and allowing bulk power transfers between utilities. The bulk power system has evolved into three major networks—the interconnected Eastern, Western, and Texas power grids—that provide a partially unified network for the U.S., most of Canada, and part of Mexico. This basic layout of the domestic power grid and the presence of transmission constraints define key regional boundaries within U.S. power markets.

In 1965, a major blackout in the northeastern U.S. left New York City in the dark for almost two days. The Great Northeast Blackout, as it came to be known, gave rise to a renewed emphasis on power system reliability. The result was the formation of the North American Electric Reliability Council (NERC) and regional councils, of which there are now 10. Since these regional councils were designed to conform to the domestic transmission system, they form the boundaries of where competitive power markets will likely evolve, at least initially. The NERC regional councils are shown in Figure 5–17.

The volume of wholesale trade in the electric power industry, which was formerly limited by the absence of universal access to transmission capacity, has been increasing. This trend is reflected in Figure 5–18, which shows the rise in utility power

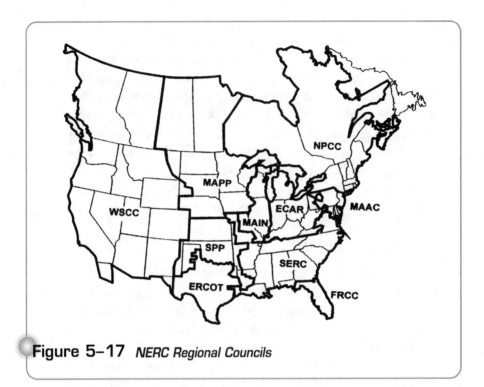

Figure 5–17 *NERC Regional Councils*

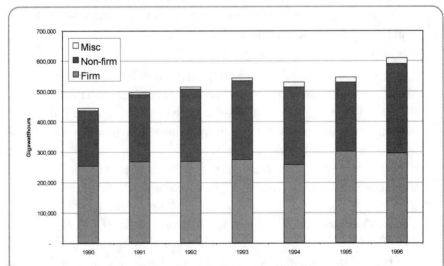

Figure 5–18 *U.S. Wholesale Trade (Utility Sales for Resale)*

Source: Energy Information Administration, *The Changing Structure of the Electric Power Industry: Selected Issues, 1998;* DOE/EIA–0562(98)

sales for resale. Both the volume of electricity changing hands and number of participants doing deals have grown since FERC mandated open access to transmission capacity. Approximately half of all electricity generated is purchased in the wholesale bulk power market before being sold to ultimate consumers.[20]

Wholesale transactions include (1) bilateral contracts, (2) spot market transactions, and (3) power exchanges, generally between vertically integrated utilities. Bilateral contracts are two-party contractual arrangements and can be on a wide variety of terms, ranging from "day ahead" or "balance of week" to "full requirements" deals. Spot market transactions are consummated off of organized exchanges like the California Power Exchange and the New England ISO exchange (ISO-NE), or "over-the-counter" through trading hubs such as Cinergy or Palo Verde. Competitive wholesale auctions of electricity occurred for the first time in the U.S. during 1998, in the California and PJM markets. Power exchanges involve in-kind trades of power when supply and demand conditions are mutually advantageous and reversible for the participants, commonly resulting from seasonal excess capacity or diversity in generating resource requirements.

To facilitate the development of fully competitive, non-discriminatory power markets, independent system operators (ISO) have been established in several regions of the U.S., and other domestic markets are in the process of developing them. There are currently three fully functional ISOs operating in the U.S. These are in California, PJM, and NEPOOL—renamed ISO-NE. New York's new ISO began operations on November 11, 1999. ERCOT has an ISO, but it does not yet provide a central market clearing function, nor does it control system operations. Rather, ERCOT's ISO is currently limited to a reliability oversight role.

The role of the ISO is to operate the competitive power system. On the basis of supplier bids, the ISO determines which plants will be dispatched and when. The ISO is also responsible for maintaining system integrity, so the operations of the ancillary services markets are under the management of the ISO. In the absence of specific federal mandates regarding market structure, regional U.S. power markets have some degree of freedom to experiment with the design of the institutions that are necessary to facilitate competition. Consequently, the new ISOs and the corresponding power markets operate under similar, but not identical, market rules. California, for example, requires all incumbent utilities to purchase their energy requirements through the market clearing mechanism, the Power Exchange. This prevents these utilities from engaging in bilateral, contractual deals other than the existing obligations they have under PURPA rules. On the other hand, PJM, ISO-NE, and New York have no such restrictions. Load serving entities in these regions may use either the spot market mechanism or contract privately for power supplies for resale.

Generation

As of January 1, 1998, the U.S. inventory of power plants consisted of 15,533 generating units with a net capacity of 778,513 megawatts (MW). While utilities have historically dominated the industry, and still control nearly 90% of capacity, nonutilities (IPPs and EWGs) have begun to play a more prominent role as the opening of the transmission system and the emergence of retail competition has encouraged wholesale trade (Fig. 5–19).

Since power cannot be cost-effectively stored, additional generating capacity must be engaged, or "dispatched," so that power supply and demand are balanced at all times as usage fluctuates over daily, seasonal, and annual intervals. Failure to maintain an exact and instantaneous match between supply and demand can have serious consequences, ranging from voltage instability (which can damage sensitive equipment) to widespread blackouts. An efficient power system will therefore maintain a generation portfolio with some "base load" stations that run almost all the time, "peaking" units that are only brought into service during the highest demand periods, and "shoulder" capacity to bridge the gap between base load and peaking units.

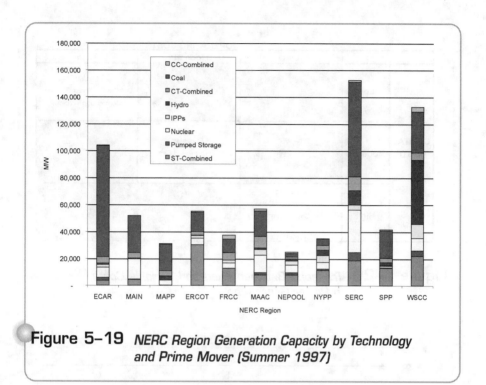

Figure 5–19 *NERC Region Generation Capacity by Technology and Prime Mover (Summer 1997)*

As illustrated in Figure 5–20, base load capacity should be highly efficient in terms of its variable costs because these plants run most of the time. These low variable costs usually require more expensive equipment, but the high relative hours of operation facilitate capital recovery. On the other hand, peakers sit idle for most of the year, so economic efficiency requires that the capital outlays for these machines be relatively low, resulting in higher variable costs of operations. Over the course of the day as well as seasonally, the price for power will rise and fall with changes in consumption, reflecting the changes in the cost characteristics of the power generating machines in use at the time. Figure 5–21 illustrates the stack of available generating capacity projected to be available in PJM in 2000. An overlay of sorted system demands—the load duration curve—shows the change in capacity requirements necessary to satisfy variations in demand.

CAPITAL COSTS		OPERATING COSTS		
		Low	Moderate	High
	Low			Peaker Old Gas/Oil Steam Turbines Combustion Turbines
	Moderate		Shoulder New Combined Cycle	
	High	Baseload New Combined Cycle Coal Steam Nuclear Hydroelectric		

Figure 5–20 *Tradeoffs Between Fixed and Variable Costs in Power Generation*

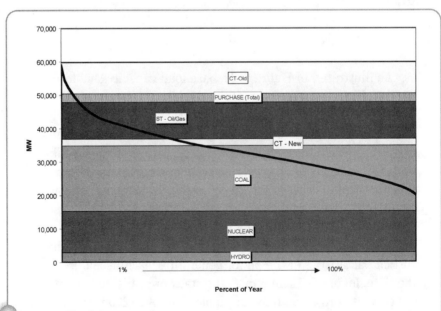

Figure 5–21 *Load Duration and Dispatch Queue in PJM (Year 2000)*

Pricing dynamics and drivers

Electricity production is a resource intensive endeavor. Power generation requires very expensive machinery, often costing hundreds of millions of dollars for a single power plant. The presence of high fixed costs, including both sunk capital recovery costs and "going forward" maintenance costs, in combination with high outage costs and the lack of long-term storage or suitable substitutes, create a potentially volatile pricing environment for electric power.

Since electric energy cannot be stored on a large scale, the availability of spare generating capacity (reserve margin) is a central determinant of price. The value of productive capacity from time to time depends on its availability and likely need. In surplus periods and during the off-season, this value may be low. During peak demand periods characterized by low reserve margins, prices may be quite volatile, effectively increasing the capacity value.

As a consequence, an economically efficient spot power market has a highly significant temporal component, *i.e.*, market prices must clear over relatively short time intervals, typically on an hourly basis in U.S. spot power markets. Also, suppliers are limited in how far they can transmit electricity, and the physical properties of power mean that "load pockets" frequently occur in metropolitan areas where demand exceeds the local supply of generating capacity. Therefore, power prices may periodically have a geographic attribute. This is giving rise to the development of zonal or nodal pricing schemes in the more established domestic spot power markets, notably California, PJM, NEPOOL, and NYPP.

As previously noted, low-operating-cost base load generating capacity is often not available in sufficient capacity to offset the more extreme daily and seasonal imbalances in electricity supply and demand. Indeed, it would not be economically prudent to meet all energy requirements with base load capacity, owing to unrecoverable fixed costs associated with a surplus capacity market. Available buffer capacity may be limited to typical seasonal and time-of-day swings in power demand in a given market area. In this event, the pricing process itself becomes a clearing mechanism for short-term supply-demand imbalances in the power market. A shortfall raises prices, coaxing additional, higher-priced generating capacity into production. When prices fall, generators may continue to operate, but at levels that just cover variable costs owing to the cost associated with ramping a plant up and down in a timely manner.

Due to the physical limitations to power storage, and the lack of ready substitutes, the cost of power interruptions or "unserved energy" can be very severe, especially for large commercial end-users and community services customers, including health, fire, and safety. Indeed, the cost of interruption may be as high as the opportunity cost of their productive or public services being shut down, including their associated damages exposure. As a result, the contractual penalties placed on firm power service contracts contribute to making power a commodity with a very volatile price if market events threaten to interrupt service.[21]

A rise in power prices reflects an underlying concern about the availability of sufficient capacity to meet load. Given the high penalties associated with unserved load, load-serving entities and power marketers with obligations to them have in the recent past taken any measures necessary to secure requisite power supply. This behavior has caused prices to be bid up very rapidly on signs of shortage. Indeed, the rush to "cover" one's position leads to further increases in power prices, whereby the value of capacity rises as a function of its perceived shortage. At critical points, namely when system-wide generation and transmission capacity approach full utilization, extreme price volatility may develop, as a shortage of supply forces prices upward to clear the market. Supply-induced volatility is reinforced by the relatively inelastic demand for power relative to other fuels, which customers can more easily find substitutes for.

Because of the relationships between fixed and variable costs and their relative impacts on power prices, competitive power prices are generally considered to have two components—an energy component and a capacity component. These terms are not very descriptive of the way power is sold in competitive spot markets, but refer to the two-part pricing mechanisms typically used in power purchase contracts. The energy part specifies a price to be paid for every megawatt-hour of power purchased, sometimes indexed to fuel prices, and is designed to compensate suppliers for their variable production costs. The capacity part specifies a fixed periodic fee to be paid for the right to buy power, usually within a given notification period, and is designed to compensate suppliers for their fixed costs, which are incurred even if no power is produced.[22]

The energy component of price

The energy component of price refers to the generation stage of production, and is determined by the short-run (*i.e.,* variable) marginal cost of production. In other words, the energy component of price is determined by the short-run variable operating costs of the last, most expensive, generating station dispatched.[23]

Power demand rises and falls over the course of the day, as well as seasonally. Figure 5–22 illustrates a typical daily pattern of power consumption. During the overnight period, particularly in the spring and fall when neither space heating nor cooling are required, demand for power is relatively low. Over the course of the day, lighting demand, appliance usage, and other residential end-uses increase, along with commercial and industrial applications of power. At day's end, consumption falls off again, and the cycle repeats itself. During summer months, as temperatures rise, power demand grows with the need for increased space cooling.

Consequently, the energy component of price rises and falls with a fairly predictable daily and seasonal pattern as power demand fluctuates. During the low demand, overnight periods, base load generating stations with very low variable costs—usually coal-fired, nuclear, and hydropower technologies—are prac-

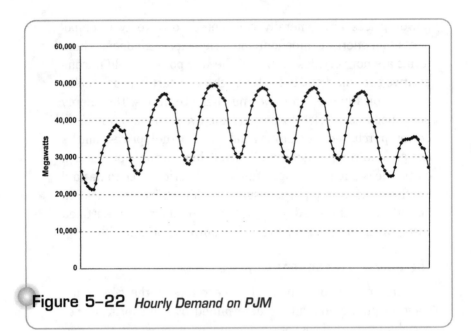

Figure 5-22 *Hourly Demand on PJM*

tically all that is needed to maintain an adequate instantaneous supply of electricity. However, as demand increases during the day, additional generators with higher operating costs are dispatched, resulting in higher short-run marginal costs and an increasing energy component of price. The opposite occurs as demand falls and the more expensive machines are shut down first, leaving progressively less expensive technologies on the margin setting prices, which fall accordingly.

THE CAPACITY COMPONENT OF PRICE

In a competitive market, the price for power should reflect the need for additional generating capacity. In the absence of effective price signals, potential suppliers will have no way of knowing that additional generating capacity is needed. More importantly, without high prices reflecting the need for more capacity, potential suppliers will have no incentive to build additional generators in competitive power markets.

Under equilibrium conditions, the revenues that incremental suppliers receive will provide a return on equity just equal to their opportunity cost. In other words, investors and developers will build new generating stations—incremental capacity—only if they expect to receive a fair return on their investment. If their returns exceed their cost of capital, they will continue to build until the price for power is driven low enough to eliminate the incentive for further additions to capacity. This means that power prices must reflect the current supply-demand balance.

The energy component alone is insufficient to either compensate incremental capacity or provide a strong signal regarding the status of supply relative to demand. While early results from competitive power markets indicate that prices will be based on short-run marginal costs—the energy component—most of the time, during the higher demand periods prices have been observed to rise above the variable costs of the last station dispatched. Figure 5–23 shows the rise and fall of representative average hourly prices in PJM resulting from the combination of the energy component and the capacity component. The observation that prices during the higher demand periods are too high to be explained by short-run variable costs alone suggests that a capacity component as defined here is occasionally present in competitive spot power prices.

The market drivers that characterize the capacity component of price are more difficult to define than those for the energy component. The instantaneous supply-demand balance indicates when the capacity component will become manifest, *i.e.*, as the supply of generating capacity approaches its limits, prices rise above short-run marginal costs. However, the magnitude of the expected capacity component is difficult to quantify in advance (Fig. 5–23).

There are four methods commonly used for estimating the capacity component of power prices, each with distinct advantages and shortcomings:

Capacity cost method. This approach adds the fixed costs of a simple-cycle combustion turbine machine, a proxy for pure

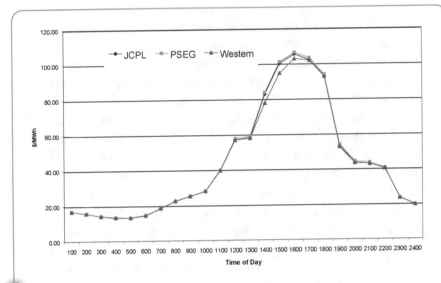

Figure 5–23 *Average Time of Day Prices in JCPL, PSEG, and Western Hub*

Data Source: PJM LMP (April 1999 – July 1999)

capacity, to the energy component of price. The idea is that the combustion turbine represents a no-frills cost for capacity, and adding its costs on top of the energy component provides cost recovery for new peakers. Under equilibrium conditions, incremental capacity required for system reliability, including peakers, should achieve full cost recovery.

While the pure capacity method is appealing in its simplicity, it has significant limitations in explaining both short- and long-run market price behavior. This is because there is no non-arbitrary way to allocate the peaker's costs across the hours of the year. Generating capacity is more highly valued during the higher demand periods, and capacity values change from year to year with changes in available supply resources. The capacity component of price should be the primary driver of higher prices during periods where capacity is in short supply, and should diminish or disappear when excessive development or mild weather creates an oversupply.

Furthermore, it is likely that incremental peakers will not be on the margin during all hours where they are running. Older simple cycle machines and inefficient early-model steam generators may sometimes be dispatched after the new peakers, creating opportunities for the new peakers to earn revenues above their variable costs even if there are no capacity values embedded in power prices. These additional revenues will provide some fixed cost recovery to incremental peakers, making it unnecessary for them to add their total fixed cost requirements to their bids.

Consumer value method. This is similar to the approach used in the United Kingdom (U.K.) spot market to calculate the capacity payment. It incorporates an estimate of the value that capacity provides to consumers—the value of lost load in the U.K. system. By quantifying the reduction in expected outages or unserved energy that results from each additional kilowatt of capacity and integrating an expected cost of outages, the consumer value of capacity can be estimated.

This calculation is designed to capture the value of capacity that is attributable to its contribution to reliable power and the value that consumers place on that reliability. Changes in the relationship between the supply of generating capacity and the demand for power alter the expected unserved energy and the probability of a loss of load. As these estimates of the likelihood and/or duration of outages change, the capacity component of price also varies, rising when supply is tight and falling to zero when there is little chance of an outage.

The practical application of the consumer cost method is complicated by the challenge of estimating the value of load losses—or cost of unserved energy—which is not directly observable and varies both over time and across customer classes. Empirical estimates of the value of lost load or the value of unserved energy vary widely and are affected by the type of customer, the timing and duration of service curtailment, and whether or not the curtailment is anticipated.

Equilibrium model method. A third approach to determine the capacity component of power prices is to simulate bidding strategies that result in an equilibrium solution using production-costing models. For example, base load generators—hydropower, nuclear, and coal-fired—would likely bid their variable costs only since there is intense competition for dispatch at this very low portion of the dispatch queue. As demand on the system grows, and a larger percentage of total generating capacity is brought on-line, competition for dispatch time is limited to a smaller number of available suppliers. At some point, the reduced level of competition allows generators to bid some of their fixed costs into the market. During the very highest demand periods, when there are very few uncommitted generators, those who still have available capacity are able to command very high prices. By simulating the operations of a power market with bidding strategies assigned accordingly, peak period bids can then be adjusted to determine where an equilibrium solution is achieved.[24]

Options pricing method. Owners of capacity, or holders of capacity rights, can be viewed as holding the "real" option to call upon that asset to generate power if market conditions are favorable for them to do so (*i.e.,* their capacity is "in the money"). This approach exploits that similarity by applying valuation formulas similar to those used to price conventional financial options. While the options perspective is useful for identifying determinants of capacity value, standard option pricing methods such as the Black-Scholes model must be carefully calibrated to account for unique features of power price probability distributions.[25]

Power summary

Electric power cannot be stored, it is subject to transportation restrictions, and it is a highly valuable commodity with no readily available substitutes. In combination, these attributes give power unique price characteristics, including the potential for extreme volatility.

The energy component of price, based on the short-run marginal production costs, varies within a relatively narrow band as demand for power rises and falls over the course of the day and by the seasons of the year. On the other hand, the capacity component can exhibit extreme volatility and is highly dependent on the supply of generating capacity relative to the demand for power. A tight supply of generating capacity gives rise to higher prices, and a very tight supply can result in price spikes into the thousands of dollars per megawatt-hour.

Limitations on transporting power mean that the U.S. is divided into regional power markets, each with its own characteristics. Regional characteristics are defined by the regional supply-demand balance, as well as the regional mix of generating capacity types, as defined by fuel and technology, and the limitations on moving power into or out of the particular market area.

Power traders and marketers must be intimately familiar with the region in which they strike deals, possessing a fundamental understanding of supply resources and potential weather-related demand impacts. Price forecasting tools must be used with care because the standard models for pricing commodities, such as the Black-Scholes model, may not capture power's unique price characteristics. Prudent restrictions on trading parameters such as "value at risk" limits must be carefully determined. While price volatility may indeed offer greater profit opportunities, it comes with a substantial increase in risk.

Notes

1. "Bark" spreads refer to the price of primary raw paper products relative to energy prices, so that a unit of energy's price is tied to the value of the intermediate paper product manufactured. "Spark" spreads are calculated as the difference between wholesale power prices and delivered fuel prices, with fuel prices converted to a $/MWh value on the basis of a specified heat rate (*i.e.*, MMBtu/MWh). "Arc" spreads represent the spread between energy prices delivered to a furnace (for raw metals production) and the value of the intermediate metals product output.

2. A common approach is to express commodity price movements as the dependent variable within a multi-variable regression equation. This equation is subject to a "best fit" to historical prices and evaluated for its explanatory power on an overall and variable-specific basis. Such econometric relationships must be updated regularly in order to adapt to new market dynamics, and foresight is required to anticipate how future price relationships will differ from past patterns.

3. Inflation and interest rates will also exert a long-term impact on oil prices, primarily through their influence on exploration and infrastructure development, but have very little influence in the short term. More immediate effects result from fluctuation in the strength of the dollar relative to other currencies, as oil is priced in U.S. dollar terms globally, so that a rising dollar tends to encourage incremental output, while dampening demand.

4. The notion of "primary petroleum supply" avoids double counting of crude oil that is subsequently converted into finished products in domestic refineries.

5. Furthermore, over half of net product imports were miscellaneous products such as asphalt, gasoline blending com-

ponents, naphtha, unfinished oils, and waxes. Net imports of motor gasoline and distillate fuel are a relatively small, yet still important, marginal component of the overall supply pool.

6. Including Iraq's reported (extra-quota) production of 2.5 MMB/D, OPEC output averages around 27 MMB/D.

7. Starting from a base level of approximately 28 MMBD (including Iraqi production), in March 1998, OPEC voted to reduce output by 1.245 MMBD effective April 1998, by 1.355 MMBD effective July 1998, and by 1.7 MMBD effective April 1999. A number of non-OPEC producers also announced output cuts during that period, including Mexico, Norway, Oman, and Yemen.

8. Combined with the expected growth in U.S. oil demand, the decline in U.S. production implies continued increases in U.S. oil imports.

9. The crack spread is measured as the wholesale market price or weighted average grouping of one or more refined products relative to the price of crude oil, expressed in $/barrel. Thus, if the wholesale price of heating oil equals $0.40/gallon (*i.e.*, $16.80/barrel at 42 gallons per barrel), and the price of crude oil equals $12.00/barrel), then the 1:1 heating oil crack spread is $4.80/barrel.

10. In the case of crude oil, daily consumption, is given by refinery inputs, while for refined products, apparent consumption is given by disappearance of supply, measured as domestic production plus net imports minus change in primary inventories. Thus, a reduction in inventory levels from one week to another is taken as an increase in apparent consumption or "disappearance."

11. A common limitation of these measures is that they are exclusively backward looking and do not incorporate any information that might alter the relationship between future and historical stock levels.

12. Secondary inventories refer typically to petroleum product stocks held in the distribution infrastructure, downstream of the refinery and major pipelines, but prior to end-user (*i.e.,* tertiary) storage. Bulk storage terminals and distributor-owned or leased terminals account for most of the secondary storage capacity.

13. Prices are also quoted for numerous other zones by trade publications such as *Gas Daily* and *Inside FERC*.

14. Liquified natural gas (LNG) is imported into the Northeast U.S. by Cabot Corporation, with storage in Everett, Massachusetts; by Panhandle Eastern into Lake Charles, Louisiana; and recently by Columbia Energy into Cove Point, Maryland. Additionally, the Elba Island, Georgia, terminal has been converted to receive LNG. However, the volume of LNG is quite small and typically is used for peaking requirements, as its delivered costs are normally higher than indigenous natural gas.

15. Heating degree days (HDD) are the number of degrees per day that the daily average temperature is below 65° F. Cooling degree days (CDD) are the number of degrees per day that the daily average temperature is above 65° F. High degree days (either HDD or CDD) generally lead to higher energy consumption.

16. The term "days supply" should not be taken literally, since a certain amount of "working gas" is required to maintain delivery pressure and is therefore not available for consumption. However, this indicator does capture how inventories compare to demand in a relative sense. Note that use of weekly rather than monthly data would highlight price dynamics more effectively.

17. The major new systems from Canada include the expansion of the Trans Canada line and the new Alliance pipeline into the U.S. Midwest.

18. A heat rate of 7,000 Btu/Kwh, corresponding to a new combined-cycle plant, was utilized to convert gas prices from

$/MMBtu to $/Mwh. Alternative heat rate assumptions will shift the spark spread profile down or up, but not alter the degree of volatility.

19. For example, utilities that choose to stay in the "wires business," providing distribution services directly to customers, are often required to divest their generating capacity to avoid the possibility of unfair self-dealing.

20. The actual increase in wholesale transactions is greater than these data suggest since it does not include broker/dealer transactions.

21. Firm contract obligations in power distinguish between firm physical supply, which means that the suppler must demonstrate access to available generating capacity, hence allowing the ability to deliver physical power, vs. firm financial supply, which means that the supplier will honor the financial obligations to the other side of its transaction (i.e., make the other side financially whole) in the event that it cannot fulfill its physical supply obligations.

22. Of course, whether costs are variable or fixed depends on a time reference. Over the very short term, the next hour perhaps, only the cost of fuel and a very little bit of mechanical wear and tear are variable. All other costs are fixed. In the very long term, say more than 50 years, the capital costs of the plants themselves may be considered to be variable. For the purposes of spot power pricing, the very short-term definition is most appropriate.

23. Technically, the energy component of price is determined by short-run "incremental," rather than marginal, production costs. Marginal costs are "at the margin," having no size or volume consideration, while incremental costs are constrained by the capacity of the last dispatched generating station or the size of the capacity block that is bid into the market. Incremental and marginal costs are not equivalent because the cost to produce power is not constant over the entire range of a generating station's potential output.

24. Results from this method are entirely consistent with the previous approaches using the estimates of the value of lost load and loss of load probability. At the lower demand levels, the loss of load probability approaches zero and the capacity component of price should therefore also be zero. This means that prices are equal to the energy component, so base load units are expected to bid their variable costs only. At the very highest demand periods, when there are very few uncommitted generators, those who still have available capacity are able to command very high prices. Again, this is entirely consistent with the loss of load probability approach because the loss of load probability becomes quite high as the available supply of capacity reaches its limit, resulting in a high capacity component of price.

25. The Black-Scholes model infers a log normal probability density function. Power prices exhibit this property to a degree, but exhibit much more of a "leptokurdic" (fat tail) probability density function. A leptokurdic distribution means that power price fluctuations are typical for commodities up to a point, but with electricity there exists a possibility that prices will "roar up" under certain conditions. This is not just theory, as such events occurred during the summers of both 1999 and 1998 in the Midwest and parts of the East Coast. With the confluence of extreme weather conditions, unexpected plant outages, and limitations on transmission capability, prices for power skyrocketed from the usual $40 to $50/MWh into the thousands of dollars per MWh.

AN INTRODUCTION TO TECHNICAL ANALYSIS

by **Bruce Kamich**

The use of technical analysis in the investment decision-making process has grown. It is more commonplace in the equity arena as sophisticated investors often have a charting package or get input from sell-side firms. In the area of commodity trading, including energy and power, because of the fast moves and leverage involved, it is rare to find a trader who does not refer to the charts or various technical indicators before entering or exiting a trade. Even old-line bond firms will pay some attention to charts. Despite its use upstairs in trading rooms or down in the pits, there remain critics of and misunderstandings about technical analysis.

There are several definitions of technical analysis but the best one is found in the Constitution of the Market Technicians Association:

> *Technical analysis is the study of data generated by the action of markets and by the behavior and psychology of market participants and observers. Such study is usually applied to estimating the probabilities for the future course of prices for a market, investment or speculation by interpreting the data in the context of precedent.*

"Fundamental analysis" is concerned with the company—and its sales, earnings, products, management, etc.—or the commodity or other asset. "Technical analysis" is concerned only with the stock of the company and the changes in the supply/demand relationship for that stock, commodity, or other instruments in the market place.

There are many factors that surround and affect financial markets. Economic factors including recession, expansion, inflation, deflation, etc., always surround the markets. Fundamental factors such as supply, demand, substitutes, exports, imports, etc. will affect prices. There are factors that cannot be quantified, such as political factors—which party is in power? Sociological factors and psychological factors such as riots and problems in Washington, D.C. also affect markets. Lastly, technical factors also surround and affect the markets—price, volume, and in the case of futures markets, open interest. These are the statistics produced by the market place—and the area with which technical analysts are concerned.

There are a few basic assumptions one should accept to support the technical approach. First, market action or prices discount "everything." Said another way: the markets are barometers rather than thermometers. "Buy on the rumor and sell on the news" is one of the oldest sayings on Wall Street and symbolizes the discounting mechanism. Just as old is the saying, "The news follows the tape." There are plenty of examples in which the market will rally ahead of bullish news or decline before bearish news is announced.

Second, prices move in trends. Before these trends are established technicians believe markets go through a period of accumulation—making a base before an uptrend is established and a period of distribution marking a top before declining. Third, technicians believe that history tends to repeat itself due to the understanding that basic human nature remains unchanged through the years. Lastly, technicians have observed that market movements usually have a relationship to one another. Small consolidations are usually followed by short-term moves and larger consolidations can produce larger moves.

THE HISTORY OF TECHNICAL ANALYSIS

Technical applications in the U.S. can be traced back to the 1880s with the development of the Dow theory. Charles H. Dow published the first stock market average on July 3, 1884—consisting of 11 stocks, of which nine were railroads. The average was not split into industrials and rails until 1897. Point and figure charting seems to have begun around the turn of the century. *The Game in Wall Street and How to Play it Successfully*— apparently, the first book on point and figure—was published in 1898. Bar charting appears to have become popular in the 1910s according to copyrights. Indicators like the Advance-Decline Line have their origin in the 1920s. The Barron's Confidence Index dates back to 1932. However, books on fundamental security analysis became more numerous only after the Securities and Exchange Commission Acts of 1932 and 1933. *Security Analysis* by Graham and Dodd did not appear until 1934!

In Japan, candlestick charts date back to the mid 1700s with the writings of Munehisa Homma, a wealthy rice trader. Homma's trading principles in the rice market evolved into the "candlestick method" used in Japan. Students of the Japanese markets often read about Sakata's Rules, which actually refer to Homma (who lived in the port city of Sakata).

Several approaches to charting have developed over the years and each approach has its own features, benefits, and drawbacks. These approaches include line charts, bar or vertical bar charts, point and figure, candlesticks, market profile, and others.

Line charts are very easy to construct and still have a place among today's sophisticated electronic and digital approaches. Line charts are best used to track a single statistic, which can be a price or an economic release. This could be a daily price "fixing" for a cash commodity or a weekly data point like API stocks or even a monthly economic release like housing starts or industrial production. If available, volume can be shown along the bottom, and moving averages can be added. Trendlines can be drawn to illustrate and identify the trend. Line charts are often found in periodicals and can quickly show a trend that would be hard to discern from a table of data.

Barcharts. While a line chart only requires one data point per day—week or month—a bar chart or vertical bar chart needs three pieces of information—high, low, and close. Because the bar chart shows the range of trading it displays more information. Traders can look at bar charts across a range of time frames. Day traders with an on-line charting system can look at 1-, 5-, 15-, 30-, and 60-minute bar charts—really, any time frame. Short-term traders can construct daily bar charts and position traders may look at weekly and monthly charts for major price moves. Both line and bar charts can be used with volume and open interest plotted at the bottom to confirm and support pattern recognition and potential reversals.

Bar chart patterns cover a wide spectrum, so putting them into categories is the best way to understand them. When grouped into major tops and bottoms, continuation patterns, reversal patterns, and gaps, these patterns are easier to grasp.

Major tops and bottoms. Major patterns that mark the beginning of a significant markup or rally—or the start of a decline—should take several months to unfold. These patterns are reversals of major trends. While the "head and shoulders top pattern" might be the best known chart pattern, let us first examine *double tops and bottoms*—two patterns more likely found and generally easier to identify.

Double tops and bottoms are often compared to M or W patterns. After a significant rally, the price of the stock or commodity reaches a level where there is enough supply put on the market to stop the advance and to start a downward reaction. The market pulls back—at least 5% from the peak—until bargain hunters or short-term traders and others begin to buy the stock or commodity. The market then rallies back to the first high where sellers who did not liquidate on the first move now take the opportunity to sell. This creates the second peak of the double top. Supply again appears in addition to the liquidation by the longs and prices decline back through the previous reaction low. Volume is usually heavy around one or both peaks. The distance—points—traveled between the reaction low and the twin peaks can be projected down from the reaction low to determine a price objective. Double tops—and bottoms are the inverse—may not top exactly at the prior high, but experience suggests one should look for a second peak anywhere from 1 to 2% below the first peak to 1 to 2% above the first peak.

Another major pattern is a variation on a double top. *Triple tops*—and bottoms—will involve the same market action and volume characteristics but a third peak or bottom will be formed. (Sometimes the stock or commodity will hesitate a while after the double top or bottom and the price action may resemble a platform.) In addition to double and triple tops and bottoms there are also saucer and line patterns. *Saucer patterns* are rounded turns. Prices curve gradually upward in a bottom or downward in a top. Volume declines until the turning point of the pattern, then builds and is often heavy when the market breaks out. A *line pattern* is similar to a saucer except prices hold in a narrow range and volume is low until the breakout.

The famous *head and shoulders top pattern* does resemble the real thing. It can be easily described as a triple top where the second rally reaches a higher point than the other two peaks. The smaller third peak is the early warning sign that the uptrend may have come to an end. The volume on the first peak—or "left shoulder"—should be the heaviest. The reaction should be on light volume followed by a second rally on good volume, but less than the first advance. This rally carries to a new high but another reaction sets in, but holds around the first low. The third rally stops short of the second peak on still lighter volume and prices begin to retreat again.

When the price breaks below the two prior lows, the decline should see an increase in volume, as the top pattern should be evident to more traders. The inverse applies to bottoms, but volume builds through the base instead of diminishing. Sometimes a brief return move occurs after the neckline is broken. Prices rebound—or pull back—to the neckline and then resume their trend.

Variations of this pattern or a complex head and shoulders might also be found. These complex patterns might have two left shoulders or two right shoulders or both, or even two heads—a double top within the pattern. Head and shoulders patterns also give us a price measurement using the distance traveled from the peak of the head to the "neckline" connecting the two lows. This distance is projected down or up from the "neckline" for an initial objective. If the decline or rally passes this objective you can double the first target.

Continuation patterns are just that. They describe patterns normally seen as prices and continue in the same direction established before the pattern formed. These include rectangles, triangles, coils, wedges, flags, and pennants.

Rectangles (or boxes) occur over several weeks when the market is trapped between equally strong support and resistance levels or zones. The market eventually breaks out from the pattern, usually in the direction of the preceding trend.

Triangles will also form over a period of weeks and can take three basic shapes: ascending (or bullish), descending (or bearish), and equilateral. A bullish triangle is usually formed in an uptrend. Prices rise to a level where buying dries up, profit taking develops, or strong supply is encountered. A reaction develops until new buying is encountered. A rally back to the first peak develops and fails again. Fresh buying interest develops, but at a slightly higher level than before. This continues with supply being encountered near the same level and demand becoming more aggressive, until eventually prices break out on the upside. Volume usually diminishes through the formation, but should expand on the breakout.

A descending—or bearish—triangle is the opposite of the bullish pattern. Prices find a lower support line, with offers to sell becoming more aggressive until a downward breakout. In an equilateral—or symmetrical—triangle one sees the peaks and dips converge to an apex with a balance of supply and demand. The equilateral triangle can appear in a bull or bear phase and can break out in either direction; however, they usually continue the trend in force. A closer examination of the consolidation area on a point and figure chart can often give one a clearer warning of the direction of the breakout. Even candlestick charts may reveal clues on the direction of the breakout through an examination of the upper or lower shadows.

With all triangles, the length of the move from the first peak to the first low can be used as a price target from the breakout.

Coils are a sub-category of triangles. They look like flatter equilateral triangles that get closer to the apex of their formation.

Wedges come in two varieties. Falling wedges usually appear in up-trends, and rising wedges are usually seen in downtrends, often at the end of a decline. Rising wedges might be seen within a double bottom pattern. Volume tends to diminish through the wedge. Prices often get close to the apex of the pattern and then sharply correct all or most of the rally. Falling wedges are usually seen near tops, and the volume also diminishes through the pattern. With rising wedges, the market does not quickly rally to the prior high but tends to slowly firm up or make a saucer pattern.

Flags and *pennants* are short-term continuation patterns that last a few days. Flags take the shape of a parallelogram slanting downward for bull or up flags and drifting upward for bear or down flags. A flag begins with a sharp runup for a day or two on good volume. The market then drifts sideways to lower as traders take profits. Volume is lighter than on the pole. The market corrects the rally of the pole in a back and forth pattern, and eventually breaks out again to resume the trend with volume expanding. The reverse image occurs in a downtrend, with the flag drifting upward as short covering occurs.

Pennants develop just like flags except that prices form a triangular shape with a better balance between supply and demand. Bullish—or "up"—pennants look just like bearish—or "down"—pennants. Volume is stronger on the pole into the pattern and is lower during the body of the pennant.

Still shorter patterns include *reversal days.* Key reversal days can occur at tops and bottoms. At a top the market has been rising for some time. On a reversal day or key reversal day, prices push up to a new high for the move up, but they run into heavy selling. The market drops, closing down on the day and usually weak, near the lows of the session. Volume tends to be heavy, and ideally sentiment should even have reversed from bullish to bearish. The key reversal at a low or bottom is sometimes easier to identify. Tops can sometimes go unnoticed, but at bottoms the news is often bearish, and tired bulls finally throw in the towel and dump their positions. News stories about liquidation selling are easier to spot for some reason than stories about short covering at a top.

Reversals may also occur over two days. Two-day reversals involve a high start with a strong close near the highs of the day—perhaps at a new high for the move during day one. On day two, the market opens nearly unchanged, seeming to indicate no real follow-through buying from day one. Then prices retreat during the day to close weak—retracing most of the prior day's gains. Over the two-day period, sentiment tends to switch sharply from bullish to bearish. The mirror image can be seen at bottoms—a weak close followed by a strong close.

One short-term trading tool that implies a reversal is the "close below the low of the high day." The reverse also works at bottoms—"a close above the high of the low day." A high is made on day one. On day two the market does not exceed day one's high and closes below the low of day one. Another short-term tool used by some floor traders is to buy the first up day after a string of declines. This tool is very subjective in its application. What is a string of declines—four days? Five? Six days down? Does it need to be a sharp correction? One needs to examine the actual market involved to see how well this works. Outside days and higher closes and outside days with lower closes also act like a two-day reversal pattern. Sometimes these outside days will also be bullish and bearish engulfing patterns when looking at candlestick charts.

Gaps or *price voids* can occur in trading, and some of these gaps can tell you a lot about the strength of the market. There are common gaps that can occur in a trading range of an inactive stock or instrument that is thinly traded, so a large order can cause a wide swing. Common gaps should be used with caution because they usually do not occur because of a shift in supply or demand. Breakaway gaps generally occur after a pattern has been completed and prices break away on expanding volume as the market reacts to some unexpected or overnight news. A runaway or measuring gap can occur after a move has begun. This gap can mean more traders are jumping on the trend. Sometimes these gaps appear in the middle of a major advance, thus the length of the first advance to the gap can be projected upward for a target for the second advance after the gap begins. An exhaustion gap is easy to identify because it is usually close to the end of an advance or decline, and prices soon retreat or bounce to fill the gap.

Constructing point and figure charts

With line and bar charts, time is indicated along the x-axis of the chart. This is one of the big differences between these charts and point and figure charts. Point and figure charts are simpler as they are only updated when price movement of a certain magnitude occurs. Time and volume do not appear on point and figure charts, but some practitioners allow for time by putting in MTWTF(riday) for the first daily entry of active markets or JFMAMJJASOND(ecember) for less frequent updates.

The price level of the stock or commodity and the volatility will influence the number of price reversals in a given period of time. Point and figure devotees contend this method of charting is the most logical and organized way of recording supply and demand. Because doing point and figure charts properly can be time intensive, it has a relatively small following. Techniques like point and figure fell out of favor in the 1950s and 1960s, but individuals like A.W. Cohen, Michael Burke, Alan Shaw, Anthony Tabell, and Thomas Dorsey have kept it alive and demonstrated its value. Though point and figure was originally used to follow individual stocks and commodities, it has been applied to market averages and indexes, indicators, and industry sectors.

Constructing a three-point reversal chart is commonly done using Xs for the entries—some prefer to use Xs for upticks and Os for downticks. Starting at the left side of the chart, a first X corresponds to the current price of the stock or commodity. If the commodity (such as crude oil) moves up one full dollar, a second X is entered in the next-higher box in the same column. This continues as the commodity trades. A reversal to the downside would need the commodity to decline at least $3 (hence the 3-point reversal). A reversal earns an O in the next column to the right, one box below the last "up X."

Various adjustments need to be made to successfully use point and figure charts. Low priced stocks (under $20) and commodities that might be temporarily depressed in price may be plotted better with smaller increments like a $1/2$ point or 50 cents. High-priced stocks (those more than $100) and high-priced commodities with wide swings could use $5 as a minimum increment. In the 1979-80 bull market in precious metals, even larger price increments made sense. Increment and reversal size can also vary with one's trading horizon. Day traders and floor traders will use smaller box sizes as they try to capitalize on smaller intra-day moves. The "count" (or price objective) draws its pattern from the extent of the lateral consolidation. The larger the price base, the bigger the rally, and the larger the top formation, the greater the correction to the downside. The "count" is often made by counting the number of Xs in the pattern that occurs along the price level with the most activity. This count is added to the base to reach a target.

Patterns also exist in point and figure charting and they have descriptive names. Some names are similar to bar charts—head and shoulders, saucers, and V tops and bottoms.

Others are called fulcrums, compound fulcrums, and delayed endings.

Candlestick charting

Japanese candle charts are that country's most popular technical analysis method. They are so named because the lines resemble candles. While traditional bar charts require just three pieces of information—high, low, and close—a candlestick chart needs four pieces of information: the high, low, close, and the opening. The price action is shown on a vertical line with a box— or real body—that shows the relationship between the open and close. If the opening is higher than the close then the real body is colored black and is bearish. If the close is higher than the opening the bulls are in charge and the box is white or empty. The highs and lows—if they extend beyond the open and close— are called the upper and lower shadows.

Candlestick lines can be drawn for all time frames. An hourly candle chart uses the open, high, low, and close for each 60-minute period. A weekly chart uses Monday's open, Friday's close, and the high/low range for the week. Because the real body is open or colored, one can quickly see if the bulls are in charge—a white or empty real body—or the bears, with a black real body. Some candles have no bodies. This is where the open and the close are the same or nearly the same. These are called doji and represent indecision—a market that is losing its breadth, or one that is getting tired.

There are 50 or 60 patterns of 1, 2, or 3 candles, but much can be learned from a single candle line. Some candles and patterns have Japanese names.

A *long opening bozu black line* occurs when the market makes its high on the open and closes much lower. This line is also called by a sumo wrestling term, yorikiri. The height and color of the real body can quickly tell you who is in charge—the bull or the bear. Though the real body is the most important part of the candle pattern, the length and position of the shadows is also important. A long lower shadow shows how a market has rejected the lower prices and a long upper shadow shows how higher prices have been rejected. Shooting stars, hammers, hanging man, and doji are examples of one-bar patterns. Bullish and bearish *engulfing patterns* and *dark cloud covers* are two-bar patterns, while morning stars and evening stars are three-bar patterns.

Candle gaps are called *windows*. A *down gap* is a falling window and an *up gap* is a rising window. Windows can act as support or resistance until there is a close below or above the window.

Candles should be used in conjunction with other techniques. They mostly mark reversals and do not give you price projections. Bar charts or point and figure charts are needed for objectives other than old support and resistance levels. Trendlines and moving averages can also be added. Reversals, where moving averages are turning, can convince one to add to positions.

Market profile

In the mid 1980s, a trader on the floor of the Chicago Board of Trade, J. Peter Steidlmayer, developed an approach to the markets called market profile. A profile chart is created from 30-minute ranges of the price action plotted on a vertical scale. Letters—A, B, C, etc.—denote each period. In subsequent periods new highs and lows are reflected in letters in the far-left vertical extremes of the chart. If prices overlap prior periods, the letters are placed to the right of these previous strikes. A bell-shaped pattern tends to develop for markets that are consolidating. The pattern will be skewed when a trend develops. A market profile has a set of rules to apply to actual trading, which lends itself to two approaches— picking tops and bottoms or buying and selling breaks.

Volume and open interest

Nearly all technicians follow volume and consider it important. Many futures traders consider open interest important, as well. Volume is the turnover or the number of contracts traded, while open interest is the number of outstanding or open contracts—the total longs or shorts but not both added together. Official volume and open interest data are reported a day late with futures, but electronic trading could change that in the near future. Open interest will display some seasonality—a tendency that can be found by looking at the average of the past five years or longer. Analysts need to look at changes in open interest vs. the average. A simple table is the best way to see the interplay of volume, open interest, and prices.

Prices	*Volume*	*Open Interest*	*Market*
rising	up	up	strong
rising	down	down	weak
declining	up	up	weak
declining	down	down	strong

A strong up market is one in which prices are rising along with volume and open interest—more participants are coming into the market. Volume can be used to confirm the price patterns discussed in the earlier section on bar charting.

Moving Averages. Moving averages are widely used in the commodity arena. Moving averages are just a mathematical trendline, a smoothing device. They can be calculated over any time period using three types: simple, weighted, and exponential. Besides moving averages of price, some analysts smooth out volume data with moving averages.

All entries are treated equally with a *simple moving average*—the most common. One adds up the number of days under question and divides by the number of days. To "move" the average, a new item is added and the first one is subtracted. Averaging the data smoothes out the line and makes it easier to view the trend. Random variations and erratic price changes tend to cancel out and a general underlying trend becomes visible.

Moving averages by definition lag the market. A short moving average will be more volatile than a longer one. Traders often average the closing prices or settlement prices, but averages of the highs or lows are also done in downtrends and uptrends. Some prefer to use a price band of two moving averages of the highs and lows separately. Others use a midpoint value of the day's range divided by two. A crossover of the commodity's moving average identifies changes in the commodity or index trend. This procedure can reduce the subjectivity of looking at patterns. A flattening of the moving average can be a sign of a change in trend.

Moving averages can be set for any time span but should make some logical sense. With commodities, this can be a 200-day moving average—this was the annual silver inventory required by Kodak. A 4-month moving average on soybean oil makes sense because it is the shelf life of margarine, according to Lever Bros. Fidelity Investments uses a 21-day moving average—the number of business days in a month. Five-day, 21-day, 13-week, 26-, and 52-week average make sense for a lot of economic data that may be released weekly, monthly, quarterly, or annually. The 200-day moving average is very popular with equities and fixed income securities. In the early 1960s, Joseph E. Granville listed eight basic rules for using the 200-day moving average.

Some argue that simple moving averages are inadequate and believe a heavier weight should be given to the recent prices. *Weighted* and *exponential moving averages* put more weight or emphasis on the more recent price data. There are many ways to weight the days. A 5-day weighted moving average would be constructed by taking the current day and multiplying it by 5, the day before by 4, and so on. The final sum is divided by 15 (5 + 4 + 3 + 2 + 1).

The exponential moving average (EMA) is a quick way to get a form of a weighted moving average. Today's price and the prior day's EMA are utilized. One first must determine a smoothing constant to use in the daily calculation—divide the number 2 by 1 plus the number of days to be smoothed. For a 10-day EMA, 2 is divided by 10+1 (11) to get 2/11=.18. One multiplies the constant by each day's closing price minus the prior day's EMA and then added to the prior day's EMA to result in the new EMA.

Using moving averages

A trader can use one moving average or two (10 and 40-day) or more averages (4, 9, 18-day system). We noted earlier that a crossover of the average could identify changes in the trend of the commodity by the commodity. A declining market is signaled when the market moves below its moving average. Traders who use moving averages contend they are fairly reliable, but their success depends a lot on the moving average selected. Keep in mind that the moving average tends to act as support and resistance. The commodity will tend to find support at the moving average in a rally and resistance in a decline.

Breaking a moving average warns that a change in trend may have occurred. Like other things in technical analysis, the longer the moving average the more significant a crossover signal when the moving average is broken. Breaking a 200-day moving average is more important than breaking a 40-day average. Using two or more moving averages tends to reduce whipsaws. Trading signals are given when the shorter average moves below the longer one and the longer one is declining. This would be a strong sign that the trend was down. An uptrend would be signaled when the shorter average moved above the longer and both averages were rising. The signals (by definition) occur after the peak or bottom in prices and will be more of a confirming indicator. Other indicators can be watched to reduce whipsaws in broad sideways markets.

Sentiment

Sentiment indicators are a useful tool to technicians and traders. They can be used to determine a consensus or majority opinion from which a contrary market position can be taken. If 70, 80, or 90% of traders are bullish on a market and have taken positions, who else is left to enter? When sentiment gets to a bullish or bearish extreme it often can mark a turning point.

In the equity market there are many measures of sentiment. The NYSE members' short index, public specialists' ratio, the short interest ratio, insider trading figures, mutual fund cash levels, margin debt, and advisory services are some. In the futures markets, we can only make use of three surveys of advisory services for what people are saying and *The Commitment of Traders (COT) Report* and put/call ratios for what people are doing. Market Vane, Consensus Inc., and MBH Commodities compile sentiment numbers. Calculating a four-week moving average can smooth the weekly numbers out. Low readings on the four-week moving average often coincide with market lows, and high readings with tops.

The best way to use this tool is to wait for a turn in sentiment as high or low readings can persist for a while. With on-line trading quickly becoming the norm, new sentiment surveys may be forthcoming from the Internet—*e.g.,* a ratio of market orders to limit orders could be tracked on-line to create a different kind of put/call ratio.

The Commitment of Traders Report is published and used by the CFTC to monitor market positioning. *The COT Report* breaks down open interest for commercial longs and shorts, non-commercial longs and shorts, and small trader longs and shorts. *The COT Report* groups information weekly, but the report is only released every other Friday. One way to use *The COT Report* is to generate buy and sell signals based on historical patterns. Looking at the history of the data has shown that commercials are right more often than non-commercial traders, especially at major turning points. It is also smart to see how commercials react to the markets that are rallying. For example, the rally in energy prices during 1995 and 1996 found commercials buy on any pullbacks and even buying on strength during the early stages of new rallies.

Put/call ratios (p/c ratios) are another useful way to indicate when traders are too bullish or too bearish. There are many ways analysts have worked with option data, but the simple approaches are often the best. The p/c ratio is calculated on a daily basis by taking the total volume of put options divided by the total volume of call options. The p/c ratio is used as a contrary indicator—*i.e.,* a high p/c ratio signals excessive pessimism among traders and investors. The best signals generated by the p/c ratio are not by day-to-day fluctuations, but when the ratio registers extreme readings. To smooth out the peaks and troughs, we like to use a 10-day moving average of the daily p/c ratio. Readings above 1.2 on the 10-day moving average indicates a strong bearish market sentiment, whereas a ratio below .8 indicates a strong bullish sentiment.

LOOKING AHEAD TO THE FUTURE:
NEURAL NETWORKS ENABLE WEIGHTING OF MULTIPLE PREDICTORS

Neural networks are mathematical modeling tools that are able to learn and generalize about complicated relationships from example. If several indicators are found to be predictive by themselves, neural nets will enable these indicators to be merged together and weighted. The neural net training process may even find beneficial relationships between predicators that were overlooked. The use of a neural net is the last phase of predictor development. Poor network training occurs when either the inputs are not predictive on their own, or training is allowed to continue for too long, resulting in memorization (curve-fitting). When used properly, neural nets are extremely powerful tools.

Technical analysis was developed by repeated observation of market phenomena over time. Technicians have long been criticized for believing that what happened in the past can condition the probability of certain future outcomes. It took deep conviction to be a technician, since they could only point to past examples for support. But auction markets were never random or fully efficient. A market would only be random for a few seconds if the memories of all its participants were simultaneously erased. Instead, the participants' willingness to buy or sell on whatever time scale they choose is ever changing, and based to some extent on recent events, recent price movements, or perceptions of value. The market does have a memory. The multi-level feedback loop that develops makes auction markets what mathematicians call a "non-linear system." Chaos theory explains the dynamics of these non-linear systems, and so technical analysis is really just the application of chaos theory to capital markets.

Conclusions

Because many of the tools of the technician are subjective, experience counts. If one wants to include this analysis into their decision-making process, one needs to work at it, test it, and monitor it. Every market has its own "personality," and time should be taken to see what works best for the time frame in which you operate. Remembering that markets are barometers and that "news often follows the tape" will help you keep one eye on the price action and the other on the fundamentals.

If you find yourself unable to successfully recognize the patterns on the charts, you might depend more on the mechanical approaches of moving averages, etc. Like many things in life and the markets, continued success comes to those who do the research and analysis, and apply discipline and money management techniques. Consider this chapter only a brief introduction to the subject and not enough to be proficient. Serious students can find more in the suggested readings.

Where to learn more?

The following books are recommended and should be read by serious students of technical analysis:

Cohen, A.W., *How To Use The Three-Point Reversal Method of Point & Figure Stock Market Trading,* Lachmont, NY, Chartcraft, 1984

Colby, Robert M. and Thomas A. Meyers, *The Encyclopedia of Technical Market Indicators,* Homewood, IL, Dow Jones

Irwin, 1988. An extensive study of more than 100 technical market indicators.

Edwards, Robert D. and John Magee, *Technical Analysis of Stocks Trends,* Boston, MA, John Magee, Inc, 1981. A comprehensive explanation of bar chart patterns, "The Bible".

Fosback, Norman G., *Stock Market Logic,* Fort Lauderdale, The Institute for Econometric Research, 1976, NY, John Wiley & Sons, Inc. A good overview of market timing indicators.

Granville, Joseph, *Strategy of Daily Stock Market Timing,* N.J. Prentice-Hall, 1960.

Murphy, John J., *Technical Analysis of the Futures Markets,* New York, New York Institute of Finance, 1986. Probably the best single book you can buy to get a complete "course" on technical analysis.

Nison, Steve, *Japanese Candlestick Charting Techniques,* New York, New York Institute of Finance, 1991. This is the standard for students to learn about candlestick charting.

Peters, Edgar E., *Chaos and Order in the Capital Markets, 2nd Edition,* New York, John Wiley & Sons, Inc., 1996

Pring, Martin J., *Technical Analysis Explained, 3rd edition,* New York, McGraw-Hill, 1991. A well written book on indicators and the theories of technical analysis.

OPTIONS STRATEGIES

by Maureen Lynch

Trading in energy options began in the mid-1980s, and market activity has expanded quickly in succeeding years. Energy options are a valuable extension of the underlying markets—physical, futures, swaps—because they offer a new approach to trading and hedging with an entirely different risk/reward structure. In the volatile energy markets, options are another mechanism for companies to manage price risk or capitalize on market opportunities. Today, petroleum, natural gas, and electricity options are an integral part of trading and risk management for all segments of the energy industry. With dramatic growth in options trading volumes at the New York Mercantile Exchange (NYMEX). Figure 7–1 demonstrates the level of industry acceptance and widespread use of options.

Although options are a derivative instrument of the underlying physical or futures market, the risk/reward structure and the distinct nature of options trading strategies constitute a whole new approach to the markets. In the realm of energy trading and risk management, options are most definitely the horse of a different color. Despite the differences, options serve the same fundamental purposes of allowing commer-

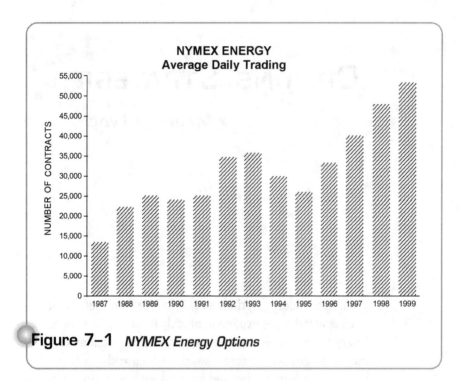

Figure 7-1 *NYMEX Energy Options*

cial companies to manage the price risk inherent in the energy business and enabling traders to take advantage of potential profit opportunities in the energy markets.

FUNDAMENTALS OF OPTIONS

A futures, physical, or forward transaction in the energy markets represents an obligation to buy or sell the commodity by some fixed date. The obligation to perform is a fundamental element of these contracts and represents the key difference between futures/physicals and options transactions. Options, by definition, are the right of choice—a holder of an option has the right to choose whether or not to effect a particular transaction by a certain date.

There are two types of options—*call options* and *put options*. A call option is the right to buy the commodity (whether futures or physicals) at a specified price by a certain date. Conversely, a put option is the right to sell (either futures or physicals) at a specified price by a certain date. The product specified in an option is referred to as the *underlying instrument* or *underlying commodity*. The purchase price referenced in a call option or sale price specified in a put option is called the *strike price* or *exercise price*. An option contract will also include the established time by which the owner must elect to either use (exercise) or not use the option—the expiration date or maturity date. Depending on the designated exercise date, options are referred to as "American" or "European." American options can be exercised at any time prior to expiration, but European options can only be exercised on the maturity date. Asian options are another category, but the term has nothing to do with any exercise restrictions. Instead, the profit/loss of an Asian option is determined by comparing the option's strike price with an average of the underlying commodity prices over a period of time—*e.g.,* a monthly average of crude oil prices. Asian options are also called average price options, or APOs.

As an example, a company that holds an American call option for May WTI crude oil with a strike price of $18 that expires on April 8 has the right, but not the obligation, to buy May WTI crude oil at $18 on or before April 8. A holder of a put option with otherwise the same specifications has the right, but not the obligation, to sell May WTI crude oil at $18 before April 8. The holders of these options are not required to exercise the option to buy and sell. However, after the expiration date, the rights conferred by the option no longer exist, and the unused option is said to have expired or lapsed. An option holder may also resell the option prior to its expiration in the market, just as he or she can resell a futures or forward position before the termination of trading. The owner of an option has three alternatives with which to dispose of the option—exercise the option, allow the option to expire unused, or sell out the option before expiration.

An *option holder* is a person or company who has purchased an option. Obviously, an option can be bought only if some person or company is willing to sell that option. The seller of an option is also referred to as the grantor or writer of an option. The buyer of a call option has obtained the right to buy the underlying commodity (*e.g.*, natural gas) from the seller of that option. If the buyer chooses to exercise the call option, the seller of the option is obligated to sell natural gas to the buyer. If the buyer of a natural gas put option exercises the right to sell, the seller of that option is required to buy natural gas from the holder of the option. For both puts and calls, the buyers of options gain rights, while the sellers of options incur potential obligations.

Since there is no requirement to exercise an option, it will only be used when it is a profitable alternative. The owner of a call option on June heating oil with a strike price of $0.60/gal will only exercise that right to buy if June heating oil prices are at least $0.60/gal. If heating oil prices were lower (*e.g.*, $0.50/gal), the owner of the $0.60/gal option would be better served by letting the option expire unused, and buying June heating oil directly at a considerably lower price. Even if the price of June heating oil were only slightly lower than the strike price of the option (*e.g.*, $0.5950/gal), the option holder would be better off purchasing directly rather than exercising the option to buy at a higher price. The ability to use the option when it is beneficial, or allow it to lapse when the current price is more favorable, is a market advantage that comes only at a cost.

The price of an option is called its *premium*. Energy options are priced in the same denomination as the underlying commodity. Petroleum product options—heating oil, gasoline—are priced in cents per gallon, crude oil options are quoted in dollars per barrel, natural gas options as dollars per MMBtu, and electric power options in dollars per megawatt hour (MWh). A premium of $0.20/MMBtu for a natural gas option for 10,000 MMBtu of gas represents a total cost of $2,000.00 for that option. The buyer of the option pays the premium to the seller when the option is purchased.

The total value (premium) for an option has two components—intrinsic value and time value. The intrinsic value of an option is the value to the holder if the option was exercised immediately. When current prices for crude oil are $18/bbl, a $17 (strike price) call option on crude oil has an intrinsic value of $1/bbl. If the owner of that option exercised the right to buy at $17/bbl, he or she could resell the crude oil at $18/bbl and earn $1/bbl on that transaction. Given the same market for crude oil, a put option with a strike price of $19 also has an intrinsic value of $1/bbl. In this case, the put option holder could exercise the right to sell at $19/bbl and purchase crude oil at the prevailing market price of $18/bbl, netting $1/bbl. Options that have positive intrinsic value are said to be *in-the-money* options.

For calls, in-the-money options are those options with a strike price below the current market price of the underlying instrument. Exercise would allow the option holder to buy at a lower price and sell at a higher price. Conversely, *in-the-money put* options have strike prices above the market price for the underlying instrument. Exercise would allow the option holder to sell at a higher price (via the option) and buy at a lower price. Options that are in-the-money on the expiration date will normally be exercised because it is profitable to do so.

Not all options have intrinsic value. Depending on the relationship between the strike price and the market price, options can also be *at-the-money* or *out-of-the-money*. At-the-money options have a strike price that is the same as the current market price. When electricity is trading at $32/MWh, a call option with a $32 strike price is an at-the-money option. In practice, options with strike prices that are close to the market price (not necessarily the same) are referred to as at-the-money options. Out-of-the-money options are the opposite of in-the-money options in that they have no intrinsic value. For calls, out-of-the-money options have strike prices above the market price. For puts, out-of-the-money options have strike prices below the market price. When electric power is trading at $25/MWh, a call option with a strike price of $30 is an out-of-the-money option. This option would not be exercised, since the holder would rather buy power directly for $25/MWh than use the option to buy at the higher price of $30/MWh. Table 7–1

	Call Option Strike Prices ($/bbl)	Put Option Strike Prices ($/bbl)	Current Market Price ($/bbl)
In-the-money	17	19	18
At-the-money	18	18	18
Out-of-the-money	19	17	18

Table 7–1   *In-, At-, and Out-of-the-Money Options*

summarizes the relationship between strike prices vs. market prices and the terms of in-, at-, and out-of-the-money oil options.

Besides intrinsic value, time value is the other factor that determines the premium for a particular option. Time value (sometimes called *extrinsic* value) is the value to an option owner that comes from the potential for favorable changes in the market price before the expiration of the option. The probability of a beneficial price move is greater with more time left before option expiration and more price volatility. Given sufficient time for a substantial price move in the underlying commodity, an out-of-the-money option can become an in-the-money option that generates a profit for the owner. At maturity, the only value in an option is its intrinsic value. The extrinsic value based on time and price volatility has evaporated since there is no longer an opportunity for a favorable price move. The time value of an option is greatest for an at-the-money option and diminishes as an option trades in-the-money option or out-of-the-money.

An option that is *deep-out-of-the-money* (e.g., a put option to sell gasoline at $.50/gal when market prices are $.75/gal) has little time value since the odds of a sufficiently favorable price move are minimal. For deep-in-the-money options, a potentially favorable price move for the buyer of the option is already reflected in the option price as intrinsic value. Indeed, there is now a significant risk that further price moves will be unfavorable to the holder of the option. The options terms we have described, accompanied by a brief definition, are reviewed in Table 7–2.

Call option	The right, but not the obligation, to buy the underlying commodity at a determined price by a specified date
Exercise price (strike price)	The price at which the holder of an option may buy (call) or sell (put) the underlying commodity
Expiration	The date and time by which an option holder must choose whether to use the option, or the rights conferred by the option will have lapsed
Grantor (writer)	The seller of an option
Intrinsic value	The value in an option if it were exercised immediately and the resulting position were liquidated at the same time—not all options have a positive intrinsic value
Premium	The price of an option
Put option	The right, but not the obligation, to sell the underlying commodity at a determined price by a specified date
Time value (extrinsic value)	That part of an option's total value that arises from the potential for favorable price changes in the underlying commodity prior to expiration

Table 7–2 *Definitions of Basic Option Terms*

Exchange-listed vs. OTC options

Over-the-counter (OTC) and exchange-listed energy options are parallel markets—separate but related. OTC options, sometimes called dealer options, are principal-to-principal, individually negotiated transactions between commercial entities. Exchange-listed options are traded on officially recognized and regulated futures exchanges (*e.g.* NYMEX), and are based on the underlying futures contracts traded at the same exchange. In either case, three basic characteristics are used to define a particular put or call option—the underlying commodity, the strike price, and the expiration date.

When an exchange lists an option for trading, it determines these elements in advance and includes them in the terms of the option contract. As a result, every exchange-listed energy option is standardized for all traders—only the price (premium) is negotiable. The same is not true for OTC energy options, in which every element of the option contract (*i.e.,* the underlying market, strike price, expiration, and premium) is subject to negotiation. The combination of both exchange-listed and OTC options results in a broad array of trading opportunities in energy options.

Exchange traded commodity options are options on futures contracts. When these options are exercised, the option holder will have engaged the right to buy (call) or sell (put) futures contracts. NYMEX has options contracts based on all their energy futures contracts. In London, the IPE lists options contracts based on their gas oil and Brent crude oil contracts. The expiration date established in these contracts is always several days prior to the termination of trading in the underlying futures contract. Exchange options contracts also specify the exercise prices that will be available for trading by establishing the intervals between strike prices. For example, strike prices for the crude oil options contract are fixed at intervals of $.50/bbl, such that options are listed with strike prices at $15.50, $16, $16.50, and so forth. Exchange option contracts are standardized for the same reason that futures contract terms are standardized. Each option bought or sold is then interchangeable with every other option, which makes them easily transferable, thus allowing for the development of an active, liquid market.

OTC options (or *dealer options* for petroleum) are not standardized contracts, but are separately negotiated between the principals to the trade. The principals are the actual counterparts to the trade, similar to any physical or forward energy transaction. An OTC energy option can be based on any market (*e.g.,* Brent crude oil, Gulf Coast gasoline, or regional natural gas market). Strike prices are also not predetermined and can be set at any level. Buyers of dealer options based on WTI could use a strike price of $16.30/bbl instead of the half-dollar strikes of exchange-traded WTI options. The expiration date and time are also subject to negotiation.

The differences between options traded on exchanges and OTC options, outlined in Table 7–3, are important for both the option buyer and seller. The advantage of exchange-listed options on futures is the generally superior liquidity in the market—the disadvantage is that the contract terms are rigid. The reverse is true for OTC options. The terms of the option can be tailor-made to the objectives of the option customer, but it is not always as easy to trade in or out of these options. Both exchange and OTC options serve their purpose in the marketplace and are a complement to each other. It is up to the buyers and sellers of options to determine which vehicle is most appropriate, given their trading needs or goals.

Exchange Options	OTC Options
Traded by open outcry on an exchange floor	Traded principal to principal
Available only for a limited selection of underlying markets	Available for a wide variety of underlying products
Uniform, standardized contracts	Individually negotiated contracts
Credit/default risk vs. the exchange's clearinghouse	Credit/default risk must be evaluated and monitored for each customer

Table 7–3 *Differences Between Exchange-Listed Options and OTC Options*

Risks and rewards of basic option trading strategies

The risks and returns of basic option trading strategies are different from long and short positions in the underlying market. Figure 7–2 depicts the profit and loss profile of a buyer of crude oil at $18/bbl. For every dollar increase in price, the buyer profits by $1/bbl. As prices fall, the buyer loses money—dollar-for-dollar with the drop in crude oil prices. The total profit or loss is limited only by the boundaries of practicality, in that crude oil prices will never be less than zero, and probably won't trade as high as $100/bbl anytime soon. The profit/loss profile of the buyer of a call option (Fig. 7–3) presents an entirely different picture of potential gains and losses. (Note: The graphs show the potential earnings and losses if the option is held to expiration. For ease of comparison, all the examples will be based on crude oil options.)

In this case, the call option has a strike price of $18/bbl and a premium of $0.50/bbl. The buyer of a call option profits as

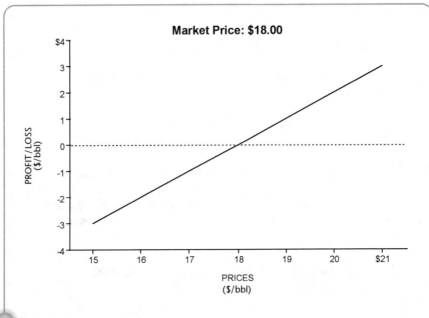

Figure 7–2 *Long Position, Profit/Loss Profile*

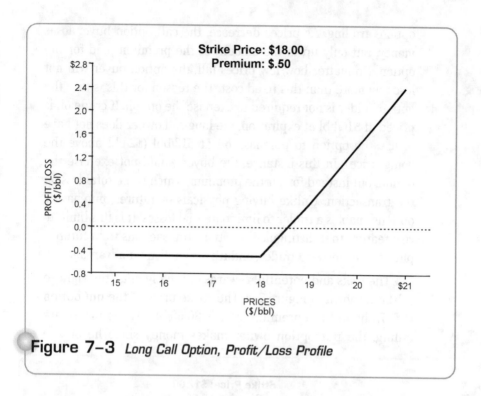

Figure 7-3 *Long Call Option, Profit/Loss Profile*

prices increase. The holder has purchased the right to buy crude oil—a right that will become more valuable as the price of oil increases beyond the strike price. However, since the cost of owning the option is $0.50/bbl, the holder will not show a net profit on the position until futures prices rise beyond $18.50/bbl. As prices increase, the option holder's potential profit is the difference between the strike price (purchase price for oil) and current market price (sale price to liquidate the position), less the cost of the option. For example, if crude oil prices are $19/bbl at expiration, the holder of this call option can exercise the right to buy oil at $18 and sell out this position at $19. The $1/bbl gain on the oil trade less the premium paid ($.50/bbl) results in a net profit of $.50/bbl on the whole transaction.

Potential profit is the motivating force for any trade. However, it is the other half of the call option graph (depicting potential losses) that illustrates a fundamental principle of options trading. As prices decrease, the call option buyer loses money, but only up to the amount of the premium paid for the option. No matter how low prices fall, the option buyer will not lose any more than this fixed cost. The reason for this is that the option holder is not required to exercise the option. If crude oil is priced at $16/bbl at expiration, the long-call owner does not have to use the option to purchase oil at $18/bbl ($2/bbl above the going price). In this instance, the buyer would not exercise the option, but instead forfeit the premium, which is the total loss on the transaction. Unlike buying physicals or futures, purchasing options enables a trader to limit potential losses. It is this limited-risk feature that distinguishes options transactions from futures, physicals or forward trades, and it's also a distinct advantage.

The risks and potential rewards of buying *puts* (the right to sell) are shown in Figure 7–4. The strike price of the put option is $17/bbl and the premium cost is $0.60/bbl. When prices are falling, the put option owner makes money since he or she

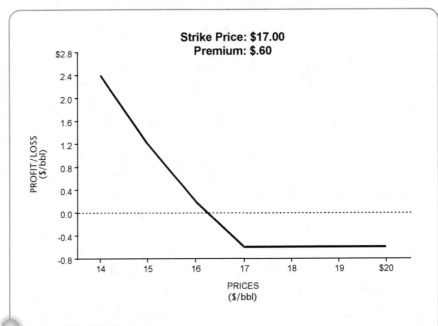

Figure 7–4 *Long Put Option, Profit/Loss Profile*

holds the right to sell at a higher price. Again, the potential profit in this transaction is the difference between the strike price (sale price for oil) and the market price (purchase price), less the cost of the option. If crude oil prices at expiration are $15/bbl, the option holder could exercise the option to sell at $17, and buy back the position at $15/bbl. In this instance, the trader makes $2/bbl on the oil transaction less the premium of $0.60/bbl for a net profit of $1.40/bbl on the trade. As prices increase, the total loss on the transaction is limited to the premium. Should futures prices rise to $19/bbl at expiration, the owner of the put with a $17 strike price would not exercise the right to sell below the market price.

The seller of either a call or put option has an exactly opposite risk/reward structure from the buyer of options. Figure 7–5 illustrates the position of a writer of a crude oil call option with a strike price of $20.00/bbl and a premium of $1.25/bbl. The seller of

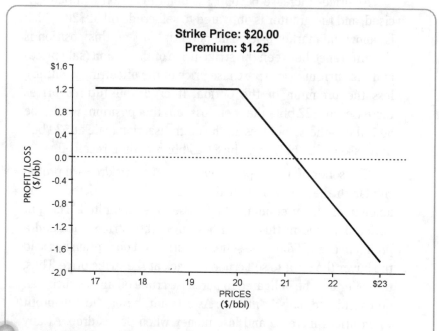

Figure 7–5 *Short Call Option, Profit/Loss Profile*

a call option has incurred the potential obligation of selling crude oil to the option buyer and in this respect, the seller is *short-the-market*. Although the nature of the call option seller's position is quite different from an outright seller of futures or physicals, they hold in common the fact that as prices fall, both positions make money, and as prices increase, they both lose money.

As the market price falls below $20/bbl in this example, the buyer of the option will not exercise the right to buy at a higher price, and the writer of the option keeps the premium of $1.25/bbl as the profit on the trade. Regardless of how low prices fall, the seller of this option can never earn more than the premium—the only money received in connection with the trade. Unlike the buyer, the seller does not have the right to exercise the option in order to earn additional money from a beneficial trade. Only the buyer can exercise an option, which he or she will do only when it is favorable and consequently, unfavorable to the seller.

As prices increase beyond $20/bbl, the option will be exercised, and the grantor is obligated to sell crude oil at $20, which is below the market price. The potential loss on this position is the difference between the strike price of the option (sale price) and the current price (purchase price of the offsetting position), less the premium of the option. If crude oil futures prices increase to $22/bbl, the net loss on the position would be $0.75/bbl—the $2/bbl loss on the oil transaction (sale at $20/bbl, purchase at $22/bbl), less the $1.25/bbl premium received.

The seller of a put option (Fig. 7–6) has a risk/reward profile similar to the call writer in that the profit is restricted to the amount of the premium, while losses are unlimited. The put option depicted in this graph has an $18/bbl strike price and a premium of $0.75/bbl. The seller of a crude oil put option has sold the buyer the right to sell crude oil back at the strike price. Thus, the seller may be obligated to purchase crude oil and as such, can be considered *long-the-market*. As a result, he or she will profit when prices increase and lose money when prices drop. At any price above $18/bbl, the buyer of the put option will not exercise the right to sell at a lower price, and the seller keeps the premi-

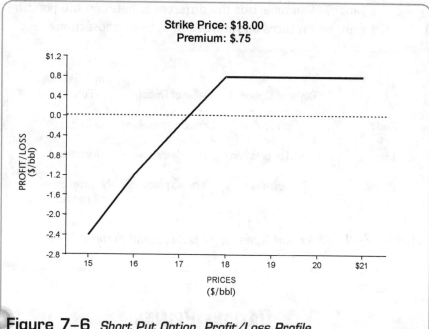

Strike Price: $18.00
Premium: $.75

Figure 7-6 *Short Put Option, Profit/Loss Profile*

um received at the initiation of the trade. Should prices fall to $16/bbl, the buyer will exercise the option to sell at the higher price ($18/bbl) guaranteed by the option. In this instance, the option seller will have to buy crude oil at $18/bbl and resell it at $16/bbl (a $2/bbl loss), resulting in a net loss of $1.25/bbl. The $0.75/bbl premium was not enough to offset the loss on the oil trade, but at least it cushioned the blow to the bottom line.

As these cases demonstrate, the financial risks/rewards of options trading are exactly opposite for the buyers and sellers of options. The buyer of an option must pay a premium for the right to limited losses and unlimited profits on the transaction. The seller, on the other hand, receives the premium to compensate for the possibly unlimited losses associated with only a limited profit. From these examples, buyers and sellers of options can be further distinguished from the buyers and sellers of futures or forwards in that there is no limit to profits or losses and no premium paid or received for futures transactions.

Table 7–4 summarizes the differences between the potential gains and returns on futures and options transactions.

	Buyer of Options	Seller of Options	Buyer/Seller of Futures
Profit	Unlimited	Limited to premium	Unlimited
Loss	Limited to premium	Unlimited	Unlimited
Premium	Pays premium	Receives premium	No premium in the transaction

Table 7–4 *Risks and Rewards of Options and Futures Trading*

OPTIONS PRICING

Option premiums are the costs buyers are willing to pay and the revenue sellers are willing to accept to engage in options trading. The option price is based on the characteristics of both the particular option (*e.g.,* strike price, time to maturity) and the underlying instrument (*e.g.,* type of commodity, price volatility). These factors will determine the value of an option at the time the trade is initiated and also influence the behavior of option prices over the life of the option.

The ability to benefit by holding a position in the underlying commodity—whether long or short—is the source of an option's value. The fact that an option is a right, but not an obligation, confers an additional value to the option. From the buyer's perspective, he or she has gained the right to profit from favorable price moves in the underlying commodity, but is insured against any loss (beyond the premium paid) resulting from unfavorable price fluctuations. Accordingly, the buyer is willing to pay a premium for an option that reflects not only the profit potential but also the insurance value inherent in the option. The option grantor, on the other hand, has gained the sole benefit of the premium and is subject to unlimited losses resulting from unfavorable price moves in the underlying commodity. From the seller's viewpoint the premium must be sufficient to compensate for the risk assumed in insuring the buyer against losses.

The determinants of the price of the option are largely a matter of common sense. Indeed, some of the elements that form the basis of an option's value were implied in the description of basic options strategies. The four factors that affect options prices are:

- relationship between the market price and the strike price

- time to expiration

- price volatility of the underlying commodity

- interest rates

Relationship between market price and strike price

As the option matures, the difference between the strike price of an energy option and the current market price is the primary factor in the value of an option. At expiration, the relationship between the market price and the strike price will determine whether or not the option is an in-the-money option and therefore profitable to exercise, or an out-of-the-money option that will expire unexercised. Even prior to maturity, this relationship has a pronounced impact on options pricing and establishes a minimum value for the price of an option. When oil prices are $18/bbl, the price of a crude oil call option with a strike price of $17/bbl must be at least $1/bbl. If the premium were less—$0.90/bbl—a trader could buy the option, exercise it, and make $0.10/bbl on the trade ($1/bbl profit on the crude oil deal, less the $0.90/bbl premium cost).

The immediate risk-free profit for the buyer would mean an immediate loss for the option grantor, which is why options are never sold for less than their intrinsic value. If prices are rising, a call option would increase in value as it went deeper in-the-money (more intrinsic value) and thus be more profitable upon exercise. Conversely, as prices are falling, a call option would lose value as it fell out-of-the-money. If prices sunk to $10/bbl, the $17 call option would become a deep out-of-the-money option with little prospect of profitable exercise. The relationship between the market price and the strike price is unique in that it is the sole measure of an option's intrinsic value (if there is any)—the only value in an option at expiration. All of the remaining factors influence the time value of an option, which is only relevant prior to maturity.

Time to expiration

Logic dictates that an option's value will increase the more time available prior to expiration. A four-month option (the expiration date is four months away) is more valuable than a two-week option, because the extra time increases the chances for a favorable price move in the underlying commodity. However, as time ticks away, an option loses value, a phenomenon called *time decay.* The decline in value, attributable to the passage of time, is gradual at first, but then accelerates as the expiration date nears. A few days less doesn't matter much for an out-of-the-money option when there are four months remaining for prices to move in the holder's favor. Those same few days can make a big difference for the holder of an out-of-the-money option when expiration is only a week away.

Price volatility of the underlying commodity

This refers to the variability of prices in the commodity over the life of the option. Since an option's value to the buyer is the ability to profit on such price changes, the more the price can move in his or her favor, the greater the ultimate potential earnings on the trade. Accordingly, as price volatility increases, the value of an option increases. Suppose that crude oil prices have only traded between $17/bbl and $19/bbl for the last two years. In these circumstances, buying a three-month call option with a strike price of $22/bbl would seem to be a long shot, and the buyer of such an option would probably be willing to pay only a modest premium. If, however, oil prices had traded in a range of $15/bbl to $25/bbl, the same option would seem to offer a higher probability of profitable exercise, and the buyer of such an option would be willing to pay a higher premium. The more prices move over the life of the option, the greater the profit potential for the holder of an option, and the greater the risk for an option seller. As a result, the buyer will pay more to acquire the option, and the seller will demand more for writing the option.

Relevant price volatility for an option. This is the range of prices that occur over the life of the option. No matter how prices behaved in the past, it is their behavior from the initiation to the expiration of the option that will determine the profit in the trade. The fact that oil prices have traded in a wide range in the past (*e.g.*, $12-$22/bbl) will not help the buyer of an $18/bbl call option if subsequently, oil trades in a range of $15–$17/bbl. Unlike the relationship of the strike price vs. market price and the time to expiration, price volatility is not a specified term of the option contract and cannot be precisely determined at the time the option is purchased. The fact that future price volatility is an unknown variable distinguishes it from the other elements that affect options pricing.

Price volatility can generally be defined as the variability of the prices in the underlying commodity. In other words, price volatility describes how much prices move up or down. As a result of its importance in determining the price of an option and its variable and unpredictable nature, volatility is the primary focus of attention for professional options traders. As a consequence, option professionals have developed a precise mathematical formula to describe price volatility. For options traders, volatility is the standard deviation of price changes expressed in annual percentage terms. The equation for volatility is shown in Equation 7-1.

Deciphering this equation is not a requirement for a reasonable understanding of volatility and its importance to

Equation 7–1
Volatility

$$\sqrt{\frac{A}{n-1}\sum_{i-1}^{n}\left(x_i - \bar{x}\right)^2}$$

Where:

A = number of trading days in a year

n = number of observations

$x_t = L_n \dfrac{P_t}{P_t - 1}$ where P_t = price at time t

$\bar{x}$ = arithmetic means of x_t's

options. The results of volatility calculations are expressed in percentage terms (annualized) for a defined period of time covering the number of observations included in the calculation. Option traders will refer to a 30-day volatility of 30%, a 60-day volatility of 28%, or a 10-day volatility of 35%.

Figure 7–7 demonstrates option volatilities for crude oil since 1993. Between 1993 and 1998, oil option volatility was valued as low as 15% and as high as 53%. At the same time natural gas implied volatilities ranged from 20% to more than 100%.

To put these volatility levels into perspective, they can be compared to the range of volatility levels seen in other actively traded options. During the same period, the S&P 500 Index option volatility has traded between 9% and 32%, and Deutsche mark options have seen a range of 5% to 22%. Energy option volatilities are substantially higher than most other commodities, foreign exchange, or securities instruments—which is no surprise to anyone who has traded the energy markets. When options trade with high volatility numbers, they reflect the market's general view that prices are going to trade in a wide range. Lower option volatilities mean that market expectations encompass a narrower price range for the underlying commodity. In this way, option volatilities are a reflection of the uncertainty surrounding future price levels. The greater the uncertainty, the wider the band of possible prices—the higher the volatility, and the more expensive the option premiums.

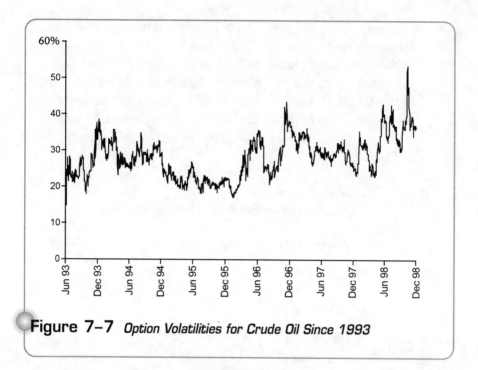

Figure 7–7 *Option Volatilities for Crude Oil Since 1993*

Interest rates

The last and definitely least important factor in pricing commodity options is the prevailing interest rate. Changes in the interest rate have only a minimal effect on the price of an option compared to the other three factors. The relationship between interest rates and option prices is based on the financing cost/earnings associated with the option premium payments. In theory, when interest rates increase, premiums decline, and when rates fall, premiums increase. But the impact on premiums is so minor that traders generally ignore interest rate fluctuations when evaluating shorter-term option strategies.

Option-pricing model

So far, we have generally discussed the factors that determine options' prices. Clearly, options traders need to define the impact of these elements more precisely in order to arrive at a particular price at which they are willing to buy or sell options.

The formula to generate a particular option's price—which incorporates all four elements—has been developed and is available to any options trader. The option-pricing model was originally developed by Professors Black and Scholes for stock options. Later, Professor Black made necessary adjustments to the model to derive premiums for commodity options. The formula to calculate the price for a futures call option is presented in Equation 7–2.

Equation 7–2
Option-Pricing Formula For Call Options

$$C = e^{-rt}\,[FN(q_1) - EN(q_2)]$$

$$q_1 = \frac{Ln(F/E) + s^2\,t/2}{s\sqrt{t}}$$

$$q_2 = q_1 - s\sqrt{t}$$

Where
  C = call premium
  r = short-term interest rate
  t = time to expiration
  F = futures price
  E = option strike price
  s = volatility measure
  e = base of natural logarithm
  Ln = natural logarithm
  $N(\ )$ = cumulative normal density function

As with the equation for calculating volatility, mastering the algebra involved in this formula is not a prerequisite for options trading. An option trader only needs a basic understanding of the purpose and results of the model. Black and Scholes' approach was to derive a premium price to sufficiently compensate an option grantor (with no market view) for the risk of the position, but no more. To control market exposure an option writer would "delta hedge" the option—a process discussed in more detail later—by either buying or selling the underlying commodity. In the Black-Scholes model the option premium equates to the theoretical cost of delta hedging the option. The formula for calculating option prices was developed to determine a theoretical value, often referred to as fair value, for a given option.

The theoretical (fair value) of an option is the price that favors neither the buyer nor the seller of the option. Over the long run, if buyers and sellers consistently bought and paid the fair value of options, they could expect to break even on their trades—no net profits, no net losses. Obviously, this is only the theory underlying the development of the equation, not the expectation of option traders who use it.

Option-pricing characteristics

In addition to computing the fair value of the option, the formula in Equation 7–2 also provides some useful by-products that define the behavior of option prices over time and as market conditions change. In addition to the option premium, Greek letters refer to other calculated results of the formula.

Delta. As a result of the special properties of options, option premiums do not move penny-for-penny with the prices in the underlying market. The delta of an option is a quantification of how option prices move in relation to price changes in the underlying commodity. Specifically, the option delta is the change in premium value per unit change in price for the underlying commodity. A crude oil option with a delta of 0.50 means that the option premium moves by $0.50/bbl for every dollar-per-barrel change in crude oil prices. In the option pricing model, deltas are a general measure of the probability that an option will expire in-the-money. At-the-money options have deltas that are valued at roughly 0.50—the option price moves only half as much as the underlying market price. Deep-out-of-the-money options have deltas that are near zero—the option's price hardly moves as the underlying market price changes. On the other hand, deep-in-the-money options have deltas approaching 1.00, such that the premium moves almost dollar-for-dollar with the underlying market price. The premium of these options is almost entirely made up of intrinsic value with hardly any time value. Thus, their price fluctuates with the changes in the value of the underlying commodity.

The delta of an option is not a static feature. As we observed, at-the-money, in-the-money, and out-of-the-money options all have different deltas. When prices are rising, the delta of an out-of-the-money call option will be constantly increasing towards a full delta of 1.00 as the option trades to substantially in-the-money. The delta of an option doesn't change much when options are either deep-in-the-money or deep-out-of-the-money. For these types of options, the deltas tend to hover around 1.00 and 0, respectively. The deltas of at-the-money options (0.50) are more variable as the option trades in- or out-of-the-money. Option deltas are the most extreme and volatile when expiration is imminent.

An option trader who has a call option on a futures contract with a delta of 0.50 holds a position that earns and loses money just as if he or she was long one-half of a futures contract. If the same trader bought another futures call option with a delta of 0.50, he or she would now hold a position that is equivalent to a whole futures contract. The deltas of options are additive—that is, an option trader who owns 20 futures call options with 0.50 deltas has a position that is equal to buying 10 futures contracts. The delta value of an option can be positive or negative, depending on whether the option position is fundamentally *long-* or *short-the-market.* A long-call position or short put position is long-the-market—the position's value increases as the market price rises)—and these options have positive delta values. Short calls and long puts have negative deltas since these positions are essentially short-the-market. The same is true for long and short positions in the underlying commodity—the delta value of a long position in the underlying market is 1.00 and a short position is -1.00.

Since deltas are additive, it's possible to calculate the combined delta of a num-ber of options. The result is a measure of the equivalent position in the underlying commodity. Traders can thus monitor their exposure to price changes, and also create "delta neutral" strategies or portfolios. For example, an option trader who is long by 10 calls with a combined delta of 5.00 (10 options x 0.50 delta) can offset the position by selling five futures contracts (combined delta of -5.00). As prices rise, the value of the option premiums increases, but a similar amount of money is lost on the short futures position. Should prices fall, the premiums will lose value, but the futures contracts will show a profit to offset these losses. Of course, this example ignores the potential effects of time and volatility on the premium that will not be balanced by the position in the underlying contract. Nonetheless, the options trader has taken the first step in insulating the position against the effects of a change in the market price. The same effect can be accomplished using either an opposing market position in the underlying commodity or in other options whose delta sign is opposite to the initial options position. In the example above, the combined delta of the long call options was +5.00 and the combined delta of the short futures position was -5.00, resulting in an overall delta of 0 for the total position.

When an options trader establishes two offsetting positions whose combined deltas are equal and opposite, the overall position is said to be *delta neutral*. However, since option deltas are dynamic, a position of this sort is delta neutral only over a limited range of prices. If prices increased significantly, the individual delta of each long call option would increase from 0.50 to 0.75 as these options trade further in-the-money. The combined delta of the 10 long calls would increase to 7.5 futures-equivalent-positions. With only 5 short futures positions (combined delta of -5.00), the overall position is no longer delta neutral, but has a market exposure equal to being long 2.5 futures contracts—the difference between the deltas of the option position and the futures position.

The variation in delta values based on market price movements is important for options traders for two reasons:

- The change in delta(s) can be beneficial or harmful to an outright options position.

- The change in delta(s) affects market exposure for trading strategies designed to be "delta neutral."

The dynamics of option deltas work to the advantage of option buyers and to the detriment of option sellers. The buyer of an at-the-money call option on futures with a delta of 0.50 is essentially long one-half of a futures contract. In the event prices increase, the buyer will not only benefit by half the amount of the price rise, but also because the delta will increase as the option trades into the money. If the delta is now 0.65, the call option's value will then increase by $0.65 for each dollar increase in the underlying commodity. The buyer of the call option is now long almost two-thirds of a futures contract. Thus, when prices increase, the buyer of a call option is the beneficiary of an increasingly favorable position. In the case of a price fall, the same at-the-money option delta will eventually decline to 0.40 or lower. At this point, the buyer is now long less than half a futures contract, and a dollar decline in the market price will result in only a $0.40 decrease in premium value. As prices decrease, the call option holder is not quite as long-the-market—a more desirable position in a falling market—and the negative impact on the option premium is diminished.

The tables are turned for the seller of a call option whose option delta is negative, reflecting the fact that he or she is short-the-market. When prices climb, the same delta change for the buyer from 0.50 to 0.65 is a change from -0.50 to -0.65 for the seller. Therefore, the seller is getting increasingly short in a rising market, which is not usually the path to riches. As the market falls, the seller's option delta changes from -0.50 to -0.40. The option now reflects a smaller short position. Just when the short position is advantageous (falling prices), the benefit to the seller is diminished.

Delta changes can also disrupt a delta-neutral options trade. The fluctuations in delta values means that a delta-neutral trade today is not likely to be a delta-neutral position tomorrow. For the options trader trying to minimize the market-price risk of an options trade, the changing deltas can result in unintentional market exposure.

Gamma. Quantifying the potential moves in option deltas is quite useful to option traders and is another feature of the option-pricing model. *Gamma* measures the rate of change in deltas in relation to changes in the underlying commodity price. The gamma of an option reveals how much the delta will increase or decrease based on a unit change in the underlying market price. At-the-money options have the highest gamma since their deltas are the most variable, and deep-in-the-money and deep-out-of-the-money options have the smallest gamma because their delta values are fairly stable. The gamma of an option increases as the time to expiration nears, reflecting the increasing volatility of deltas at that time. Like option deltas, the gamma of an option can be positive or negative. Option gammas are positive for long-option positions (long call, long put) and negative for short-option positions (short call, short put). Long options have positive gamma because the changes in delta are beneficial to the positions, and the negative gamma associated with short-option positions reflects the fact that delta changes have the opposite effect on these positions. Positive gamma means that the options position of the trader will become progressively long-the-market as prices rise and increasingly short-the-market as prices decline. Option positions with negative gamma don't offer this advantage, but grow increasingly short-the-market as prices rise and long-the-market as prices fall. Price moves (price volatility) are advantageous to long option positions with positive gamma, but traders who have short option positions with negative gamma are better served by a stable market.

Theta. Options are a wasting asset in that their value erodes as time passes. The measure of the time-decay of an option, *theta*, is another property of the option-pricing model. Theta quantifies the daily decline in the option premium attributable only to the passage of time. The effects of theta are the most pronounced as an option nears expiration when each remaining day counts. Short options (short call, short put) have positive theta, and long options (long call, long put) have negative theta. For traders who hold long options, theta works against the value of their position because premiums decline over time. Short options positions benefit from time decay as premiums fall. Unlike the other factors that influence options prices, time decay is a one-way street. The time-to-expiration can never be increased to enhance the value of an established option position.

Kappa. The impact of price volatility on option prices has also been quantified, thanks to the option-pricing model. The *kappa* of an option measures the change in premium value for each 1% change in price volatility, or in more general terms, the sensitivity of the option's price to changes in volatility. Sometimes, this statistic is also called *sigma* (another Greek letter) or *vega* (not a Greek letter at all, but perhaps named for the star or the GM car model that went out of production years ago). Kappa values are positive for long-option positions (long call, long put) because an increase in volatility causes the value of option premiums to increase as well. Short-option positions have negative kappa, because an increase in volatility causes an increase in option premiums and is detrimental to these positions.

The effects of volatility and time on an option's value are exactly opposite. Long options suffer the effect of time-decay, but their values appreciate with an increase in volatility. Time is on the side of short options, but an increase in volatility works against these positions. In the terms of the option-pricing model, long options have negative theta and positive kappa, and short options have positive theta and negative kappa. The two elements, time and volatility, which comprise an option's extrinsic value, can never favor the same option position, but are constantly at odds. Depending on the position, the options trader hopes that the effects of the one factor will outweigh the impact of the other. In the end, however, time always wins out. The volatility of an option is irrelevant at expiration because time has simply run out.

As we have discussed, volatility is different from the other factors in options pricing because it is prospective in nature. Only the historical price volatility is known, but to calculate the value of an option, a volatility assumption for the future must be included in the option-pricing model. The volatility input is a forecast of the expected range of prices in the underlying commodity over the life of the option. Predicting volatility is as difficult as predicting any other future event. Luckily, the option-pricing model relieves a trader from relying solely on soothsaying abilities and allows him or her to ascertain the market's expectation of volatility. Instead of inputting the four ingredients of option prices into the model to determine the premium, the calculation is reversed. The options' price is already known and the other factors (*i.e.*, time, strike price, market price, and interest rate) are determined as well, so the model calculates the remaining variable, volatility. This calculation returns the volatility implied by the option price, and the result is called *implied volatility*. This is the measure of volatility most commonly used by option traders. Since the implied volatility of an option is just the market's forecast of volatility, option prices can vary based on a change in the market's expectations regarding volatility, without any change in the underlying market price. In addition to providing a ready reference for expected price volatility, implied volatility is also used as a yardstick for determining which options are priced higher or lower on a relative basis to other similar options. Knowing the different options' implied volatilities, and thus which options are relatively expensive or cheap compared to like options, or in relation to past pricing behavior, is valuable trading information.

To review, then:

- The factors that determine an option's price and their more precise quantification in the option-pricing model are summarized in Table 7–5, with a specific example presented in Table 7–6.

	Definition	Value for Long Options (Long Call, Long Put)	Value for Short Options (Short Call, Short Put)	Comments
Delta	Rate of change in premium value per unit change in underlying price			The delta's value, positive or negative, is related to whether the option position is fundamentally long or short the market. Long calls and short puts have positive delta. Short calls and long puts have negative delta.
Gamma	Rate of change of option delta per unit change in underlying price	Positive	Negative	At-the-money options have the highest gamma values. Gamma increases as the time to expiration decreases because delta values are more volatile.
Theta	Daily decrease in value of premium related to time decay	Negative	Positive	Theta values are highest as the option expiration nears because time decay has accelerated.
Kappa	Change in premium value for each 1% change in expected volatility	Positive	Negative	

Table 7–5   *Quantifying Variables in the Option Pricing Model*

- The Greek letters refer to the elements that comprise an option's value and isolate the impact of these factors.

- In the real world of options trading, all these variables are changing at the same time and their separate effects on premiums don't happen in isolation.

Underlying commodity:	WTI Crude Oil
Type of option:	call option
Term to expiration:	three months
Strike price:	$18/bbl
Current market price:	$18/bbl
Volatility:	30%
Premium:	$1.05/bbl

Delta:	0.52	The option price will change by $0.52 for every dollar change in crude oil prices.
Gamma:	0.15	The delta will change by this amount for every dollar change in crude oil prices.
Theta:	0.006	The option premium will decline by $0.006/bbl on the next day as a result of time-decay.
Kappa:	0.035	For every 1% change in volatility, the option premium will change by $0.035/bbl.

Table 7–6 *Option Value Statistics*

- Monitoring the changing values of these statistics, their relation to each other, and their effects on option premiums has been made much easier by option pricing software.

More important, however, is a conceptual understanding of the components of an option's value and how they work for and against an option position.

The Black-Scholes options pricing model has been a valuable tool for options traders, with some limitations. Underlying the model are assumptions that aren't always an accurate reflection of the real world. For example, the model assumes continuous, no-gap pricing in the underlying commodity, a condition that is notably absent from the energy markets at times. During the 1990 Gulf War, prices were anything but continuous. Crude oil prices jumped by $8/bbl in a single day after Iraq's invasion of Kuwait. Also, energy prices tend to be more volatile than other commodity or security prices. The electricity market can hum along for weeks between $20-$30/MWh and prices will then spike up to thousands of dollars per MWh. Oil, natural gas, and electricity options have all traded at prices that reflect implied volatilities of over 100%. When options trade at extreme levels of volatility, the market doesn't fit neatly into the model anymore, and the equation's results are no longer as reliable. At that point, traders become more concerned about being positioned on the right side of the market than any output from an options pricing model.

Basic Options Trading Strategies

Options are very flexible trading instruments. Compared to the underlying markets, they offer a much greater assortment of trading strategies. In addition to choosing whether to buy or sell, the options trader can elect to use puts or calls and can select the particular strike price that meets his or her objectives. Different options can be combined in many ways to fashion a position that reflects almost any type of price or volatility forecast and risk/reward tradeoff. The following options trading strategies can be divided into two broad categories:

- Strategies based on directional price movements

- Strategies based on the stability or volatility of price movements

This section offers examples of both types of strategies using options on crude oil. All the examples will be for three-month options with 30% volatility, and (unless otherwise noted) the options' strikes will be at-the-money. The graphs illustrating each example will be the profit/loss profile at expiration, ignoring transaction costs.

Strategies based on directional price movements

Trading strategies based on the expected direction of price movements can be either bearish or bullish. With options, these types of trades can be further refined to reflect a moderately bullish or moderately bearish price forecast. The strategies also differ on whether premiums are paid or collected and how much risk is associated with the position.

Bullish options trades are designed to take advantage of rising prices. The simplest example of a bullish option position is the long call, which we reviewed earlier in the chapter. Figure 7–8 illustrates the risks and returns for three different long-call positions when the underlying price is $18/ bbl—an at-the-money $18 call, an in-the-money $17 call, and an out-of-the-

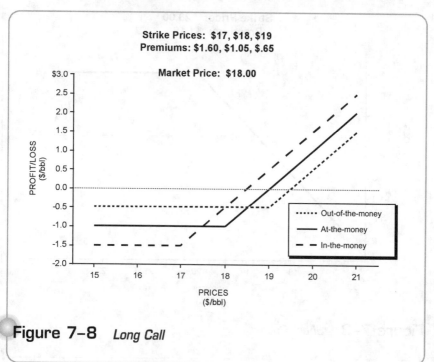

Strike Prices: $17, $18, $19
Premiums: $1.60, $1.05, $.65

Market Price: $18.00

Figure 7–8 *Long Call*

money $19 call. The maximum profit for these positions is unlimited, while the maximum loss is confined to the amount of their respective premiums—$1.05/bbl, $1.60/bbl, and $0.65/bbl. The in-the-money option has the highest premium cost (largest potential loss), but, as prices rise, shows a profit sooner than the other options. The out-of-the-money option has the least downside risk (smallest premium cost), but futures prices will have to climb from $18/bbl to almost $20/bbl before there will be any real profit in this trade. Like any other type of investment, the biggest risks are associated with the greatest rewards. One of the advantages of options trading is the ability to choose different strike prices whereby the trader can structure the trade based on his or her specific market outlook conditioned by acceptable risk parameters.

If a trader has a more moderately bullish view, selling a put is an alternative (Fig. 7–9). In this instance, the short put has a $20 strike price and a premium of $1.16/bbl. The profit/loss pro-

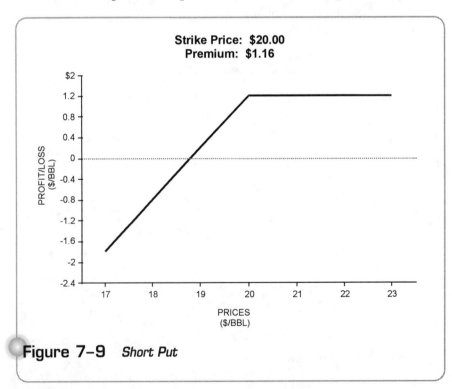

Figure 7–9   *Short Put*

file shows gains, limited to the size of the premium, as prices rise and unlimited losses as prices decline. The essential difference between long options and short options is the greater risk of loss associated with short options. This strategy is only moderately bullish in that the seller of a put option has limited profits to a fixed number, no matter how high prices eventually climb. The trader would forfeit this profit potential only if he or she doesn't believe that a major price increase will happen. Granting puts is a trade designed to take advantage of stable to slightly rising prices.

A bull-call spread is another transaction that reflects a mildly bullish view. This spread involves the purchase of a lower strike-price call and the sale of a higher strike-price call. The price of the purchased call will always exceed the premium received for the sale of the other call, because the lower strike call is more in-the-money and carries a higher value. In the example in Figure 7–10, the purchased call has a strike of $19 and a

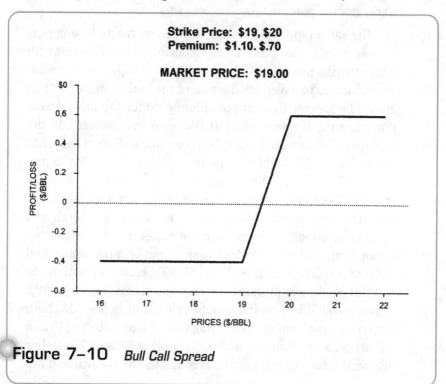

Figure 7–10   *Bull Call Spread*

premium of $1.10/bbl. The short call has a strike price of $20 and a premium of $0.70/bbl. The net cost of the transaction, or net debit, is $0.40/bbl—the difference between the premium paid and the premium received. As prices fall below $19, both calls are out-of-the-money and will not be exercised. The total loss on the transaction will be the cost (net debit) of initiating the position, $0.40/bbl. As prices rise to $19.75/bbl, the trader will be long at $19, via the long call, but the profit in the oil market will be diminished by the net cost of the transaction. After prices trade up beyond $20, both calls will be in-the-money, resulting in a long position at $19 and a short position (the exercised short call) at $20/bbl. The dollar profit less the $0.40/bbl net debit leaves a total profit of $0.60/bbl on the transaction. This is the potential profit in the trade even if prices trade up to $25/bbl. Again, the trader is moderately bullish and therefore is willing to limit the upside potential. In contrast to the short-put position, however, the downside risk is limited as well. This is a more conservative trade, but the potential profit is also smaller.

The same type of trade can also be constructed using puts instead of calls. The bull-put spread involves buying a put with a lower strike price and selling a put with a higher strike price. The premium received for the sale of the higher strike put will always be greater than the premium paid for the lower strike put, since the higher strike put is deeper in-the-money. In the example illustrated in Figure 7–11, the high strike put ($19) has a premium of $1.10/bbl and the low strike put ($18) has a premium of $0.65/ bbl. At initiation, the trade generates a net credit of $0.45/bbl, the difference between the two premiums and the maximum profit. When prices are above $19, both put options are out-of-the-money and the trader retains the net premium. If prices fall to $18.60, the short put is in-the-money and the trader will be long at $19. The $0.40/bbl loss on the oil trade is offset by the net premium received such that the trader still shows a $0.05/ bbl profit. Should prices fall below $18, both options are in-the-money, resulting in a long position at $19 and a short position (courtesy of the long put) at $18/bbl. The dollar loss on the futures transaction is mitigated by the original net

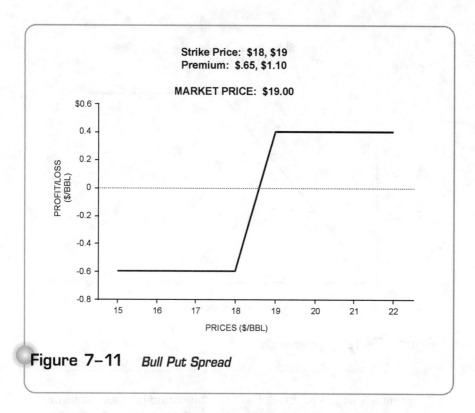

Figure 7–11   *Bull Put Spread*

credit on the trade ($0.45/bbl), and the total loss is limited to
$0.55/bbl. The maximum profit and loss on a bull-put spread is
known at the outset of the transaction. While losses are restricted, profit potential is also limited.

The covered call is our last example of a mildly bullish
option strategy. A covered call is a combination of a short-call
position with a long position in the underlying commodity. The
call, in this instance, is referred to as a covered call to distinguish
it from naked calls, which are short calls with no balancing position in options, futures, or forwards. Figure 7–12 illustrates the
profit/loss profile of a short call with an $18 strike price and
$1.05/bbl premium coupled with a long position at $18/bbl. The
premium received, $1.05/bbl, for the short call is the maximum
profit for this trade. At $18 and higher, the trader is both long
and short (by way of the short call) at the same price, $18/bbl.
The positions are exact offsets, and the trader keeps the

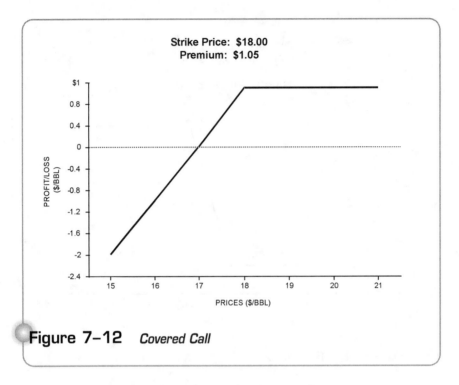

Figure 7–12 *Covered Call*

premium as the profit. Below $18, the option component of the trade is out-of-the-money and the trader retains premium, but the long position is losing money. The losses in the underlying market are cushioned by the premium received, but as prices drop, these losses eventually exceed the amount of the premium for an overall net loss on the trade. Covered calls have limited profits, but there is no limit to the amount of potential losses. Normally covered calls are the result of adding a short call to an already established long position. In these circumstances, the trader has modified the outright bullish view as he or she is willing to forfeit the unlimited profit potential in the original trade for some downside protection (the amount of the premium).

Options can also be used to establish positions that reflect a bearish market forecast. These strategies can encompass the full range of market viewpoints—from the mildly bearish to the strongly bearish. In all cases, they are designed to benefit from falling prices. Since these transactions are simply the opposite of the bullish option strategies, we will limit the discussion to just a few examples.

The long put, depicted in Figure 7–13, is an outright bearish position. In this case, the put has a $20 strike price and a premium of $1.16/bbl. The total risk to the position is the premium forfeited if prices are above $20/bbl. The potential profits in the trade, when prices fall, are unlimited. The buyer of a put must have a sufficiently bearish view that the expected price change will be greater than the initial cost of the trade. Similar to long calls, the risk/reward levels of a long put can be adjusted by selecting a strike price that is in-, at-, or out-of-the-money.

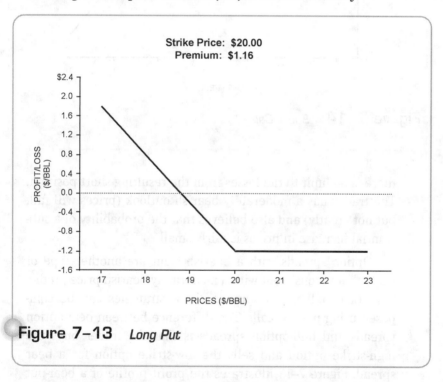

Figure 7–13 *Long Put*

The short call is the mildly bearish counterpart to the mildly bullish short put. The strike price for the short call used in Figure 7–14 is $18, and the premium is $1.05/bbl. The seller of a call collects the premium, which is the maximum profit in the position if prices are stable or falling. When prices increase

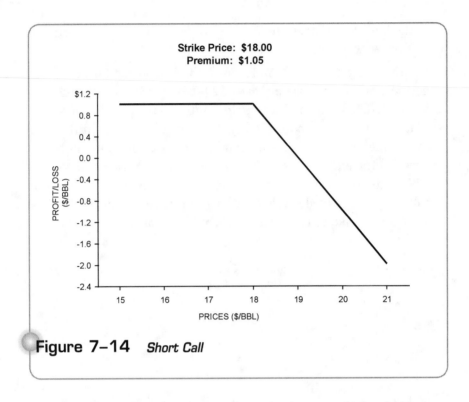

Strike Price: $18.00
Premium: $1.05

Figure 7–14   *Short Call*

there is no limit to the losses from the resulting short position. The trader has a moderately bearish outlook (prices will fall, but not greatly) and also believes that the probability of a substantial increase in prices is fairly small.

Option spreads with a bearish slant are another type of trade that is consistent with a moderately bearish price prediction. Like bull-option spreads, these strategies can be composed using puts or calls. The difference between bear-option spreads and bull-option spreads is that the trader buys the high-strike option and sells the low-strike option for a bear spread. Figure 7–15 illustrates the profit profile of a bear-put spread. The trade involves buying a high-strike ($19) put for $1.10/bbl and selling a low-strike ($18) put for $0.65/bbl. The cost of the transaction is $0.45/bbl, the net premium paid to establish the two option positions. If prices are higher than $19 at expiration, both puts are out-of-the-money, and the total loss

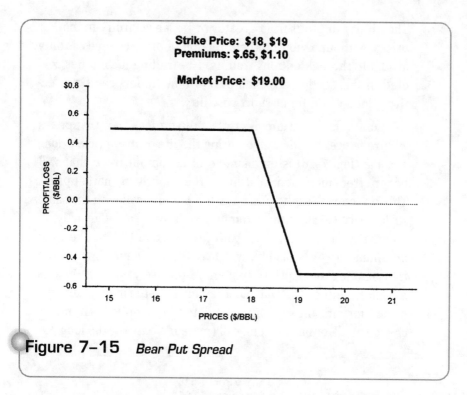

Strike Price: $18, $19
Premiums: $.65, $1.10

Market Price: $19.00

Figure 7–15   *Bear Put Spread*

is the net premium ($0.45/bbl). When prices fall between $18 and $19, the high-strike long put is in-the-money and the trader is effectively short at $19/bbl. The profit from the short position is reduced by the initial cost of the trade. Below $18, both options are in-the-money, and the trader is now short at $19 and long (via the short put) at $18/bbl. The dollar profit in the positions is offset, in part, by the net premium paid ($0.45/bbl), resulting in a maximum net return of $0.55/bbl. This bear-put spread is designed to take advantage of a limited price fall, but with protection against a substantial price increase. The reduced risk is balanced by the modest profit potential.

Strategies based on price volatility

The second category of options-trading strategies includes trading techniques that are not based on bearish or bullish price forecasts, but whether prices will be stable or volatile.

The ability to profit from greater or lesser volatility in market prices, without a view on the direction of price changes, is only available through options trading. The trading techniques covered in this section are examples of how traders can be effectively long-volatility or short-volatility.

Long-volatility strategies reflect the trader's view that prices will trade over a wide range during the life of the option. A *long straddle* (Fig. 7–16) is an example of an option trade that will benefit from increased volatility in the underlying market price. This trade involves the purchase of a put and call with the same strike price ($18). In this example, we have assumed exactly at-the-money options that are both priced at $1.04/bbl. The total premium cost is $2.08/bbl, which is the maximum loss on the transaction should prices remain at precisely $18/bbl. In this instance, neither the put nor the call is in-the-money and the trader forfeits the premium paid for both options. If prices change at all, either the long call (price increase) or the long put

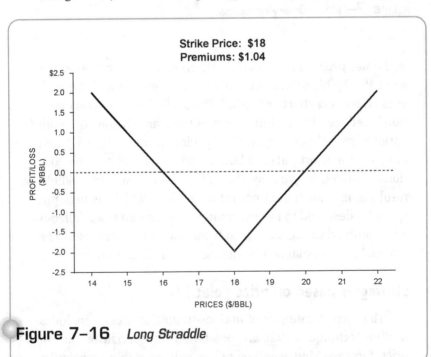

Figure 7–16 *Long Straddle*

(price decrease) will be in-the-money. However, until the market trades at least $2.08 higher or lower, the profit from the exercise of the in-the-money option will be outweighed by the initial premium cost. Should the market see a major price rally or collapse, the profit potential is unlimited. The long-straddle position benefits from increased price volatility. The trader believes that prices will change dramatically, but doesn't know if the expected price move will mean higher or lower prices. Skeptics of this strategy argue that it is the rare trader who doesn't have a market bias, and, therefore, this trade has limited application.

But, the viewpoint inherent in this trade is not unheard of. For example, technical analysis refers to breakout points in the charts, but these signals don't always indicate which direction prices will move, only that there will be a substantial price change. The long straddle may be an appropriate position in these cases or whenever a trader is bullish on volatility, but is undecided about market direction.

Option traders can also use options to profit from price stability. Figure 7–17 is the profit/loss profile of a short strangle. Strangles are like straddles in that they are the purchase or sale of both a put and a call. The difference is that straddles are composed of a put and a call with the same strike price, while strangles use puts and calls with different strike prices that are usually both out-of-the-money initially. In the given example, the short strangle is the sale of a high-strike price ($20) call with the sale of a low-strike price ($18) put. The premiums for these options are $0.70/bbl and $0.65/bbl, respectively, resulting in a net premium credit of $1.35/bbl. When prices are between $18 and $20, both options ($20 call, $18 put) are out-of-the-money, and the trader keeps the combined premium, which is the maximum profit. Above $20, the short call is in-the-money and the trader will be short at $20/bbl in a rising market. Below $18, the short put is in-the-money and the trader will be long at $18/bbl as the market is dropping. Potential losses on this trade are unlimited as crude oil trades well above $20 or well below $18/bbl. The object of the trade is to capitalize on an expected

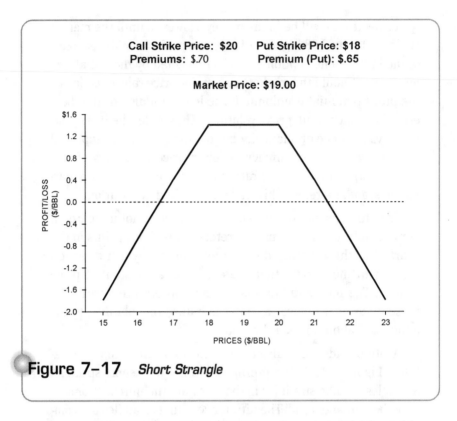

Figure 7-17 *Short Strangle*

narrow price range of $18–$20/bbl, a forecast of fairly stable prices. Unlike straddles, the maximum gains or losses for strangles do not peak at one price, but are consistent over a range of prices. The wider band of prices at which the maximum profit is achievable is an advantage to the trade, but the total potential profit in a strangle is less than that for a straddle.

Another options strategy that benefits from stable prices is the butterfly, but this is a more complicated position than the strangle. A long butterfly (Fig. 7–18) is the combination of one in-the-money long call, two short at-the-money calls, and one out-of-the-money long call. The illustrated case shows calls with an $18 strike price (premium of $1.60), $19 strike premium (premium of $1.10), and $20 strike price (premium of $0.70). The premium received for the sale of the two medium-strike calls ($2.20/bbl) largely, but not completely, offsets the amount paid ($2.30/bbl)

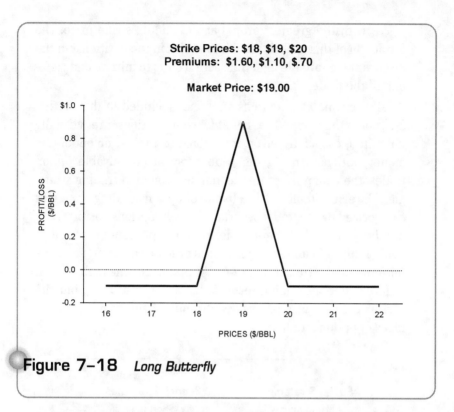

Strike Prices: $18, $19, $20
Premiums: $1.60, $1.10, $.70

Market Price: $19.00

Figure 7–18   *Long Butterfly*

for the low-strike and high-strike calls, resulting in a net premium paid of $0.10/bbl. A long butterfly always has at least a small net debit. When prices are lower than $18, all the calls are out-of-the-money and the trader loses the amount of the net premium. Between $18 and $19, the low-strike call is in-the-money and the position is long at $18/bbl. The difference between the current market price and $18, less the amount of the net premium, is the profit in the trade. That profit is maximized when futures prices are exactly $19/bbl. Above that price, the two short calls are in-the-money, which means that the trader is then long one contract of crude oil at $18 and short two contracts at $19/bbl. The short positions are losing money twice as fast as the one long position, but above $20 the final long call balances the scales. At these higher levels, the profits and losses on the resulting positions offset each other, and the total loss on the trade is the net debit of $0.10/ bbl Clearly, this trade is based on a forecast of stable prices with the greatest profits at the middle strike price. The attraction of this trade is the minimal risk in the position, but the disadvantages are the high transaction costs to initiate and close-out all the trades.

The examples of options strategies included in this section are not exhaustive. The possible combinations are virtually unlimited, especially given the choice of in-, at-, or out-of-the-money options. Among the wide array of conceivable option trades, the examples in this section are common trading strategies. To review, Table 7–7 is a listing of options trading strategies categorized by the trader's market outlook. Options positions can also be grouped by whether there is a net premium received or paid (Table 7–8) and whether profits or losses are defined at the initiation of the trade (Table 7–9). At first blush, the multitude of different options-trading techniques can be confusing, but the vast assortment of strategies is also one of the primary advantages of options trading.

Bullish Strategies	Bearish Strategies
• Long futures	• Short futures
• Long call	• Long put
Moderately Bullish	**Moderately Bearish**
• Bull-call spread	• Bear-call spread
• Bull-put spread	• Bear-put spread
• Short put	• Short call
• Covered call	• Covered put
Stable Prices	**Volatile Prices**
• Short straddle	• Long straddle
• Short strangle	• Long strangle
• Long butterfly	

Table 7–7   *Classification of Trading Strategies by Market Outlook*

Net Debit (Net Premium Paid)	Net Credit (Net Premium Received)
• Long call	• Short call
• Long put	• Short put
• Bull-call spread	• Bear-call spread
• Bear-put spread	• Bull-put spread
• Long butterfly	• Covered call
• Long straddle	• Short straddle
• Long strangle	• Short strangle
	• Covered put

Table 7–8   *Net Debit and Net Credit Options Positions*

Defined Loss Positions (Limited Risk)	Defined Profit Positions (Limited Reward)	Defined Profit-and-Loss Positions (Limited Risk and Reward)
• Long call	• Short call	• Bull-call spread
• Long put	• Short put	• Bear-call spread
• Long straddle	• Short straddle	• Bull-put spread
• Long strangle	• Short strangle	• Bear-put spread
	• Covered calls	• Long butterfly
	• Covered puts	

Table 7–9   *Options Strategies and Defined Risk/Reward Limits*

OPTIONS AND RISK MANAGEMENT

Options are also an important element of commercial companies' risk management programs. The vast selection of put/call, at- and-out-of-the-money options allows an energy company to construct a hedging strategy that closely matches the firm's market expectations and risk parameters. Options are not the only, or necessarily optimal, hedging method, but they are a valuable alternative in the portfolio of risk management techniques. The option hedging strategies included in this section are regularly used by both energy producers and consumers.

Purchasing options to hedge an opposing position in the underlying commodity can be compared to buying price insurance. In exchange for the premium payment, the company is protected against the consequences of an adverse price move. Long options can be used to protect against rising or falling prices. For a natural gas producer, buying a put would establish a minimum, but not maximum, sale price based on the strike price and the premium of the option. For buyers of electricity, a long call would fix a maximum purchase price determined by the strike price and the premium of the option. Depending on market view, risk tolerance, and available capital, the option hedger can choose to use at-the-money or out-of-the-money options. At-the-money options cost more, but they provide more protection than out-of-the-money options. If a crude oil producer buys a put option with a strike price of $18/bbl when current prices are $20/bbl, the price protection offered by the option is only relevant if the market trades lower by $2/bbl. The difference between the current price and the strike price is analogous to the deductible in an insurance policy. In this example, the producer is willing to accept the penalty of a $2/bbl fall in prices, before the price insurance is effective, in exchange for a lower premium cost. It's a situation similar to any kind of insurance—the bigger the deductible, the lower the premium. The following examples will generally use at-the-money options for illustrative purposes, not because they are always the optimum strategy when hedging with options.

The first strategy is a long call option to protect a utility's power purchases against rising electricity prices. The utility is concerned that prices and load requirements will likely increase based on a forecast of an exceptionally cold winter. Consequently, the company would like to establish a maximum price for any incremental power purchases, but not lock-in a fixed purchase price in case the local meteorologist's forecast turns out wrong. By purchasing a long call, the utility can guard against rising prices, yet still take advantage of stable or lower electricity prices. In this case the utility buys a January-February call based on daily electricity prices with a strike price of $35/MWh and a premium of $5.75/MWh. Figure 7–19 shows the effective purchase price for electricity at different market prices. Above $35/MWh, the utility would exercise the

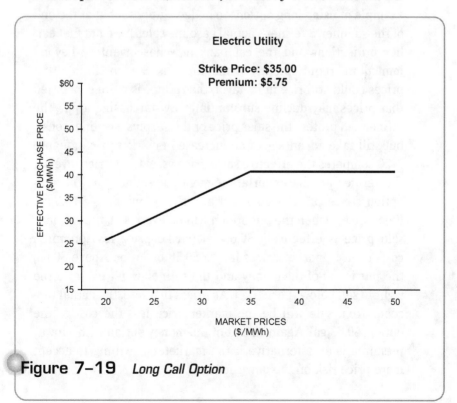

Figure 7–19 *Long Call Option*

option ($35 call) in order to purchase electricity below the market price. No matter how high market prices climbed, the effective purchase price (strike price plus premium) would never be higher than $40.75/MWh. Below $35/MWh, the utility would allow the option to lapse in order to take advantage of lower prices. The effective purchase price would be the current market price plus the amount of the premium (*e.g.*, $30.75 if electricity prices were $25). A utility could also elect to buy an out-of-the-money option for a smaller premium. In this instance, the effective purchase price would be lower if the market declined (due to the smaller premium), but a higher purchase price (because of the higher strike price) if market levels increased. This is the trade-off in choosing an out-of-the-money option, *i.e.*, greater participation in a favorable price move vs. less protection when prices are unfavorable.

Buying puts to protect the value of inventory is another example of using long options to hedge. Suppose that at the end of the summer, a refiner's actual gasoline sales have not met earlier projections and the company now has inventory beyond immediate requirements. While there is the possibility that prices could still rise in its favor, the refiner is more concerned that prices may decline substantially. By purchasing a put, the refiner can protect the sales price of the surplus gasoline stocks, but still take advantage of an increase in market prices. Figure 7–20 compares the effective sales price vs. market price levels if the refiner purchases an at-the-money gasoline put. The put-option strike price is $0.68/gal and the premium is $0.03/gal. Below $0.68, when the put option will be exercised, the refiner's sale price is effectively $0.65/gal (strike price less premium cost) even if market prices fall to $0.58 or lower. Above $0.68, the put is out-of-the-money and the refiner won't exercise the right to sell below the market. As prices increase, the actual proceeds from sale will be the market price less the cost of the option, $0.03/gal. Again, an out-of-the-money option with a lower premium is an alternative if the marketer is willing to accept more price risk on the downside.

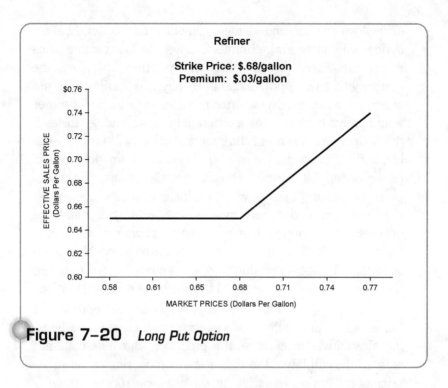

Figure 7-20   *Long Put Option*

Long-option hedge strategies are usually employed when there is considerable uncertainty about the direction of prices, and the hedger wants defined price protection. Also, some traders prefer to buy options as a hedge when implied volatility is low and premiums are relatively cheap. The advantage of long-option hedges is that they offer price protection, but the hedger can still benefit from a favorable price move. The major difficulty with long-option strategies is that they are capital intensive. Commercial entities often complain that the premiums are too high, and depending on the situation, the price protection may not be worth the cost.

Selling options as part of a company's risk management program results in an entirely different risk/reward structure. As we already know, the total gain from a short-option position is limited to the amount of the premium. This fact doesn't change even if the short option is combined with a physical or forward position. The premium is the total cash amount that can be used to offset losses in the underlying commodity. Consequently, short options only offer limited protection against unfavorable price movements based on the underlying position. Therefore, the company that sells options against its physical position does not anticipate a major adverse price move, or the company's trader would probably elect to use a different hedging strategy. Instead, the hedger believes that future market prices will be fairly stable, and the premium income can increase the financial return on the underlying position. Those companies not usually predisposed to hedging their physical positions also use short-option strategies. These firms are more interested in the additional income from the option than in the potential price protection. In their view, the risk inherent in the underlying position is an acceptable business risk that they are prepared to tolerate, and the premium is just incremental income to an existing position.

The earnings of a natural gas producer are susceptible to a fall in prices, and selling calls against production is one hedging alternative. In essence, the producer who sells calls has granted the call buyer the right to buy production at the strike price of the option. In exchange, the producer receives the premium income. If prices rise beyond the strike price, the buyer will exercise the option—if prices fall, the option will expire unused. From the producer's perspective, if the option is in-the-money, he or she is obligated to sell at a price (the strike price) that is lower than current market prices, but the premium represents additional income to the trade. When prices fall, the producer still retains the premium, but the subsequent sale of the natural gas is now at a lower market price. The premium may be only a partial offset to the loss in the value of the production. Figure 7–21 is an illustration of the effective sales price of natural gas if a producer has sold a winter (November-March, monthly settles) call option with a strike price of $2.75/MMBtu and a premium of $.15/MMBtu. As prices rise, the call is in-the-money and the producer effectively sells the natural gas at the strike price plus the value of the premium, or $2.90/MMBtu. If prices fall, the option is not exercised and the return from the natural gas sale is the current market price plus

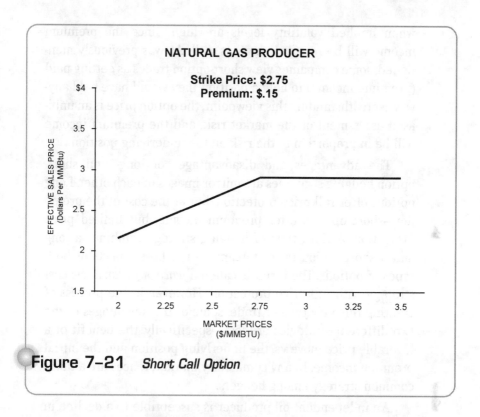

Figure 7–21   *Short Call Option*

the premium received ($.15/MMBtu). When selling at-the-money calls, the producer, in return for the premium, has given up the opportunity to profit from a major increase in prices and risks potential losses if prices fall. The natural gas producer could also choose an out-of-the-money call option with a strike price that is a target sale level. There is no guarantee that prices will rise to the level of the strike price, but if they do, the producer has already determined that he or she is satisfied to sell the production at this price. Should prices decrease, the downside protection of an out-of-the-money call is reduced since the premium received is less.

Short-option strategies do not provide full price protection. The income from the premium can only mitigate the losses on the underlying position in the event of an adverse change in prices. Commercial option hedgers may prefer this strategy when implied volatility levels are high, since the premium income will be relatively high as well. As was previously mentioned, some companies view short-option trades as getting paid (premium income) to hold a position they would have held anyway. Notwithstanding this viewpoint, the option price is an unbiased assessment of the market risk, and the premium income will be in proportion to the risk on the underlying position.

The advantages and disadvantages of long- and short-option hedging strategies are mirror images of each other. Long options offer full price protection, but at the cost of the premium—short options offer premium income, but limited price protection. A third type of hedging strategy combines a long and a short option to try to capture the best aspects of both types of options. The result is called a *fence* or *collar,* a low-cost strategy with full price protection. However, in the process of creating this new type of trade, some of the advantages of the two different strategies are lost—specifically, the benefit of a favorable price move vs. the underlying position and the initial premium income. In any commodity market, fences are a fairly common strategy among hedgers.

An independent oil producer is susceptible to a decline in the value of crude oil. Assume that the producer has decided to hedge this downside risk using crude oil options, but wants to avoid the premium cost of a simple long-put strategy. In this situation, the refiner could purchase puts to protect against falling prices, but also sell call options to finance the cost of the price insurance. The results of this type of strategy are pictured in Figure 7–22. In this example, the market value of the crude at the initiation of the trade was $18, and both of the options were equally out-of-the-money. The short calls have a strike price of $19 and a premium of $0.65/bbl, and the long puts have a strike price of $17 with a premium of $0.60/bbl. The lower premium for the purchased options means that the options' portion of the trade has actually generated a net credit of $0.05/bbl. As prices fall below $17, the producer would exercise the put and sell production a dollar lower, offset only by the very small premium income ($0.05/bbl). The effective sales price

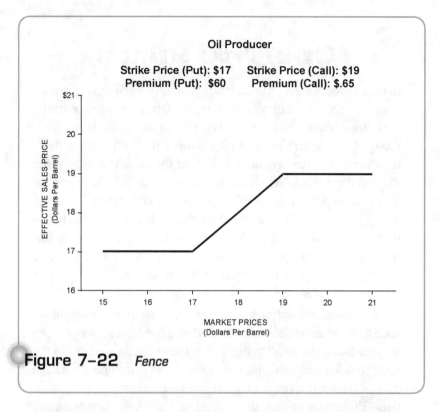

Figure 7–22 *Fence*

will never be lower than $17.05/bbl. If prices increase beyond $19, the in-the-money short call will be exercised and the producer is obligated to sell at $19. The small net premium ($0.05) plus the dollar increase in crude oil prices is the maximum sales level possible with this position. The net proceeds from the crude oil sale can never be higher than $19.05, even if market prices are considerably higher. In between $17 and $19, the options are irrelevant since they are both out-of-the-money, and the effective sales price is the market price plus the small net premium. This strategy has established a minimum sale price (at lower values) and a maximum sale price (at higher prices) for the producer's crude oil. In general, a fence can be designed to limit the downside risk of a cash position while allowing limited participation in any upside potential.

COMPLEX OPTION STRATEGIES

In recent years, new options strategies have been developed for both traders and commercial hedgers. Often these new strategies are called exotic options or complex structures even though most aren't really that complex or exotic. What these structures do have in common are that they don't fit neatly into the standard Black-Scholes option pricing model. The complexity of these options comes in valuing the strategy and managing the position. The following examples are option strategies that are typically used by the energy industry. The charts in this section depict the payout of the different structures, separate and apart from any underlying position and exclusive of premium costs/revenue.

Swaptions are options to buy or sell a swap. The only difference from other options is the underlying instrument, a swap. *Call swaptions* are the right to buy a swap, and *put swaptions* are the right to sell a swap. In addition to the strike price and expiration date of the option, the contract terms will include the swap duration—the start-and-end dates for swap pricing. Swaptions are often based on strips of futures contracts—January-June of the next year or a whole calendar year of contracts.

The maturity date of the option precedes the swap pricing period—*e.g.,* December 15, 1998 for a calendar 1999 swap. A longer duration for the underlying swap (calendar year vs. first quarter of the year) or a more forward start-date after the option's expiration (June 1, 1999 rather than January 1, 1999) will reduce the relative cost of the swaption. Swaps with a longer term or later start-date incorporate pricing in the more distant future, and forward prices are not as volatile as near-term prices. The reduced volatility of the underlying swap lowers the swaption price.

Binary options—sometimes called *digital* options—are another new alternative for energy traders. The difference between binary options and standard options is the payout at maturity. In-the-money binary options pay a fixed amount to the buyer regardless of the spread between the market price and the strike price. The agreed payout of a binary option is the same whether the option is barely in-the-money or deep-in-the-money at expiration. The holder of a call binary option, with a strike price of $20/bbl and a fixed payout of $1.50/bbl, will receive $1.50/bbl whether market prices are $20.01/bbl or $30/bbl. Below the strike price, the binary option is out-of-the-money and pays nothing. Binary or digital options get their name from the all-or-nothing, on/off nature of such options that is pictured in Figure 7–23. In this graph of the call binary option described above, the payout is zero until market prices are above the strike price. At that point the option holder receives the full payout ($1.50/bbl), which doesn't change as prices increase.

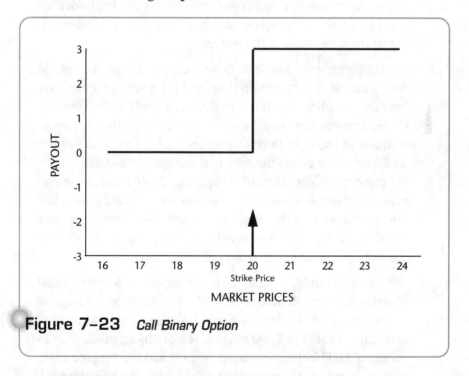

Figure 7–23 *Call Binary Option*

The difference in the payout profile alters the valuation and pricing of binary options. In our discussion of delta, we stated that this statistic was a rough measure of the probability that an option would expire in-the-money. Using the delta of a standard option with the same strike price and maturity, the value of a binary option is the fixed payout multiplied by the delta. In other words, the premium for a binary option is calculated as the odds that the option will be profitable multiplied by the potential profit. Traders of binary options generally have a very defined market view.

Though they are all called swaps, the next four strategies are really a combination of option and swap. Embedded in each swap structure is an option that, when exercised, will significantly alter the original swap position and economics. The optionality in the trade can have a major impact on the swap pricing. All the strategies may be utilized by companies with exposure to either falling prices (producers) or rising prices (consumers), and the trades are often referred to as producer swaps or consumer swaps depending on the orientation of the hedger.

Double-up or *variable volume* swaps function as normal swaps, except that at certain threshold price levels the contract quantity (number of bbls or MMBtus) is automatically doubled. Either party to the swap, buyer or seller, can be the grantor or recipient of the right to double up the trade. If the seller of the double-up swap grants the option, the volume is doubled if market prices are higher than the swap price. In this trade (referred to as a *producer double-up*) the seller has not only sold a swap, but also a call option. If the swap buyer grants the option (*consumer double-up*), the volume is doubled if market prices are lower than the swap price—in effect, a put option is exercised.

As an example, a crude oil producer sells a 6-month 3,000 bbls/day producer double-up at $20/bbl. In any month when the average price of oil exceeds $20/bbl, the swap volume is automatically doubled to 6,000 bbl/day. The producer, in addition to selling a 3,000 bbl/day swap, has sold a $20/bbl average price (Asian) monthly call option for 3,000 bbl/day. The benefit to the producer is the higher price for a double-up swap, $20/bbl vs. $19.50/bbl for an equivalent standard swap.

The double-up swap is a combination of a standard swap and an average price option for the same contract volume with a strike price equal to the swap price. The value of the option is incorporated into the swap price, and therefore double-up swaps are priced differently than standard swaps. The seller of a producer double-up (sells the swap and grants a call option) is paid a higher swap price to compensate for the embedded option. Likewise, a consumer double-up buyer (buys the swap, sells a put option) pays less because the standard swap price is reduced by the value of the put premium. In the example above, the double-up swap price paid to the seller included a premium of $.50/bbl for the call option.

Extendable swaps are also a fusion of swap and option, but it is the duration of the swap, not the volume, that may be changed. In an extendable swap, one counter-part to the trade (buyer or seller) has the option to extend the termination date of the swap (the price and volume would remain the same). For instance, a natural gas consumer could buy a swap for the winter period (November–March), and grant the swap seller the right to extend the swap through the summer (April–October). As with double-up swaps, the incentive for the option grantor, the natural gas consumer, is to improve the base swap price. In this case, the original swap price would be reduced by the value of the put swaption granted by the buyer.

An extendable swap is the combination of a basic swap with a swaption for the extension period. The important elements to these transactions are the initial swap structure (price, volume, term), the expiration date for the option to extend the swap, and the term of the extended swap. The value of the swaption in an extendable swap will determine the price discount or premium vs. a standard swap with similar specifications.

Range swaps are a form of swap where payments are only exchanged within a predetermined market range. If the market price reaches a specified level (knockout price), the swap ceases to exist and payments stop. For producer range swaps, payments are discontinued at a pre-determined price below the swap level, *e.g.*, the producer sells a $19/bbl crude oil range swap with a $15/bbl knockout price. For consumer range swaps, payments quit above the swap price—*e.g.*, the consumer purchases a $1.80/mmbtu natural gas range swap with a knockout price of $2.40/mmbtu.

Figure 7–24 shows the payout profile of the producer range swap. Similar to standard swaps, the payments to the producer increase as prices decline. However, when the knockout price is reached ($15), swap payments are discontinued. Below the knockout price, the producer no longer has any price protection vs. the physical production. The tradeoff for this risk is the better pricing available through range swaps ($19/bbl vs. $17/bbl for a basic swap). The payments from the producer range swap are more than a basic swap over the specified price range because the producer range swap price is greater than the basic swap price.

The range swap structure consists of a swap and two theoretical options—a binary option and a standard option, both struck at the knockout price. In our example, the producer has

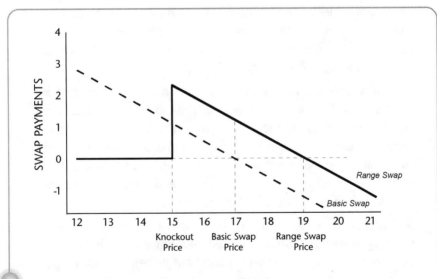

Figure 7–24   *Range Swap Payout Profile*

sold a swap, and effectively, also granted the buyer a binary put option and a standard put option with strike prices equal to the knockout price. The binary option's fixed payment is the difference between the initial swap price and the knockout price, and the other put option begins paying below the knockout price. When the market trades below the established knockout price, the buyer's payout on the two put options is equal to what would have been the buyer's swap payments to the producer. The theoretical payment obligations of buyer and seller are exactly offset, and no payments are made below the knockout level. Because the premiums for the two put options are included in the swap price, the producer range swap is priced higher than a basic swap. The advantage of the improved swap price is countered by the risk that the hedge will disappear just when it is increasingly valuable. As a result, range swaps tend to be used by commercials with a strong market view that prices won't trade below (producers) or above (consumers) a certain level.

Reset swaps are yet another form of swap with an embedded option combination. Similar to range swaps, the initial payments are exchanged over a defined market range. Unlike range swaps, when the market reaches a predetermined price (the reset price), the swap doesn't completely disappear. Instead the swap's fixed price is changed to the reset price, and payments continue based on the revised price level. For a producer reset swap, the reset price is lower than the original swap price, and for consumers the reset price is higher than the original swap price. In a producer reset swap, the producer sells an $17.50/bbl swap with a $15/bbl reset price. As the market trades below the reset price, the swap price is adjusted down to $15/bbl, and swap payments are now based on the revised swap price. A reset swap is different from a range swap in that the producer or consumer doesn't totally lose the price hedge outside of the designated market range. Price protection begins anew at a lower level for producers and higher level for consumers.

Figure 7–25 illustrates the payout for the producer reset swap. Swap payments increase as prices decrease until the mar-

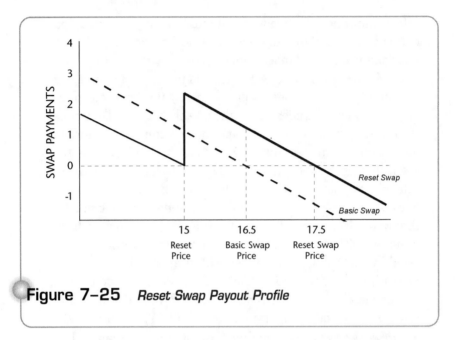

Figure 7-25 *Reset Swap Payout Profile*

ket reaches the reset price. At that level, the swap's fixed price is lowered and payments are now exchanged based on the reset swap price. Reset swaps are used by producers and consumers to improve the original swap price relative to a basic swap structure. In exchange for the better swap price, the commercial company is willing to give up some price protection. The pricing advantage of the reset swap is less than a range swap, but the downside risk is reduced as well.

A reset swap is comprised of a basic swap and a binary option. The strike price of the binary option is the reset price, and the payout of the binary option is the difference between the original swap price and the reset price. For our reset swap example, the producer has sold a swap, and also granted a binary put option to the buyer. At the reset level (strike price of the option), the buyer's swap payments are reduced by the amount of the binary option payout. Swap payments are resumed, but from a lower level, the reset price. Reset swaps are priced at better levels than a standard swap because the premium for the binary option is included in the price.

Consequently, the payout over the initial price range is more than a basic swap (Fig. 7–25). Reset swaps are generally used by commercials with a market view about the range of prices.

CONCLUSION

The energy markets have seen dramatic price fluctuations over the course of time. The abrupt and sizable changes in price have meant both increased risk and opportunity—more risk for the commercial companies who buy and sell energy, and more opportunity for those traders who seek to profit from the changes in the value of oil, natural gas, and electricity. Energy options provide an additional means for hedging and trading, an extension of the underlying markets—physicals, forwards, futures, and swaps. The benefit of options is that they present a wholly new way of trading energy with an entirely different risk/reward structure.

Clearly, options trading can be more involved than trading futures, physicals, or forwards, and the myriad of alternatives may initially be overwhelming. To take advantage of the additional opportunities requires more thinking and planning prior to initiating a trade. In the first place, the trader must decide on the best alternative trading or hedging mechanism. If the decision is to use options, there are still a wide variety of alternative strategies. In selecting the appropriate position, the trader must decide not only the direction of prices, but the expected magnitude of the price change, the relevant time frame, and the acceptable risk levels. However, if the trader can sort through these decisions, options provide a means for tailoring a strategy that closely reflects the trader's views and objectives. The sometime confounding complexity of options is balanced by their superior flexibility in designing an optimal trading strategy.

REFERENCES

Bookstaber, Richard M. *Options Pricing and Investment Strategies.* Chicago: Probus Publishing Co., 1987

Colburn, James T. *Trading in Options on Futures.* New York: New York Institute of Finance, 1990

Fink, Robert E., and Feduniak, Robert B. *Futures Trading: Concepts and Strategies.* New York: New York Institute of Finance, 1988

Kamins, Harold. *Volatility Concepts (presentation).* New York: Morgan Stanley & Co., Incorporated, 1997

Labuszewski, John and Sinquefield, Jeanne Cairns. *Inside the Commodity Option Markets.* New York: John Wiley & Sons, 1985

Mayer, Terry. *Commodity Options: A User's Guide to Speculating and Hedging.* New York: New York Institute of Finance, 1983

Natenberg, Sheldon. *Option Volatility & Pricing.* Chicago: Irwin Professional Publishing, 1994

Ryan, Robert P. "Deciphering Implied Volatility." *Energy in the News.* New York: NYMEX, 2nd quarter, 1987

Sullivan, Joe. *NYMEX Crude Oil Options* (videotape). New York: NYMEX, 1987

DEVELOPMENT AND INTEGRATION OF HEDGING STRATEGIES

by Robert Boslego

Energy price volatility ruled the 1990s. Crude oil prices soared as high as \$40/bbl during the Gulf War and dropped as low as single digits in 1998 and 1999. They were at 10-year highs as this book went to press. Natural gas prices experienced as much—or even greater—volatility as changes in temperatures increased and decreased the size of the "gas bubble." These wild swings in energy commodity prices wreaked havoc on the bottom lines of many energy producers, refiners, marketers, traders, and end-users.

One outgrowth of these market developments was the sprouting of energy price risk management programs throughout the energy industry. For a few companies, the experience was a highly visible financial disaster owing to the misuse—or misunderstanding—of the use of derivatives in so-called "hedging" programs. For the vast majority of companies, success in energy price risk management was mixed. As a result, comprehensive, enterprise-wide risk management programs are still not widespread throughout the industry.

From my experience analyzing energy risk management programs since 1979, there are several key reasons why there are relatively few really successful energy price risk management programs. First and most fundamental is the failure to properly establish an important and sustaining rationale for the hedging program. In every company, there will be wide-ranging opinions as to whether the company should be hedging, and if it does, what results should be expected.

A second critical reason is the failure to properly analyze and quantify the company's portfolio risk exposure on a continuous basis. Clearly, if the risk is misdiagnosed, like a disease, it cannot be properly treated or controlled.

A third crucial reason is lack of a systematic strategy properly designed to address the company's portfolio risk. Few companies have what I consider to be a formal strategy, with decision rules. Many that do have rules based on physical rather than financial events.

A fourth major reason is the lack of structure and discipline in the implementation of the risk management process. Often, expectations are not set or, again, vary widely among executives. Evaluations of results, if they take place at all, are often inconsistent with risk reduction objectives.

In this chapter, I shall try to provide a general overview for how these issues should be addressed.

To hedge, or not to hedge

For hedging to gain lasting acceptance in any company, it must be seen as a means by which the company can better attain its corporate strategic or financial goals. Such goals may include meeting or exceeding a budget, protecting against a drop in cash flow that could threaten debt ratings or payments, or better enabling a company to have a competitive cost or price. In short, it must provide a viable alternative to simply accepting the market risk and its impact. It is management's responsibility to set the proper objectives for risk management and the proper evaluation criteria.

In my view, there are at least two valid hedging objectives:

- to achieve the highest risk-adjusted return on capital employed

- to reduce the risk of unacceptably low returns on capital employed

Over the years, I have heard many reasons why executives believe their companies should not hedge. Some believe that their companies are being rewarded in the stock market for taking energy market risks. Even for those companies that are oriented toward accepting the market's energy price exposure, I believe hedging is still logical. Why? Because companies should take risks that have the highest risk-adjusted expected returns.

Why take risks on exposures that are expected to lose money? If an unhedged portfolio has market exposures with negative expected returns, those exposures should be hedged. By hedging those exposures, the company can afford to take additional risk on exposures with positive expected returns. This is simply the most logical method to allocate risk capital. Whether the outcome of such capital allocation is favorable or not, the company would at least be making a more rationale risk management decision than taking exposures with negative expected returns.

Portfolio risk

Before addressing the questions of what to hedge, when to hedge, or how much to hedge, the company needs to know the nature and magnitude of its price risk. The lessons learned about its price risk are often as valuable in making other business decisions as they are in making the determination of whether to hedge—e.g., refinery optimization and inventory management.

The application of portfolio theory to businesses, and not just stock portfolios, began to take hold in the latter part of the 1990s. Many financial firms, and even some industrial firms, embraced the concept of managing the "enterprise" or "global" risk of their business portfolio.

A *business portfolio* is a group of assets—such as a company's oil reserves, refineries, or inventories. A *financial portfolio* may be a group of oil futures contracts, swaps, and/or derivatives. Each has its own set of risk/return characteristics, depending on what a portfolio includes. When a financial portfolio is combined with the firm's business portfolio, the combination (or total portfolio) will have new risk-return characteristics, or market exposure, than either one separately. Diversification of risk enables the total portfolio to have lower risk than either the business portfolio or financial portfolio has separately. Controlling the risk of the financial portfolio separately is inconsistent with managing the risk of the total portfolio.

It is this portfolio framework that one must apply in the construction of hedges. Otherwise, determining the proper portfolio is just guesswork that may lead to a result the opposite of what is expected.

The Financial Accounting Standards Board (FASB) has defined commodity price risk as *the sensitivity of a firm's income to changes in prices.* Many large oil companies are exposed to changes in literally thousands of prices,[1] and so the problem of price risk identification and quantification is analytically challenging.

As a result, many firms do not conduct a comprehensive, portfolio risk assessment to identify their risk exposure. The most common mistake is that someone identifies one risk within the portfolio and the company hedges that risk.

However, a risk analysis that addresses only part of a company's portfolio (*i.e.,* a partial risk analysis) is inherently flawed. Correlations among all risk factors need to be quantified. The result of considering only part of a company's portfolio risk exposure can in fact lead to a hedging strategy that actually increases, rather than reduces, risk.

Price risk identification

The best way I have found to identify a company's portfolio risk to commodity prices is to create a model of their earnings.

The objective of building the model is to determine how the company's earnings change if "market prices" of related commodities change.

Though any number of market prices can be used in building the earnings' model, I often use NYMEX futures contract prices. The futures price curve could be viewed as an unreliable input since it keeps changing all the time. However, the benefit of this approach is that one can "lock-in" projected earnings if they are high enough, or if the downside is perceived to be great. In a sense, the "prediction" can become a self-fulfilling prophecy through hedging, no matter how the price curve changes after the hedge is established.

Earnings models

Earnings can be forecast by linking NYMEX futures prices to a company's sales prices and costs. The equations can be developed through multiple regression analysis. By inserting the current forward strip, an earnings forecast for forward months can be generated. As NYMEX prices change, new earnings forecasts can be automatically generated.

Stress tests

A stress test is a means for assessing the impact of an extreme price movement on future earnings. For example, with an earnings model, crude futures prices could be increased or decreased by $1/bbl to determine the effect such a change would have on future earnings.

Monte Carlo simulations

The drawback of stress testing is that the probability of the scenario being tested is not taken into account. To assess the likely distribution of earnings for any given month, a probability distribution for futures prices is needed. Further, the relationships among futures prices must be maintained for the resulting distribution to be realistic.

One analytical method to develop a distribution of earnings is "Monte Carlo simulation." A Monte Carlo simulation is a method by which price scenarios are randomly selected from their distribution according to their frequency in the distribution. The output of the simulation is a distribution showing the frequency of different earnings estimates (Fig. 8–1).

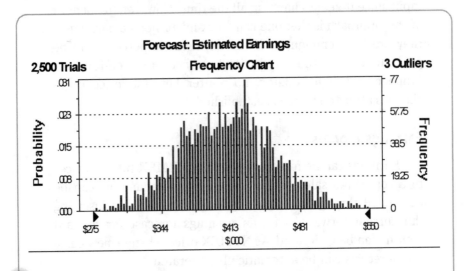

Figure 8-1 *Portfolio Risk Impact Assessments*

The standard deviation of an earnings distribution is a generally accepted measure of portfolio risk. A new standard deviation can be computed when hedge positions are included in the portfolio by running the Monte Carlo simulation. If the new standard deviation is lower, the hedge has reduced portfolio risk, and *vice versa*.

Risk limits

Creating risk limits is one of management's most important steps in the process of controlling risks and the effects of risk management activities. Unfortunately, the risk limits we have seen relate to the risk associated with the hedge positions instead of the corporation's total risk exposure. This is backwards, because the purpose of risk management positions should be to reduce the corporation's total risk exposure. Instead, the risk associated with those positions is treated as a new risk to the corporation, consistent with the view some have that hedging is speculation.

An overall limit to portfolio risk for a given time-period (month, quarter, or year) should be set for the corporation and approved by the board. The company's portfolio risk needs to be assessed on an on-going basis and reported. All proposed hedge transactions should be input to the corporation's portfolio risk model to ensure that it would reduce the portfolio's risk exposure. All positions actually taken need to be input when taken, and removed when closed to the portfolio risk model for all future calculations.

Testing proposed transactions

With an earnings model, proposed hedge or speculative transactions can be tested to determine their impact on portfolio risk. If the proposed transaction reduces portfolio risk, it is a hedge transaction. If it increases risk, it is a speculative transaction. Ideally, the expected risk/return of all proposed transactions should be evaluated before they are entered, and they should meet the pre-determined risk/return "hurdle rates" established by management.

DETERMINING IDEAL HEDGE PORTFOLIO

The risk-minimizing portfolio of hedge contracts can be mathematically derived with an earnings model. The hedge portfolio that is effective in eliminating market risk is the ideal hedge portfolio, or risk-minimizing hedge portfolio.

The hedge ratio is the relationship between the size of the hedge and the size of the position being hedged. For example, if one million barrels of crude were being hedged by 1,000

NYMEX crude contracts, the hedge ratio would be 1.0 (*i.e.*, 1,000,000 barrels divided by 1,000 contract times = 1,000 barrels per contract).

Optimal hedge ratios are rarely 1.0 in the real world. They must be determined by correlations and volatilities such as running Monte Carlo simulations within an earnings model.

Hedge index concept

The size of the hedge should be proportional to the size of the risk. Therefore, as the size of the risk changes, so should the size of the hedge.

Determining the relationship between hedge sizes and risk can be determined objectively or subjectively. Further, the hedge index can be customized to reflect management's appetite for risk.

By characterizing management's "risk preferences" at various earnings levels, it is possible to create a hedging strategy using the hedge index concept. The hedge index concept simply defines in advance the level of hedging that will take place depending on what level of earnings is forecast.

Formal corporate risk preference assessments are highly beneficial for several reasons. They:

- translate management's views to actionable decision rules

- provide the guidance needed for implementation

- reduce the time required by senior management

- ensure greater consistency in program implementation

Hedge strategy development

A hedging strategy is a set of decision rules that define when to enter the hedge, how and when to adjust its size, and when to exit a hedge.

An efficient hedge strategy specifies all key position inputs in advance, *i.e.*, the effect risk exposure will have, and the effect predicted income would have on determining the percent hedged.

Positioning programs translate the strategy to daily decisions. There is no need to reinvent the wheel everyday. Consistency, not emotion, is the key.

Simulating the actual effect of a hedging strategy is both informative in the process of developing the strategy and essential in the process of obtaining management buy-in.

Institutionalizing risk analysis, hedging strategy, and evaluation

To integrate the development of a risk management program with its implementation, it is important to develop and/or revise the company's risk management policies and procedures to reflect the company's objectives, strategy, and structure. The goal should be to provide the necessary means to enable management to successfully control the corporation's risk exposures and guide all risk management activities. All major participants should review drafts of the policies and procedures for their input, understanding, and commitment to their success.

The creation of a risk management committee (RMC) to steer the management of a company's risks is a good idea that works. Generally, there are issues that require input from numerous corporate departments, and so the timely and recurring input of each is useful. Therefore, it makes sense to keep key executives and departments informed on a regular basis. Because risk management is a financial function, the chief financial officer or treasurer should normally chair the RMC. The person acting as risk manager should be a knowledgeable manager of traders, supply or purchasing, depending on the business.

More specifically, some key elements the policies and procedures should include:

- Define an evaluation criterion that specifically measures how well the company is meeting its objectives for risk management.

- Define the methodologies that shall be used to measure portfolio risk exposures. Relate to the company's overall price risk exposures, and not be limited to controlling risks of derivatives only. Create an earnings model and risk manager's model to project portfolio risk and return.

- Require the development and implementation of a formal risk management strategy with decision rules for hedge entry, hedge size, and hedge exit.

- Identify the risk management instruments that can be used.

- Define management's responsibilities in monitoring and controlling risk measurement and management.

- Specify levels of authority, risk limits, and "red flags"—such risk limits not simply being a maximum derivative loss.

- Specify the process for quickly and effectively addressing any development that has been "flagged."

- Provide the necessary level of reporting to those responsible for managing, implementing, and monitoring risk management activities.

- Define management reports that management can understand.

- Provide clear separation between those implementing the risk management activities and those controlling the activities.

- Specify hedge criteria and establish the infrastructure for hedge accounting.

Evaluating hedging effects

Typically, most companies do not determine in advance how they will judge their hedging performance. Of course, this causes unpleasant surprises after the fact.

Most companies measure results only in terms of hedge gains or losses—the same way they would measure the success of a speculative trading program. We recommend the use of both risk and return measures.

Over time, a successful hedging program will outperform both the "blind hedge" (*i.e.*, 100% hedge) and the "unhedged" case, in risk-adjusted return.

Energy price risks are out there. You can manage them or hope for the best.

NOTES

1. Again, I characterize similar commodities sold at different locations or under different classes of trade as different exposures.

DELIVERIES, ADPS, AND EFPS

by Peter Beutel[1]

To most participants, futures contracts are financial instruments—paper barrels or paper electricity—that are liquidated before trading ends and delivery is required. However, the success of any futures contract is critically dependent on the confidence of all participants that the market will bear a predictable and reliable relationship to the physical (or wet-barrel, real kilowatt) market. In other words, that paper barrels can be turned into wet barrels should a buyer or seller so desire.

Traditionally, the simplest method of ensuring this relationship is through each futures contract's requirement for physical delivery of the specified commodity—or the cash equivalent determined by reliable indices. Therefore, all futures contracts spell out in laborious detail the terms for physical delivery. However, flexibility is allowed in the form of alternate delivery procedures (ADP) and exchanges for physicals (EFP), which we shall discuss presently.

---

1. Contributions by Virginia Cowan.

DELIVERIES

On the New York Mercantile Exchange's NYMEX Division, trading ceases in heating oil and gasoline futures on the last business day of the calendar month before the delivery month. In other words, the October heating oil contract expires on September 30 (or the last business day) and the April gasoline contract expires on March 31 (unless it falls on a Saturday, Sunday, or Good Friday).

Crude oil contracts on the NYMEX Division expire on the third business day before the 25th. Normally, crude contracts expire between the 19th and 22nd of the month prior to the delivery month. A July crude oil contract will ordinarily cease trading around June 20, give or take a couple of days.

On the International Petroleum Exchange (IPE), gasoil futures expire at noon on the business day that is three business days prior to the 13th of the month. Brent crude oil futures expire on the 10th calendar day (or the business day before that) of the month preceding delivery.

Heating oil and gasoline deliveries on NYMEX can be made by delivery into a buyer's barge, truck, tanker, pipeline, by pump-over, or by stock or book transfer. The NYMEX Division crude contract calls for delivery free on board (FOB) at any pipeline or any storage facility in Cushing, Oklahoma, with pipeline access to ARCO Cushing storage or Texaco Trading and Transport.

Material acceptable for NYMEX product deliveries must meet Colonial Pipeline specifications. Crudes deliverable against the light, sweet crude oil contract are West Texas Intermediate, Low Sweet Mix, New Mexican Sweet, North Texas Sweet, Oklahoma Sweet, South Texas Sweet, U.K. Forties, U.K. Brent Blend, Colombian Cusiana, Nigerian, Bonnie Light, and Norwegian Oseberg Blend. Other crude oils can be delivered through the use of an EFP or an ADP.

IPE uses a cash settlement system that allows traders to collect monies due them, and requires them to pay for losses accrued should they hold positions through expiration. Those who prefer to use their IPE positions in conjunction with a physical transaction may use either an EFP or ADP.

There are many additional rules that are available from brokers or the exchanges—and not all of them are listed in this book. Each delivery is different, so before taking your first delivery, it would be wise to consult an experienced broker. Let us actually walk through delivery to put things in perspective.

We will create a company, Trading Heating Oil Resellers (THOR) that wishes to take delivery of 25,000 barrels of November heating oil. On the other side is a company, Wise Oil Distributors Energy Company (WODEN), wishes to make delivery on 50,000 barrels of November heating oil. THOR is still long 25 November contracts on Halloween (October 31), while WODEN remains short 50 November heating oil contracts when the goblins come out.

They are matched by the NYMEX on 25 contracts (or the equivalent of 25,000 barrels), and WODEN is matched with a second firm, Light Oil, Kerosene & Insulation (LOKI) for the other 25,000 barrels—but let's not be led off our path by LOKI just now. The settlement for November heating oil on the last day of trading will be used as the basis of delivery. Delivery must take place between the fifth business day and the second-to-last business day of the month.

The buyer can tender delivery instructions between those dates. He must make the tender two calendar days prior to delivery, and do so before 10:30 AM or sacrifice another day. In this case, THOR tenders delivery instructions to WODEN at 9:00 AM on Tuesday, November 15. The delivery is to be by barge along the Hudson River, where THOR has storage facilities. Schedulers for both THOR and WODEN nominate a barge, arrange for independent assessment of the product, and agree on timing. In this case, it will be Thursday, November 17. The buyer is expected to pay the seller by certified check by noon the following day. In practice, this is often accomplished by letters of credit. In our example, THOR would pay WODEN for 25,000 barrels at the settlement price on October 31 at 10:30 AM, Friday, November 18.

Once the material passes the intake flange of the buyer's barge, it is responsibility. That is the definition of FOB: The seller is free of any responsibilities of ownership once it is on board the buyer's vessel.

ADP

If the buyer and seller matched by the exchange prefer to make and take delivery under terms or conditions that vary from those of the exchange, they may elect to pursue an alternate delivery procedure (ADP). Once they have given notices of their decision to the exchange, they are on their own—together—no longer under the aegis of the exchange or its clearing members. Thus, the ADP procedure offers even greater flexibility than the EFPs (to be discussed next), since EFPs require a transfer of title to physical oil, whereas an ADP does not require such a transfer.

EFPs: Midwife in the union of cash and futures

An EFP is the means for a very special type of transformation. It enables a paper futures contract to go experience a unique metamorphosis into a physical, or wet position. An EFP is a vital link between cash and futures that acts as an important stabilizing influence should one market get out of step with the other. It is an indispensable tool for hedgers wishing to use futures as both a price and supply hedge.

In order to understand how EFPs work in the oil futures market, we must first review their underlying premise. When NYMEX initiated trading in oil futures (with its heating oil contract in November 1978), it recognized the importance of linking the paper market to the wet market. Without mechanisms providing for a smooth conversion between wet barrels and paper barrels, there could be no firm mooring to an underlying commodity. Fungibility would have to be anchored to a workable and accepted method allowing for physical delivery. As the NYMEX has grown and added contracts, it has always built those new contracts around solid frameworks of physical convertibility (*i.e.,* delivery procedures that work).

Many oil contracts have been started without proper attention to the delivery mechanism. Before NYMEX tried it in 1978, there was a string of failures stretching back to 1890, when hundreds of thousands of "to arrive" barrels of oil were traded daily on the Consolidated Stock & Petroleum Exchange in Manhattan. Since 1978, other contracts have died because of poorly received delivery methods. A successful futures contract is based on an underlying physical commodity. It must have a delivery process that is flexible, responsive, and accepted.

The oil contracts that trade on NYMEX and on IPE have been built around delivery processes that fulfill the needs of the companies using them as hedging vehicles. The trade, as those companies are called, can make or take delivery against those contracts, or use them as purely financial hedges. It is their decision.

As it works out, most oil companies buy and sell their wet oil through established channels and use futures as a financial hedge for months in advance. There has been a growing trend, however, to use both of these approaches simultaneously. That method is the EFP, the exchange for physical.

How EFPs work

Sometimes, companies would rather go through the delivery process with a company with whom they have previously dealt in the cash market. Rather than taking 1,000 barrels of crude oil from a different company each day or each week—as could possibly happen by means of NYMEX delivery for light, sweet crude oil—a company can select another company that is familiar and comparable in size.

Let us say that Standard Petroleum of Illinois (SPILL) has 300 contracts long of September NYMEX crude oil about to expire. For now, let us overlook the aggregate price. That translates into 10,000 barrels per day (bpd) into the pipeline system at Cushing, Oklahoma. If SPILL elects to go through normal NYMEX delivery, there may be days with more than one supplier of the crude oil. This should not be a problem, but to avoid extra bookkeeping, SPILL decides to EFP the 300 contracts. One of SPILL's regular trading partners, the Missouri Oil Marketers & Buyers Association (MOMBA), has at least 300 contracts short of September light, sweet crude oil.

Let us focus on SPILL's 300-contract problem, rather than concentrating on both SPILL's and MOMBA's position for now. MOMBA has at least 300 shorts. The companies contact each other and agree to enter into an EFP transaction for 300 contracts, or 300,000 barrels (for September with 30 days, that is 10,000 bpd).

In the futures market, SPILL's 300 longs match with MOMBA's 300 shorts and cancel each other out. Restoring the hidden step would show SPILL selling 300 contracts to MOMBA, thereby liquidating SPILL's long position and covering MOMBA's short position. Neither company wants to be flat. To balance the equation, SPILL then buys 300,000 barrels of wet oil from MOMBA in the cash market. MOMBA will deliver 10,000 bpd (via pipeline) during September to SPILL's Lincoln City refinery. Table 9–1 shows SPILL's and MOMBA's actions.

| | SPILL | | MOMBA | |
	NYMEX	Cash	NYMEX	Cash
July	300 long	Needs 300 for refinery	300 short	Gathers bbls to sell in September
Late August	EFP with MOMBA		EFP with SPILL	
	Sells 300	Buys 300	Buys 300	Sells 300
Net position in September	Flat	Takes wet delivery	Flat	Delivers wet bbls to SPILL

Table 9–1   *SPILL's and MOMBA's Tally Sheet #1*

In table form, that is how the mechanism works. SPILL sells its 300 longs on NYMEX and replaces them with a purchase of 300 contracts in the cash market. MOMBA buys back its short commitments on NYMEX, and sells 300 contracts in the cash market in their place. Rather than execute each leg of the transaction individually, these companies complete the deal in one single trade. This is why EFPs have become the preferred mode of entering into physical delivery at both NYMEX and IPE.

We have witnessed the physical metamorphosis of paper barrels into wet barrels, but we purposely left out any prices. Let us now examine EFP's financial applications. Table 9–2 includes prices.

| | SPILL | | MOMBA | |
	NYMEX	Cash	NYMEX	Cash
April	Buys 300 @ $17.00/bbl			
June			Sells 300 @ $18.00/bbl	
July	300 long	Needs 300 for refinery	300 short	Gathers bbls to sell in September
Late August	EFP with MOMBA @ $17.50/bbl Sells 300 @ $17.50/bbl	Buys 300 @ $17.50/bbl	EFP with SPILL @ $17.50/bbl Buys 300 @ $17.50/bbl	Sells 300 @ $17.50/bbl
Net position in September	Flat	Takes wet delivery	Flat	Delivers wet bbls to SPILL

Table 9–2 *SPILL's and MOMBA's Tally Sheet #2*

In April, SPILL's traders recognize an emerging uptrend and decide to lock in their crude acquisition prices out to September. Their existing contracts with suppliers cover them for everything but 10,000 bpd of crude oil needed at SPILL's Lincoln City refinery, so they purchase 300 contracts (300,000 barrels) of September light, sweet crude oil on the NYMEX—the equivalent of 10,000 bpd for the 30-day month. In April, when they buy these contracts, the price for September barrels is $17.00/bbl.

In June, after a rise of a $1.00/bbl since May, MOMBA's traders start to feel that a temporary top may be forming in prices. Since MOMBA is a cooperative-gathering operation, the decision is made to play it safe by locking in selling prices through the rest of the calendar year. Now, MOMBA's traders are known to be both shrewd and nimble so other traders always watch their actions and second-guess them—this has made them very secretive. We cannot say with certainty how many of their barrels were sold in June, but we do know that they sold at least 300 for September delivery on NYMEX at a price of $18.00/bbl.

At any rate, come August 20, the September crude oil contract reaches expiration and SPILL still has 300 contracts long while MOMBA has at least 300 contracts short. They decide to do an EFP with each other. Fortunately, the crude oil gathered in Missouri by MOMBA is Sweet Border Blend (S.B. Blend)—a light, low-sulfur crude oil that is conveniently identical to West Texas Intermediate (WTI) in every significant aspect. There are no discounts or premiums between S.B. Blend and WTI, which can be used interchangeably by Mid-Continent refiners.

On August 20, September NYMEX crude oil finishes out at $17.50/bbl, which is the price that SPILL and MOMBA agree to use in their EFP transaction, both to close out their futures positions and to initiate their cash positions. Table 9–3 demonstrates how their futures positions square out.

They both made $0.50/bbl on their individual NYMEX trading but, more importantly, these were "hedge" positions. That $0.50 has to show up on the debit side somewhere else—and it does: When SPILL buys 300,000 barrels of S.B. Blend from MOMBA at $17.50/bbl, SPILL has to pay $0.50 more for its crude oil than it had planned to back in April, while MOMBA receives

	SPILL		MOMBA	
	Bought	Sold	Bought	Sold
April	300 September @ $17.00/bbl			
June				300 September @ $18.00/bbl
August		300 September @ $17.50/bbl	300 September @ $17.50/bbl	
Net		+$0.50/bbl		+$0.50/bbl

Table 9–3   SPILL's and MOMBA's Tally Sheet #3

$0.50 less than it had planned for in June. This is how the futures hedges paid off for both of them. SPILL pays $17.50/bbl for its wet S.B. Blend supply minus its $0.50 profit on its NYMEX hedge for a net acquisition cost of $17.00/bbl. MOMBA receives $17.50/ bbl from its cash-market sale plus its $0.50 profit from its NYMEX hedge, for a total sales price of $18.00/bbl. Both companies have succeeded in their objectives, and their trading departments have continued the corporate effort to stave the wolves from their respective doors each quarter.

EFPs as a quality hedge

EFPs have other uses. Primary among them is their use as a means of hedging varied international types of crude oil. NYMEX accepts WTI, Brent Blend, Bonny Light, and Oseberg Blend, among others, for delivery against its crude contracts. What about other crudes? How can they be hedged on the Merc or on IPE? The answer is, once again, by using EFPs. Let us look at how they can be hedged.

Let us say there is a trading company called Cross Alps Traders of Oil (CATO) based in Alpenland, Europe. They specialize in cargos of a crude oil called Hannibal Light from the Republic of New Carthage, North Africa. They ship the oil to a refiner on the U.S. Gulf, Refining & Oil Marketing Enterprises (ROME). Hannibal Light usually trades somewhere between $0.50 and $2.00 below WTI.

In December, CATO's traders decide to look into a long-term deal with the Republic of New Carthage for a monthly cargo of Hannibal Light. The price is established at the current market differential of $0.30/bbl more than Brent Blend. To lock in that price, CATO buys Brent futures on the IPE for three months ahead. CATO must lock in the sales price while ROME must lock in its purchase price. CATO and ROME enter into a to-be-priced (TOP) relationship designed around EFPs. They agree to use a differential of $1.00 between WTI and Hannibal Light, which is where it is at the time, in December.

(In this example, no allowances have been made for transportation or profits in order to keep things simple. For those who cannot bear that thought, assume either that ROME is a wholly owned subsidiary of CATO, or that New Carthage rebates CATO for transportation costs and credits the firm the equivalent of 2% of the purchase price on the next lifting.)

CATO's traders immediately sell 600 contracts of February, March, and April NYMEX crude futures. ROME's traders buy an equal amount. The prices for February, March, and April are $18.00, $17.50, and $17.00/bbl, respectively. CATO's biggest concern out to April is the relationship between Brent and WTI: Anything below $1.30/bbl means CATO will pay more for Hannibal Light based on Brent and receive less for it based on NYMEX crude. If the light, sweet crude contract is more than $1.30/bbl above Brent, CATO will receive a windfall.

Based on these numbers, CATO will be long on IPE at $16.70 $16.20, and $15.70/bbl for February, March, and April contracts, respectively, and short on NYMEX at $18.00, $17.50, and $17.00/bbl, respectively. The Republic of New Carthage has a committee reviewing futures and is still at the mercy of the market.

By early January, prices have dropped $0.50 across the board, leaving all differentials the same. CATO now lifts a cargo of Hannibal Light and pays the Republic of New Carthage

December—CATO

	Buy	Sell	Description
Dec 2	600,000 bbls/mo of Hannibal Light @ Brent plus $0.30/bbl		Republic of New Carthage sells Hannibal Light cash
Dec 3	600 contracts of IPE crude oil: Feb @ $16.70/bbl Mar @ $16.20/bbl Apr @ $15.70/bbl		IPE Brent futures
Dec 4		600 contracts of NYMEX crude oil Feb @ $18.00/bbl ($130/bbl more than Brent) Mar @ $17.50/bbl	NYMEX WTI futures
		Apr @ $17.00 600,000 bbls/mo of Hannibal Light @ WTI minus $1.00/bbl	EFP with ROME

December—ROME

Buy	Sell	Description
600 contracts of NYMEX crude oil Feb @ $18.00/bbl ($130/bbl more than Brent) Mar @ $17.50/bbl		NYMEX WTI futures
Apr @ $17.00/bbl 600,000 bbls/mo of Hannibal Light @ WTI minus $1.00/bbl		EFP with CATO

Table 9–4 *CATO's and ROME's Tally Sheet #1*

$16.50/bbl—the price of February Brent plus $0.30/bbl and $0.50 less than CATO expected to pay. But there is a catch—that $0.50 is lost on their futures position that they received cash settlement for on the IPE. The end result is a purchase price of $17.00/bbl.

By the end of January, CATO delivers its cargo of Hannibal Light to ROME. They affect their EFP on the Merc at a price of

$18.00/bbl, as the price rose $1.00 while the oil was on the water. CATO receives from ROME $1.00 less for the differential for the crude oil, as agreed to earlier. CATO has made $0.50/bbl on the physical transaction, but has lost $0.50/bbl on its short-futures positions. Similarly, ROME paid $0.50/bbl more than it had planned to for Hannibal Light, but made $0.50/bbl on its futures position.

As one can see, this was not terribly profitable for CATO—they received what they had paid for their Hannibal Light. In normal instances, they would have negotiated to take into account a certain amount of profit-after-transportation costs, but the numbers used in this example are strictly for point of comparison. In this example, the EFP allowed CATO to protect itself against adverse price movements. The EFP also dovetailed nicely with both CATO's and ROME's physical commitments to each other. What's more, there are 11 more months for their traders to earn their keep. Let us review the transactions made so far.

In actuality, CATO and ROME could initiate their futures positions through an EFP transaction, but this example is attempting to show every step of the whole deal. The effect is parallel, regardless of whether the futures position is initiated through an EFP or normally on the floor of NYMEX. An EFP could be agreed upon even when the exchange is closed, provided it does not initiate a position within the last three days of trading in the particular contract. Liquidating EFP transactions can be done until 2:00 P.M. of the trading day following a contract's expiration.

As early January arrives, CATO lifts its first cargo of Hannibal Light from the Republic of New Carthage. It simultaneously sells out its long position on the IPE in London. CATO has expected to lift the Hannibal Light at $17.00/bbl and enter January with a long position of 600 lots in February IPE Brent crude oil futures at $16.70/bbl. Table 9–5 charts CATO's January activities.

The gain of $1.00/bbl in the cash market offsets the two $0.50/bbl losses in the futures. For CATO, this has been an effec-

January—CATO			
	Buy	**Sell**	**Description**
Jan 2	Lifts 600,000 bbls/mo of Hannibal Light @ Brent plus $0.30/bbl, or $16.50/bbl		From Republic of New Carthage
		600 IPE crude oil Feb @ IPE $16.20/bbl	IPE Brent futures
Net	600 @ $16.70/bbl	600 @ $16.20/bbl	IPE futures
LOSS	$0.50/bbl		
Net	600,000 bbls @ $16.50/bbl		Hannibal Light
Jan 20		600,000 bbls @ $17.50/bbl (WTI—$1.00/bbl)	Hannibal Light sold to ROME in cash market
	600 contracts of Feb. WTI futures @ $18.50/bbl		NYMEX EFP with ROME
Net	600 @ $18.50/bbl	600 @ $18.00/bbl	NYMEX WTI futures EFP with ROME
LOSS	$0.50/bbl		
Net	600,000 bbls @ $16.50/bbl	600,000 bbls @ $17.50/bbl	Hannibal Light cash position

Table 9–5 *CATO's Tally Sheet #2*

tive hedge—had the market advanced $0.50/bbl in early January and then dropped $1.00/bbl in late January, there would have been two $0.50/bbl gains on the futures sides of the transaction and a $1.00/bbl loss on the cash position. Table 9–6 shows ROME's January activities.

ROME paid $0.50/bbl more for its shipment of Hannibal Light than it had planned to, but because the company was hedged, that $0.50/bbl increase in cost was offset by a $0.50/bbl

January—ROME			
	Buy	Sell	Description
Jan 20	600,000 bbls @ WTI minus $1.00/bbl		Hannibal Light from CATO
		600 contracts of Feb. crude oil (WTI) @ $18.50/bbl	NYMEX EFP with CATO
Net	600 @ $18.00/bbl	600 @ $18.50/bbl	NYMEX WTI futures EFP with CATO
LOSS	$0.50/bbl		
Net	600,000 bbls @ $17.50 (WTI minus $1.00/bbl)		Hannibal Light cash position

Table 9-6 ROME's Tally Sheet #2

gain on ROME's long NYMEX futures position. The net effect is that ROME paid what it had planned to pay. (Remember, there is a refined products short position in place that has locked in ROME's refining margin.)

EFP mechanics

On January 20, when CATO and ROME EFP their futures positions with each other, their traders follow a simple procedure. Both companies call their favorite brokerage houses (First Consul Securities for CATO, and Skippee, O'Frick, Cannes for ROME). The companies had already agreed upon a set price differential between WTI (as represented by NYMEX crude-oil futures) and Hannibal Light. That differential was $1.00/bbl under WTI for Hannibal Light.

When CATO's traders call their brokers at First Consul, they tell them they want to do an EFP. They say they are short 600 February crude and instruct their brokers to look for Skippee's broker on the floor (representing ROME), who holds 600 longs in February crude. CATO's traders also give First Consul the price and other details of the EFP, including the physical side.

In this case, the price on which they agree to settle out the futures position is $18.50/bbl, while their cash transaction in Hannibal Light is done at $17.50/bbl.

ROME's traders follow a similar procedure when they called their brokers at Skippee, providing mirror-image information. Floor brokers acting on behalf of the brokerage houses will find each other, check and exchange the details of the EFP, and, if everything agrees, they will then post the EFP as a completed transaction with the NYMEX. It is now an official trade—Brokers from First Consul and from Skippee call their clients at CATO and ROME, respectively, to let them know that their EFP has been posted.

What has happened is that CATO and ROME have exchanged their futures positions, in effect netting out their position in futures and substituting cash-market (or wet-barrel) positions in their place. NYMEX (or IPE, as the case may be) matches one trader's short position with another trader's long position, in this case, CATO's short with ROME's long, liquidating both. These former futures positions have been "exchanged for physical" positions. The transformation is complete.

The EFP allowed both companies to enjoy the security of exchange-regulated trading and the financial surety that attends it. Both companies enjoyed the benefits of futures and were also able to easily convert the financial hedge into a physical trade when the time was right to do so. EFPs provide all the advantages of futures and cash markets, and they are like a porous membrane that easily allows the transformation of one into the other.

EFPs are becoming increasingly popular because of their ease and convenience. In many delivery months, EFPs account for more than 80% of the closeouts in the last few days, on both NYMEX and on IPE. They can be used to either initiate or close out positions, and they help to keep a tight relationship between futures and cash.

RISK MANAGEMENT

by Daniel A. Pocius & W. Walter Green III

During the mid-1980s, chief financial officers (CFO) of energy companies attending the industry's finance conferences were greeted with a new panel topic. "Energy Risk Management" was promoted as the new financial discipline offering the CFO tools and techniques, that could redefine the role of the treasury and finance department. It built on the momentum created by the evolution of the interest rate derivative market that began in the late 1970s. Commercial and investment bankers were eager to apply these concepts to new markets.

After NYMEX opened trading of crude oil futures in 1983 and the Commodity Futures Trading Commission (CFTC) granted "safe harbor" to over-the-counter (OTC) commodity derivative trading in the U.S., commercial and investment banks rushed to establish energy derivative departments. They broadly promoted their expertise and creativity. Concepts that were previously reserved for the trading room were now available to help enhance a company's financial performance. These applications were promoted as having the potential to smooth earnings volatility, improve capital expenditures forecasting, justify an increased amount of financing, and improve shareholder value.

Like any new concept, there was great debate about the practical application of these risk management techniques. As CFOs of energy companies considered the need to balance oil price risk, interest rate, and in some cases exchange-rate risk, in order to maintain access to the capital markets, they were a willing audience. As they learned about straddles, swaptions, and other hedging techniques, many were also starting to consider and debate how these would be incorporated into their treasury organization and what other risks would arise as a result.

As the new century begins, the debate continues to rage. The difference today, vs. the late 1980s, is that all parties now have a personal experience—or in some cases, a horror story—to justify their position.

This chapter will briefly review the development of the energy derivative market and highlight some of the risks and challenges facing today's CFOs, including some recent events and experiences that offer insight. Finally, we will offer a perspective on the future of energy risk management and provide a few suggestions for an energy company CFO to consider when establishing a risk management program.

DEVELOPMENT OF OVER-THE-COUNTER ENERGY DERIVATIVES

Product development

Development of energy risk management products was expected to mimic that of more mature derivatives in interest rates and currencies. With gradual acceptance by corporations, these would eventually become mainstream risk management tools. With financial institutions serving as consultants to less sophisticated companies, much of the energy risk management business, and profits, were expected to flow through financial institutions. Banks viewed energy risk management as a credit quality enhancement that would eventually become a requirement for credit hungry energy producers. Energy consumers were also expected be a significant user as products matured and gained acceptance, and would be more likely to rely upon banks for energy risk management advice.

The Persian Gulf War gave the business a burst of momentum. Producers took value from an overheated market while energy consumers were motivated by short-term panic to hedge. Margins were substantial and the strong volume drew many new dealers to the market. Both futures and OTC derivative activity grew quickly. When the war ended, prices fell and the energy derivative business contracted rapidly. With more stability anticipated, consumers, no longer worried about supply, became hesitant to commit to a hedge program. As the Gulf War volatility became a fading memory, volume in the market slowed to a crawl.

In the aftermath, some market leaders among energy consumers began disputing the wisdom of hedging, contending that financial strength obviated the need to hedge. Some took the position that only the weak would suffer long-term harm from temporary price spikes. On the producer side, optimism outweighed risk. Producers had no interest in giving away potential upside profits with current swap prices below $20, remembering that spot prices had broken $40 just months before. In addition—and more importantly—producers did not necessarily see energy price risk as a negative. They often argued that their shareholders bought their stock in order to take a position on commodity prices, therefore they did not want to reduce their energy price exposure.

In the years that followed, the growth of energy risk management products took an unexpected path. Much of the activity was tactical or opportunistic in nature. Corporations took advantage of perceived anomalies in the market, primarily with short-term trades. Sophisticated energy companies used their market knowledge to continue trading as they had in the past, but were now able to use OTC derivatives as trading tools. Many energy companies actually became competitors for banks as they provided internal and external risk management advice and execution. The anticipated strategic applications of OTC derivatives to control market exposure, improve credit rating, or finance acquisitions were far less numerous than expected. Financial institutions, whose business plans called for the growth of the energy derivative business to parallel the growth of currency and interest rate derivatives, were disappointed.

Much of the tactical activity was conducted directly on the exchange or "went OTC" when rare market anomalies occurred. Strategic activity was often dependent upon the ability of banks to demand that hedging be in place to support the extension of credit. When the volume of business did not materialize, banks moved quickly to consolidate or abandon their energy derivative groups. This resulted in some stabilization of margins and a concentration of commodity derivative business between banks and those customers who valued their advice and rewarded their top bank relationships.

During 1993 and 1994, in an attempt to expand the applications of commodity derivatives, dealers developed new asset class—commodity-structured notes. Dealers hoped that by embedding commodity structures into debt instruments they could access customer segments not previously available. Both those who sought commodity exposure as an alternative investment, and those who could not use straight derivative structures to hedge existing commodity exposures, were potential users of these new instruments.

For those who desired to diversify an equity and/or fixed income portfolio or obtain inflation protection, several dealers created commodity indexes. Thus, with a single investment an investor could capture some of the upside of the commodity markets. Structured notes provided a convenient and flexible vehicle for this investment.

Unfortunately, the concept of commodity-structured notes never generated the volume of business that many dealers anticipated. Although the theoretical justification of a small asset allocation to real assets (including commodities) was well accepted, asset managers did generally not put it into practice. After stumbling in 1994, equity and fixed income markets resumed their upward trend, making diversification trades less interesting. Where energy investments were made, it was generally as direct investments and not through derivatives. Furthermore, inflation remained innocuous, so commodity investment as an inflation hedge created very little interest. In addition, many asset managers preferred money market instruments to real assets for inflation protection. Perhaps most importantly, the derivatives debacles of the mid-1990s (Orange County, Procter & Gamble, etc.) made structured notes a less than desirable tool for asset managers.

As a result, the focus for energy derivatives shifted back to standard risk management for energy producers and consumers. Simple swaps, caps, floors, and collars make up the overwhelming majority of all commodity derivative trades. Occasionally hedgers will use swaptions as a part of a structure. Swaptions—options to enter into a swap—are used to hedge potential exposure, such as exposure associated with a pending acquisition. Variations on the swaption include the extendable swap, whereby a producer sells a swaption to a dealer in order to obtain a higher fixed price in the swap. Other variations such as barrier structures and knockouts are also occasionally used. For the most part, except for some of the exotic structures created for commodity speculators during the structured note period, commodity derivative structures have stayed "plain vanilla."

The financial community's disappointment at the use of derivatives in the traditional oil and gas sector abated when new players started to emerge. Deregulation of the natural gas and electricity markets created new participants. As players in regulated industries compete for revenues and have to account for expenses, risk management is becoming a key determinant in their survival and success. From the ranks of the previously regulated, both sophisticated derivatives users and smaller scale hedgers have provided much of the growth. These new users have been quicker to embrace the need for risk management than many of the potential customers of the early 90s. Exploration and production companies were the prime targets for energy derivative providers when this business began, but they proved to be very reluctant hedgers. Utilities and power marketers have proved to be more risk averse and more likely to participate in the derivatives market even "between market peaks." As a result, natural gas and electricity markets show greater promise for the growth of energy derivatives.

Natural gas

Natural gas was the fuel for growth of the commodity derivative business after the Persian Gulf War. Natural gas futures and options traded on the NYMEX became substantially more liquid during 1992 and 1993. As a result, the OTC derivative business in Henry Hub natural gas grew quickly with the participation of both physical and financial market dealers. Short term hedging by both producers and consumers made up the bulk of natural gas derivative business in the early 1990s. However, the limitations of the market were soon stretched by the demands of the independent power producer (IPP) trade. Large and long-term gas trades—10 to 15 years and more—began to pass through the market with far greater frequency. Gas hedging was often a key part of obtaining financing for these projects. Growth of the basis market (natural gas hedging at locations other than Henry Hub) soon followed as the size of natural gas basis risk was repeatedly demonstrated to all that participated in this market. A key factor in the growth was the development of the inter-dealer trade in basis, which allowed those outside the physical market to compete in this very substantial part of the gas derivative business. With the continued deregulation of the electrical power industry in the U.S. and its increasing reliance on natural gas as a fuel for generation, we can expect continued growth in natural gas derivatives.

Electricity

Electricity derivatives are developing in a similar fashion to gas derivatives with one key exception—most of the early growth in electricity derivatives occurred on the physical, not the financial, side of the business. Newly created power marketers and well-established physical market trading houses are providing a broad range of electricity derivatives attached to physical supply agreements or with physical settlement.

Here we have an excellent example of the effect of the migration of derivative expertise from the financial dealers to the physical market players. In the electricity markets, much of the need for financial derivatives is being eliminated by the sophistication of well-staffed energy and power companies. There will certainly be additional growth of the financial side of electricity derivatives (if only to provide access to the credit capacity of the financial dealers), but we expect the physical side of the business to remain the dominant segment.

Certainly, too, the energy derivative business did not develop quite as we envisioned it 10 years ago. For derivative dealers—especially those outside the physical market—the business was smaller and less profitable than expected. Surprisingly to some, those with the greatest exposure to energy prices were least inclined to hedge that exposure. Crude oil, heating oil, and non-basis natural gas have rapidly become mature, slow-growth businesses. Most importantly, the energy risk management business has been flexible enough and responsive enough to survive and grow during the 1990s and continues to meet the needs of those who choose to take advantage of it.

The CFO's Challenge

Despite a decade of experience in risk management now available, an energy company CFO designing or administering a risk management program faces a complex task. Beginning with economic trends that at times appear to be competing, the

CFO's challenge is to design a risk management program that is sensitive to the needs of four groups of constituents.

Primary among these are *investors* who have an interest in the company's ability to create shareholder value. A company's reputation in the investment markets is a function of the investor's willingness to entrust management with the use of their capital. With the evolution of the concept of economic value added (EVA)—which was introduced in the 1980s and became the "true corporate faith of the 1990s"[1]—shareholders have a more convenient means of monitoring a company's ability to create wealth. Popularized by Stern Stewart & Co., EVA encompasses all the decisions associated with increasing the return on capital and promoting policies that will increase the value of the stock.

Competitors provide a perspective as to the financial practices that are the norm for the industry, as well as the rationale for those who deviate. The CFO is charged with identifying opportunities for the company to try to exploit their unique capabilities at the expense of their competitors.

The CFO has a responsibility to *management* to ensure that the capital is available to fund the business plan. This begins with an assessment of the company's strategic plan including the cash requirements and resources necessary to carry it forward. The financing decisions that follow must be tested for macroeconomics variability, as well as the possibility of extreme downside scenarios. While the mandate is "don't run out of cash," the CFO must also assure the board of directors and fellow employees that their jobs will not unknowingly be put in danger.

Finally, the CFO must be sensitive to balancing the interests of the company's *financial advisors*. This includes investment bankers, commercial bankers, accountants, lawyers, and other consultants who promote their services via a steady stream of ideas aimed at new techniques in financial engineering. The CFO must determine who is in the inner circle and whose advice is the most practicable given a company's circumstances.

While balancing the interests of these four groups is normal for any CFO, the energy CFO faces a landscape that is even more challenging given the inherent commodity volatility. Consider some of the recent industry events.

- *Capital spending has continued to rise.* According to a recent study by Arthur Anderson and John S. Herold, Inc., exploration and development expenditures by the largest upstream petroleum firms rose 30% in 1997 to more than $91 billion. Unlike prior years, 40% was spent in the U.S., which was the highest proportion in at least 5 years.

- *Crude prices have risen to their highest level in the last 10 years.* From a high in January 1997 of more than $24/bbl to prices hovering around $12–$13/bbl at the end of the decade, to highs above $30 in 2000, predicting future movements is always difficult. To what degree this will impact future capital spending is also difficult to predict.

- *Investor interest in the energy industry is surging as financing activity reaches new highs.* According to Herold's *1997 M&A and Capital Markets Review,* almost $60 billion of new capital came into the energy arena in 1997. This included a 66% increase in the use of debt, which totaled $29 billion. This record-setting total easily topped the $31.7 billion recorded in 1995 and the record $43.7 billion set in 1996.

- *This surge of debt and equity capital helped drive a record wave of mergers and acquisition (M&A) activity.* Herold reports that among the universe of companies they follow, some 467 significant transactions (with a minimum value of $10 million) fueled $149 billion in global energy M&A activity.

- *Traditional investors are taking a new perspective on the industry, resulting in debt tenors substan-*

tially beyond the standards of only a few years ago.
During the 1980s most upstream debt financing was
provided by commercial banks using a variety of
structures based on the value and life of the
reserves. As competition among the banking industry intensified—and at the same time institutional
fund managers flush with cash were looking for new
places to invest—the market developed a different
perspective. Rather than limit the tenor of the
investment to the life of the reserves, the view of the
company as a "going concern" was gaining acceptance. In June of 1990, there was a ripple of excite-
ment in the market when Burlington Resources
(rated A3 and A- by Moody's and Standard & Poors)
issued unsecured senior debt for 30 years. This issue,
however, paled in comparison to the 100-year bonds
launched by Apache in 1996—particularly since
Apache's debt ratings were Baa1 and BBB and their
reserve life was only 7–8 years.

- *New private equity investors are becoming a
  force.* In the last several years, funds have been
  flowing into private venture and leverage buyout
  funds at a record pace. In 1997, total funds raised by
  private investor firms topped $34 billion. During
  the first half of 1998, this surge continued with
  almost $29 billion of new money—virtually ensur-
  ing that this record pace would continue. While
  most of these investors are focused in areas other
  than energy, a growing number of them are dedicating investment resources in the energy market.
  Examples include firms such as SCF Partners, who
  since 1988 has raised close to $800 million for
  investments in oil field service companies, and the
  Beacon Group, whose new fund targets to raise $1
  billion. First Reserve Corporation is forming their
  eighth fund with $800 million. Natural Gas
  Partners has a $350 million fund. Texas Pacific

Group—has raised more than $3 billion since their founding in 1993 and in 1997 acquired Ohio based Beeline and Blake. Always looking for value, these firms, flush with cash, are potentially a threat to the management of any company that is not providing an adequate return to shareholders.

- *Deregulation is recasting the definition of the energy industry.* The utility industry is undergoing a massive reconfiguration. Energy trading desks are expanding as brokers try to redistribute plant capacity to new markets. The consumer is a new force in this equation. They are now being given choices as to where they will purchase their energy. New partnerships are evolving between trading companies, producers, and distributors making it difficult to differentiate between clients and the competition!

- *In the banking and finance industry, mergers and consolidations are changing the identity of the traditional suppliers of capital.* Many of the prominent energy banks of the 1980s and early 1990s are being absorbed into other organizations. Gone are previously formidable names such as Security Pacific, Chemical Bank, Manufacturers Hanover, First City, Republic Bank, and Continental Illinois. Prominent energy banking institutions such as First Chicago, Bank of America, and Citibank have been absorbed into new larger organizations.

While these are only a few recent examples, they reflect the types of volatile macro factors that typify the energy markets. The danger and challenge for the CFO are how to use risk management programs to balance these variables. For example, an attempt to take advantage of price swings to improve shareholder returns—and please investors—could unduly expose the firm's credit worthiness and diminish their ability to access the capital necessary to support management's business plan. Unfortunately, over the last couple of years a number of companies have painfully discovered that just because they were "hedged" does not guarantee their risks are mitigated or their goals assured. During the winter of 1995-96, many exploration and production companies realized that their commodity price programs had not reduced risk but instead reduced earnings, as a result of unforeseen "basis risk."

A few years earlier, Louis Dreyfus Natural Gas promoted a strategy of hedging most of their interest rate and commodity risk on the theory that because their company has fewer risks than their competitors, the equity market would reward their shareholders with premium returns. Unfortunately, because information on a company's hedging exposure is incomplete and inconsistent, equity analysts continued to treat Louis Dreyfus as they would any other exploration and production company—rewarding them when commodity prices went up, and penalizing them when they went down.

According to a report published in *The Financial Post* in October 1997, "Eighty percent of Canadian energy producers report that they lost money during the year on hedges against oil price fluctuations, and 50% lost money on derivatives to protect themselves against natural gas price fluctuations."

While these examples call into question whether risk management is worth the risk, we contend that hedging and risk management are not the problem. The question is not whether or not to hedge. Leaving a company totally unhedged only exposes the company to the whims of the market—which represents another form of risk taking! Risk management is a toolbox that potentially has value for the CFO in managing relations with investors, managers, competitors, and advisors. The challenge is to use these tools in the right way.

THE FUTURE OF ENERGY RISK MANAGEMENT

In looking to the future, it is helpful to recognize two important forces that are shaping the management of energy risk:

- the profusion and ease of use of energy risk management tools

- the rapid increase in interested and increasingly sophisticated users of these tools

Energy futures trading has become more liquid. With the availability of futures and options on an increasing number of products—and for increasing terms—exchange-traded energy risk management has become quite accessible. In addition, specifically tailored OTC energy derivatives now make it possible for both producers and consumers to turn over some—or nearly all—of the risk analysis and hedge implementation function to an expert advisor.

As the variety and liquidity of hedge instruments have grown, so has the acceptance of derivatives to control exposure to energy prices. It is now well known among senior financial managers that energy commodity risk can be controlled. As a result, many corporations have changed their approach to this exposure. Newly appointed "risk managers" are measuring and monitoring energy price risks company-wide while senior management closely scrutinizes their performance.

We anticipate those who use energy derivatives will continue to be broadly categorized into two groups. The first are the fairly sophisticated and experienced users, which include integrated majors, large independents, and larger, trading-oriented utilities. The second are those firms that recognize and attempt to control their energy risk, but whose risk does not justify the scale to manage the risk internally. This includes most energy consumers and smaller producers.

The most sophisticated users have developed extensive internal trading and risk management capabilities and will likely continue offering these services to the less sophisticated. We will see some energy and utility companies competing with financial institutions for energy risk management business. These sophisticated users also are frequent trading counter-parties for other derivative dealers, providing them with access to the physical markets (*e.g.*, natural gas basis) through financial transactions.

It is in the second category—the smaller scale hedgers—where we expect companies to make greatest use of energy risk management services provided by financial services firms. Here is where financial service firms have found the greatest potential for the future growth of their energy derivative's business. Many of these firms depend upon banks for access to capital, and in effect reward their top bank relationships with derivative and other value-added business. In return, banks provide customized analysis and advice for these selected clients. Many banks are more closely aligning their risk management groups with their corporate finance groups to improve their responsiveness to client needs. This is yet another indicator of the movement of risk management from a non-standard, stand-alone instrument to a widely accepted part of mainstream corporate finance.

Developments in the 1990s pointed the way forward for the next decade in energy risk management. The most sophisticated physical players—oil majors, large utilities, large energy and power marketers—will expand their role and dominate trading in coming years. Those financial services providers with the strongest customer bases, who remain committed to energy risk management and add capabilities as needed, will remain significant players and be the dominant "trusted advisors" to the smaller scale hedgers. Physical market knowledge and trading capabilities will sharply divide these two groups.

Deregulation will continue to create new market participants, but energy and power industry consolidation will eventually counteract this effect and slow or eliminate the growth of new participants.

New risk management products will continue to evolve to enable the management of all energy and power risks. Electricity derivatives have grown substantially over the past few years and will grow more as deregulation progresses. For instance, derivatives on temperature have been introduced and are progressing quite rapidly. Designed to hedge exposure to unexpected temperature fluctuation, these products have generated substantial interest among gas and electric utilities, fuel suppliers, municipalities, retailers, educational institutions, insurance companies, and many others. Temperature derivatives offer energy and power producers and consumers a product to hedge "volume" risk left unhedged in standard risk management programs.

Another new derivative solution to an old risk is the introduction of derivatives on the price of coal. Both OTC and exchange traded instruments address this risk. In the coming years, energy producers and consumers will be able to readily access tools to hedge the gamut of energy and power risks.

Suggestions for the CFO

Energy risk management is now a widely accepted financial tool. Senior management of any corporation or organization whose bottom line is significantly affected by energy price and demand fluctuations will be expected to have a position regarding the company's risk management position. For the CFO charged with this responsibility the following suggestions are offered:

- *Determine the level of knowledge within the organization regarding risk management.* Whereas a decade ago "derivatives" was a new concept to many senior managers, today most have some degree of familiarity. However, many CEOs and directors do

not have actual hands-on experience and/or sufficient insight to match the risks in the organization
with the proper tools. Developing a realistic understanding of management's knowledge and comfort
will help guide the remainder of the process.

- *Begin the education process early.* Regardless of
the level of existing sophistication, the CFO's efforts
will be aided by raising the degree of knowledge to
a higher level. General information on the derivative
markets and the programs of competitors—or examples of "what if we had"—will help to put the company's needs and opportunities in prospective.

- *Consider bringing in an outside consultant.* Some
corporations will be able to complete this process
without outside assistance. For many, expert and
trusted advice from an "outside expert" will help
advance the process. When selecting consultants, the
greatest consideration should be given to the consultant's experience in your industry. If a good part-
nership is formed, a close relationship with a trusted
resource can be a key part of a stable, long-term risk
management program.

- *Develop a corporation wide analysis of the company's risk profile.* All direct and indirect implica-
tions across the corporation must be considered.
Recently, J.C. Whorton, Jr. and Dan Sanford provided a roadmap in a widely read article in the *Oil and
Gas Investor.*[2] In their article they identified more
than 40 different types of potential risks inherent in
a company. While not all of these can be hedged, it
will be critical to have a view on each one.

- *Develop an inflexible list of objectives for your
risk management program.* Senior management
must honestly determine their expectations for the

program and openly state these expectations and their rationale. It is critical to determine if a risk management program is needed to meet corporate objectives. If the need is confirmed, the design of the program should be based directly upon these tenants.

• *Develop a road map for implementation.* This is the most straightforward part of the process. This is where the tools are matched with the risks and the objectives. Establishing limits, authorities, reporting requirements, due diligence requirements, bidding procedures, payment arrangements, termination events, and counter-party requirements are only a few of the elements that must be included in the program. If implementation is guided externally, your consultant must be kept well aware of your strategy and any changes that might arise.

• *Select one or two advisors to help guide the initial trades.* Initial execution may be limited to a few basic transactions to test the system. Alternatively, the company may need to complete a large volume in conjunction with a project. In either event, selection of one or two advisors—based upon a few initial trades—will generally yield far better results than ongoing discussions with a field of price competitors. Particularly for companies with limited resources or hedging needs, a close relationship with a trusted advisor can be a key part of a stable, long-term risk management program.

• *Enforce the governance program.* Initially, the CEO and directors will need frequent and complete reports on the results of the hedging activities. The more knowledge they have, the more effectively they can carry out their responsibilities. Frequent updates will also help overcome some of the concern that directors will likely have regarding some of the "mysteries" of hedging. A better sense of risk tolerance will also emerge, which may result in modifications to the original program.

- *Continue the education program.* The advance of technology can only result in more variations on traditional techniques. It will also offer the CFO the opportunity to remind management of the difference between taking risk...and mitigating risk...and where the company falls on this scale.

During the last decade, energy risk management has gone from being a novel concept to a standard element of company strategy. The CFO now has a broad array of tools to control undesirable risks. A well-designed and well-implemented risk management program provides a benefit to the corporation's management, shareholders, and advisors. It can also provide a strategic advantage against competitors. These benefits should be made clear to all parties at inception of the program and on an ongoing basis. Reduced earnings volatility, protection against financial distress, and the ability to plan future capital expenditures with greater confidence all create value for shareholders. In addition, a complete understanding of the risks and benefits will better prepare the board and shareholders for the inevitable discontent of "hindsight traders" when hedges actually limit earnings.

The keys to success are the same as they were a decade ago. The CFO, management, and the directors must understand the capabilities and limitations of risk management and properly define its role within larger corporate goals.

NOTES

1. William Smithburg, CEO of Quaker Oats in a 10/23/93 article in *Fortune* magazine

2. J.C.Whorton Jr. and Dan Sanford, "From the Trading Floor to the Boardroom," *Oil and Gas Investor,* May 1998, pp. 52-54

ACCOUNTING, TAXATION, AND INTERNAL CONTROL

by David M. Johnson, Ted E. McElroy, James E. Toups, Jr., & J. Clinton Walden

BACKGROUND

No later than December 31, 2000, all companies must have completed their implementation of Statement of Financial Accounting Standards (SFAS) No. 133. The Financial Accounting Standards Board (FASB or the Board) issued this long-awaited accounting standard on derivative instruments and hedging activities in June 1998, in response to the significant proliferation of derivative financial instruments being used by companies in all sectors of the market.

The FASB's SFAS No. 133, "Accounting for Derivative Instruments and Hedging Activities," replaces the existing accounting pronouncements and practices with a single, integrated accounting framework for derivatives and hedging activities. This statement dramatically affects just about every business—including participants in the energy business, from oil and gas producers to energy marketers.

This chapter addresses the accounting, taxation, and internal control aspects of energy derivative instruments including futures, forwards, swaps, options, and many energy contracts. Since accounting and tax requirements are continuously subject to change, readers should consult with experienced accounting and tax professionals for guidance on the treatment of specific transactions.

Accounting Considerations

Overall summary of accounting

SFAS No. 133 changes the previous accounting definition of a derivative, which focused on freestanding contracts like options and forwards—including futures and swaps. It expands to include embedded derivatives and many commodity contracts—including energy contracts. Under this standard, every derivative instrument is required to be recorded at fair value as either an asset or liability on the balance sheet. The statement requires that changes in the fair value of derivative instruments be reported currently in earnings unless specific hedge accounting criteria are met.

The new standard requires all entities to formally document any hedging relationship and the risk management objective for implementing the hedge, including the assessment of hedge effectiveness to qualify for hedge accounting treatment. Because the mechanics of hedge accounting are very complex, special accounting for qualifying hedges allows a derivative's gains and losses to offset related results on the hedged item as follows:

- In a fair value hedge, the derivative is marked to its fair value currently through earnings with an offsetting, mark-to-fair-value of the hedged item (only for the risk being hedged) through earnings

- In a cash flow hedge, the derivative is first marked to its fair value with the effective portion of the change recorded through other comprehensive income (OCI), or equity. The gain or loss on the derivative is removed from OCI and recognized in earnings in the same period as the gain or loss on the hedged cash flow

- In a hedge of a net investment in a foreign operation, the effective portion of the changes in fair value of the derivative (or the transactions gain or loss on a qualifying non-derivative instrument) are reported the same as the cumulative translation adjustment (CTA)

SFAS No. 133 (as amended by SFAS No. 137) will increase earnings volatility, as any hedge ineffectiveness will be recorded currently in earnings. This statement is effective for fiscal years beginning after June 15, 2000—or Jan. 1, 2001, for companies with calendar-year fiscal years.

Derivative instrument definition

SFAS No. 133 defines a derivative instrument as a financial instrument—or other contract—having all three of the following characteristics:

- The settlement amount is determined using an underlying (*e.g.*, a reference rate or price) and a notional amount (a payment provision).

- The initial net investment is not significant (*e.g.*, the initial net investment on most option contracts is insignificant compared to the derivatives notional amount).

- Net settlement is permitted or required, a market mechanism exists for net settlement, or the asset to be delivered is readily convertible to cash.

This definition of a derivative instrument may include contracts for natural gas and electric power sales and purchase contracts that were previously not recognized or considered derivative instruments for accounting purposes. This assumes they do not meet the normal purchases and normal sales exemption. "Normal purchase and sales provisions" relate to assets such as generation or oil and gas production—not trading activities. The "normal purchases and normal sales provision" exempts contracts from the definition of a derivative if the asset to be delivered is readily convertible to cash. However, if a contract has a net settlement provision or a market mechanism to facilitate net settlement, then the normal purchases and sales exemption do not apply.

Natural gas and electric power contracts shall be considered derivative instruments if the contract allows net cash settlement, even if net cash settlement is permitted only upon default and the parties intend to settle the contract with physical delivery. For example, the following contracts may meet the definition of derivative instruments under SFAS No. 133:

- Exchange traded futures and options contracts

- Over-the-counter (OTC) forward, swap, and option contracts

- Physical delivery contracts negotiated by an exploration and production entity for the sale of future production/reserves

- Physical delivery/purchase contract negotiated by an electric generation facility for the sale of future production or purchase of natural gas

To the extent that provisions of SFAS No. 133 do not apply to these contracts, the provisions of Emerging Issues Task Force 98–10, (EITF 98–10) "Accounting for Energy Contracts" may apply. If a company has already adopted EITF 98–10, the company must still determine if the provisions of SFAS No. 133 are applicable.

Derivative and hedge accounting

A fundamental premise of SFAS No. 133 is that all derivative instruments shall be reported at fair value as either assets or liabilities with changes in the fair value of derivative instruments recorded currently in earnings. Hedge accounting is permitted if certain criteria are met, however, hedge accounting is an election, and management may choose whether or not to designate a transaction as a hedge. This election cannot be made with the benefit of hindsight. Hedge designation must be made and documented at the inception of the contract. Gains or losses on derivative instruments shall be accounted for as shown in Table 11–1.

Hedge accounting criteria

In order for a derivative instrument to qualify for hedge accounting treatment, certain criteria must be met. Companies will need to review existing hedging strategies and determine whether those strategies qualify for hedge accounting under SFAS No. 133. It is also important for management to understand that not all activities the management considers hedging—in an economic sense—will qualify for special hedge accounting for financial reporting purposes.

Hedge designation and effectiveness

In order for a company to apply hedge accounting, a company must designate a hedging relationship at its inception (in each circumstance). It must also formally document the company's risk management objective and strategy for the hedge—including the hedged item, hedging instrument, risk being hedged, as well as the method in which it will measure effectiveness. To qualify for hedge accounting under SFAS No. 133, a derivative has to be highly effective in achieving offsetting changes in fair value or offsetting changes in cash flows for the risk being hedged. Under SFAS No. 133, all hedge ineffectiveness will be recorded in earnings currently effective.

MANAGEMENT DESIGNATION	ACCOUNTING TREATMENT
Default designation	Derivative instrument is recorded at fair value on the balance sheet with changes in value recorded currently in earnings.
Fair value hedge	Derivative instrument (hedging instrument) qualifying as a fair value hedge is recorded at fair value on the balance sheet with changes in value recorded in earnings. Offsetting changes in value of the hedged item recognized currently in earnings in the same accounting period as the hedging instrument.
Cash flow hedge	Derivative instrument (hedging instrument) qualifying as a cash flow hedge is recorded at fair value on the balance sheet with effective changes in value recorded in OCI, to the extent effective, and subsequently reclassified into earnings as the hedged forecasted transaction affects earnings.
Foreign currency hedge	The gain or loss on the effective portion of a derivative instrument designated as a hedge of a net investment in a foreign operation shall be recorded in OCI as part of the cumulative translation adjustment.

Table II–I *Accounting for Gains or Losses on Derivative Instruments*

A company must document how effectiveness will be assessed and:

- define a method that provides a "reasonable basis" for assessment. For example, spot rate changes or intrinsic value changes must explicitly define whether the time value of an option used in a cash flow hedge—or forward points on a forward contract used in a fair value hedge of the derivative—will be included in or excluded from the assessment method. The method of amortizing option time value as practiced by many companies prior to the issuance of SFAS No. 133 is no longer appropriate.

- expect the hedge to be "highly effective" in achieving offsetting changes in fair value or variability in cash flows.

- assess hedge effectiveness whenever financial statements are issued or earnings are reported (at least quarterly).

- measure ineffectiveness of the hedge and report it currently in earnings.

Embedded derivative instruments

SFAS No. 133 also includes derivatives embedded in broader non-derivative contracts. Specifically, if the economic characteristics of an embedded derivative and its host contract are not closely related, SFAS No. 133 requires that the embedded derivative be separated and accounted for like a stand-alone derivative. For example, the call option embedded in an investment in convertible debt must be broken out from the host contract for financial reporting purposes. Embedded derivatives are also typically found in volumetric production payments, and the provisions of SFAS No. 133 will apply to all parties to these types of agreements. Further guidance is available from FASB staff concerning implementation of SFAS No. 133, specifically, Question B11, "Volumetric Production Payments."

It is important for entities to determine the extent to which derivative instruments are embedded in non-derivative contracts and determine if the embedded derivative meets the "clearly and closely related" exemption of the standard. The FASB also provides financial reporting entities the opportunity for a one-time exemption for contracts that contain embedded derivatives. The requirement to bifurcate embedded derivative instruments applies to all structured notes or other hybrid instruments that were issued, acquired, or substantively modified after Dec. 31,

1997, or at the company's election, Dec. 31, 1998. An entity may choose not to apply this statement or recognize an asset or liability for derivative instruments embedded within hybrid contracts. However, the entity must be consistent with the adoption choice for all embedded derivative instruments.

Fair value hedge

The following illustrations provide examples of fair value hedges. The examples used to illustrate fair value and cash flow hedges are identical. However, in each example management designates the hedged exposure (fair value or cash flow) and the assessment of effectiveness.

Example 1. Company ABC is an energy marketer that regularly injects and withdraws natural gas into storage facilities under storage cycling programs. As such, ABC injects natural gas during the month of June and typically withdraws the gas in February. On July 1, 20X2, Company ABC decides to hedge the value of its natural gas inventory of 500,000 MMBtus at Henry Hub by selling 50 futures contracts for the month of February. The inventory exposes Company ABC to changes in fair value attributable to changes in the price per MMBtu at the Henry Hub. If Company ABC complies with the other criteria specified in paragraphs 20 and 21 of SFAS No. 133, the hedging relationship can qualify for fair value hedge accounting. Company ABC will exclude from its assessment of effectiveness the change in value of the forward contract related to the spot-forward difference. Management will assess hedge effectiveness by comparing the change in value of the futures contracts related to the change in spot prices to the change in value of the hedged inventory based on spot prices. Since the notional amount of the inventory and the futures contract are equal, the inventory is located at the same location that the futures contract is based, and the value of the futures contract was zero at inception, it is reasonable for Company ABC to assume that the hedging relationship will be highly effective.

Management should look to paragraph 65 of SFAS No. 133 for these effectiveness criteria.

At the inception of the hedge, the futures contracts have a fair value of zero since they were executed at a market-clearing price and the carrying value of the inventory is $1,000,000—cost basis of $2.00/MMBtu. On January 26, 20X3, ABC settles its futures contracts and sells 500,000 MMBtus of physical product. The futures price of natural gas at the relevant reporting dates are shown Table 11–2.

The change in fair value of the February futures contract for each reporting date is calculated in Table 11–3.

	HENRY HUB SPOT PRICE	FUTURES PRICE OF FEBRUARY CONTRACT	SPOT-FORWARD DIFFERENCE
July 1, 20X2	$2.20	$2.60	$.40
December 31, 20X2	$2.30	$2.70	$.40
January 26, 20X3	$2.65	$2.65	$.00

Table II–2 *Future Prices of Natural Gas at Relevant Reporting Dates (Ex.I)*

	JULY 1—DEC. 31, 20X2	DEC. 31, 20X2— JAN. 26, 20X3
Beginning futures price	$2.60	$2.70
Ending futures price	$2.70	$2.65
Change in price	$0.10	$(0.05)
50 contract @ 10,000 MMBtus	x500,000	x500,000
Gain/(Loss) – Fair value	$(50,000)	$25,000

Table II–3 *Fluctuations in the Future Prices of Natural Gas at Relevant Reporting Dates (Ex.1)*

	JULY 1—DEC. 31, 20X2	DEC. 31, 20X2— JAN. 26, 20X3
Beginning spot price	$2.20	$ 2.30
Ending spot price	$2.30	$ 2.65
Change in price	$0.10	$0.35
500,000 MMBtus	x500,000	x500,000
Gain/(Loss) on inventory	$50,000	$175,000

ACCOUNT	DR.	CR.
December 31, 20X2		
Earnings	$50,000	
Derivative instrument (futures)		$50,000
Inventory	$50,000	
Earnings		$50,000
(To record fair value of futures contract and change in value of inventory)		
January 26, 20X3		
Derivative instrument (futures)	$25,000	
Earnings		$25,000
Inventory	$175,000	
Earnings		$175,000
(To record change in the fair value of futures contract and change in the fair value of inventory since December 31, 20X2)		
Derivative instrument (futures)	$25,000	
Cash		$25,000
(To record settlement of futures contract)		
Cash	$1,325,000	
Earnings		$1,325,000
(To record sale of natural gas inventory [500,000 x $2.65 = $1,325,000])		
Cost of goods sold (COGS)	$1,225,000	
Inventory		$1,225,000
(To record the COGS related to the sale of inventory)		

Table II–4 *Accounting Future Prices of Natural Gas at Relevant Reporting Dates (Ex.I)*

The change in fair value of Company ABC's inventory is calculated based on changes in Henry Hub spot prices as shown in Table 11–4.

The overall effect of these entries is to lock-in a sales margin of $.60/MMBtu on July 1, 20X2 for 500,000 MMBtus or $300,000 effectively.

Example 2. Using the same information in Example 1, Company ABC could have determined that it would assess the effectiveness of the fair value hedge by comparing the entire change in fair value of the futures contracts to the change in the forward market price of the hedged commodity inventory. Table 11–2 provides the futures price of natural gas at the relevant reporting dates. The change in fair value of the February futures contract for each reporting date is calculated as shown in Table 11–5.

The overall effect of these entries is to lock-in a sales margin of $.60/MMBtu on July 1, 20X2 for 500,000 MMBtus or $300,000 effectively.

Impairment

All assets or liabilities that have been designated—and qualify as hedged items—must continue to be assessed for impairment pursuant to other applicable generally accepted accounting principles. Therefore, in the above example, a test of impairment should be performed on the inventory after hedge accounting has been applied and the carrying value of the hedged item has been adjusted.

Written options

Written options generally do not qualify for hedge treatment except in limited circumstances. Generally, in order to designate a written option as a hedge of an existing asset or liability, the combination of the written option and the hedged item must provide at least as much potential for gains as exposure to losses from an unfavorable change in their combined

	JULY 1—DEC. 31, 20X2	DEC. 31, 20X2— JAN. 26, 20X3
Beginning spot price	$2.60	$ 2.70
Ending spot price	$2.70	$ 2.65
Change in price	$0.10	$(0.05)
50 contracts @ 10,000 MMBtus	x500,000	x500,000
Gain/(Loss) – Fair Value	$(50,000)	$25,000

ACCOUNT	DR.	CR.
December 31, 20X2		
Earnings	$50,000	
Derivative instrument (futures)		$50,000
Inventory	$50,000	
Earnings		$50,000
(To record fair value of futures contract and change in value of inventory)		
January 26, 20X3		
Derivative instrument (futures)	$25,000	
Earnings		$25,000
Inventory	$175,000	
Earnings		$175,000
(To record change in the fair value of futures contract and change in the fair value of inventory since December 31, 20X2)		
Derivative instrument (futures)	$25,000	
Cash		$25,000
(To record settlement of futures contract)		
Cash	$1,325,000	
Earnings		$1,325,000
(To record sale of natural gas inventory [500,000 x $2.65 = $1,325,000])		
(COGS)	$1,225,000	
Inventory		$1,225,000
(To record the COGS related to the sale of inventory)		

Table II–5 *Accounting Future Prices of Natural Gas at Relevant Reporting Dates (Ex.2)*

fair value. Hedge accounting is prohibited for other written options.

Cash flow hedge

Example 3. This is the same example as Example 1 and 2 in the fair value hedge example, except Company ABC decides to hedge the variability in cash flows from the sale of natural gas inventory rather than the fair value of the stored commodity. Company ABC is an energy marketer and regularly injects and withdraws natural gas into storage facilities under storage cycling programs. As such, ABC injects natural gas during the month of June and typically withdraws the gas in February. On July 1, 20X2, Company ABC decides to hedge the variability of cash flows resulting from the future sale of 500,000 MMBtus at Henry Hub. Therefore, ABC sells 50 futures contracts for the month of February to effectively lock in a sales price. The hedging relationship qualifies for cash flow hedge accounting. Since the notional amount of inventory that is anticipated to be injected and the notional amount of the futures contract are equal, the anticipated inventory is expected to be located at the same location that the futures contract is based, and the value of the futures contract was zero at inception, it is reasonable for Company ABC to assume that the hedging relationship will be highly effective. Management should look to paragraph 65 of SFAS No. 133 for these effectiveness criteria

At the inception of the hedge, the futures contracts typically have a fair value of zero since they were executed at a market-clearing price. ABC settles its futures contracts and sells 500,000 MMBtus of physical product on January 26, 20X3.

The futures price of natural gas at the relevant reporting dates are as shown in Table 11–2. The change in fair value of the February futures contract for each reporting date is calculated as shown in Table 11–6.

The effect of hedging the variability of changes in cash flows resulted in Company ABC locking in a sales price of $1,300,000 (500,000 x $2.60). Any impairment of inventory

	JULY 1—DEC. 31, 20X2	DEC. 31, 20X2— JAN. 26, 20X3
Beginning spot price	$2.60	$ 2.70
Ending spot price	$2.70	$ 2.65
Change in price	$0.10	$(0.05)
50 contracts @ 10,000 MMBtus	x500,000	x500,000
Gain/(Loss) – Fair Value	$(50,000)	$25,000

ACCOUNT	DR.	CR.
December 31, 20X2		
Other Comprehensive Income	$50,000	
Derivative instrument (futures)		$50,000
(To record fair value of futures contract)		
January 26, 20X3		
Derivative instrument (futures)	$25,000	
Other Comprehensive Income		$25,000
Inventory	$175,000	
Earnings		$175,000
(To record change in the fair value of futures contract since December 31, 20X2)		
Derivative instrument (futures)	$25,000	
Cash		$25,000
(To record settlement of futures contract)		
Cash	$1,325,000	
Earnings		$1,325,000
(To record sale of natural gas inventory [500,000 x $2.65 = $1,325,000])		
Earnings	$1,225,000	
Other Comprehensive Income		$1,225,000
(Reclassify changes in fair vale of futures contracts to earnings)		

Table II-6 *Accounting Future Prices of Natural Gas at Relevant Reporting Dates (Ex.3)*

needs to be considered and the deferral of any loss is subject to impairment considerations.

Disclosures

SFAS No. 133 supercedes many previous disclosures and requires new and different disclosure requirements. The following describes the new disclosures required:

- Objectives, strategies, risk management policies for holding and issuing all derivatives

- Description of hedged items

- For derivatives (and qualifying nonderivatives) designated as fair value and cash flow hedges:

  a. Net gain or loss recognized in earnings attributable to ineffectiveness or excluded from effectiveness measurement and where that amount is reported in earnings

  b. Net gain or loss recognized for firm commitments or forecasted transactions that no longer qualify as hedges

- For derivatives (and qualifying nonderivatives) designated as cash flow hedges:

  a. Events that will trigger earnings recognition of hedge results deferred in other comprehensive income and the amount that will be reclassified into earnings in the next year

  b. The maximum period over which the company has designated a cash flow hedge (excluding cash flow hedges of floating-rate debt)

- For derivatives (and qualifying nonderivatives) designated as a net investment in a foreign operation, the net amount of gains or losses included in the cumulative translation adjustment during the reporting period

- Encouraged disclosures about entity's overall risk management profile

- In the year initially adopted, disclosure of the gains and losses reported in accumulated other comprehensive income and associated with transition adjustments that will be reclassified into earnings during the 12 months following initial application

Effective date

SFAS No. 133 is effective for fiscal years beginning after June 15, 2000 or Jan. 1, 2001 for calendar-year companies. The statement will be applied as of the beginning of the fiscal year. Early adoption of SFAS No. 133 is permitted, but only as of the beginning of a fiscal quarter that began after June 15, 1998.

U.S. TAXATION CONSIDERATIONS

Taxpayer Relief Act of 1997

This section addresses the general federal income tax considerations that apply to petroleum contracts and related derivative instruments—futures, options, notional principal contracts, etc.—used to hedge against price risk inherent in long-term supply contracts. The Taxpayer Relief Act of 1997 made substantial changes by adding §475(e) and (f) that allows dealers and traders in commodities, and commodities derivatives, to elect mark to market treatment for tax purposes.

The changes alleviate the character whipsaw that dealers in commodities and commodities derivatives were exposed to. For example, if a dealer misidentified a transaction as being a tax hedge, the gain from the transaction would be ordinary and the loss would be capital. Likewise, if a dealer failed to identify a transaction as a hedge, the gain and loss would be capital and the straddle loss deferral rules would apply. Now a dealer has certainty that if the mark to market election is made, all gains and losses will be characterized as ordinary income or loss. However, the straddle loss rules still may defer recognition of certain losses.

Definition of dealer and trader

The definition of a dealer or trader is based on numerous judicial decisions. The courts have stated that a taxpayer is a dealer or trader based on the facts and circumstances surrounding the taxpayer's commodity activities. Certain characteristics of a dealer include:

- Commodities held as stock-in-trade or inventory, primarily for sale to customers in the ordinary course of business

- Conducts an active trade or business for income or profit

- Holds certification or license with appropriate security agency (Commodity Futures Trading Commission)

- Holds self out as a dealer

- Established place of business

- Substantial, frequent, and continuous trading activity

- Income derived from short-term trading vs. passive income or long-term capital growth

- Material involvement of taxpayer's time and effort

The characteristics of a trader tend to overlap the characteristics of a dealer. A dealer must meet the characteristics of a trader, but a trader may or may not be considered a dealer. The difference between a dealer and a trader is that a dealer buys and sells financial or commodity instruments to customers. A dealer is willing to enter into either side of a transaction and will make a market in the commodities. A trader, on the other hand, does not have inventory for sale to customers and will not enter into either side of a transaction, but will make profit on short-term swings in the market.

Tax consequences of the mark to market election

In general, a dealer or trader who makes the §475 election will mark to market all commodities and commodity derivative instruments at year-end and recognize ordinary income or loss on the market adjustment. Ordinary gain or loss on the disposition of any commodities will also be recognized at year-end. There are certain items that, if properly identified, are exempt from mark to market treatment. Some of these items include commodities held for investment, commodities held in the capacity of a trader—not for sale to customers—or a hedge on a commodity exempt from mark to market.

For hedges on commodities exempt from mark to market or for dealers not electing mark to market, the hedging rules of Reg. §1.1221–2 apply. In general, a properly identified hedging transaction is ordinary in nature and is not subject to the straddle loss deferral rules. However, if the hedge fails to qualify as a tax hedge, capital gain or loss treatment may result. The advantages of making a §475 election are the guaranteed ordinary character of income and losses and the exemption from the burdensome identification rules under the hedging regulations.

§1256 contracts

§1256 governs the tax treatment for certain transactions in futures and option contracts. The provisions of §1256 are not applicable if a §475 mark to market election is made or the taxpayer properly identifies the transaction as a hedging transaction. If this provision applies, §1256 contracts (contracts traded on a regulated U.S. exchange) must be marked to market at the end of each year. Any gain or loss on contracts is recognized in that tax year, and the contract's basis is adjusted to reflect the gain or loss recognized. This gain or loss is considered to be capital in nature, and §1256 requires 40% of the gain/loss to be short-term and 60% of the gain/loss to be long-term. Since the 1986 Tax Reform Act has presently done away with the preferential rate for capital gains for corporations, the current importance of the capital vs. ordinary characterization is that capital losses can only be used to offset capital gains—they cannot be used to reduce ordinary taxable income.

On the other hand, a position in a non-§1256 contract is not taxed using mark to market. Non-§1256 contracts include all contracts not traded on a U.S. exchange (*e.g.*, Alaska North Slope crude, Brent). Gains or losses on such contracts are generally taxed when realized—either through expiration of a contract or closing it out—unless the contract is part of a straddle, in which case the loss position will not be recognized until the gain position is recognized. Such gains and losses continue to be capital in nature.

Taxation of dealer activities without mark to market election

Dealers receive ordinary, rather than capital treatment on commodities bought and sold in the ordinary course of business. Once the dealer takes title to the commodity, it becomes inventory for tax purposes. Then the inventory method elected for tax purposes will determine the timing of the recognition of gains and losses inherent in the inventory. When a futures or forward commitment is closed-out prior to taking title, realized gains and losses on such transactions are either recognized immediately or, depending on the method of accounting, treated as a component of the cost of inventory.

In addition to buying and selling in the ordinary course of business, a dealer may also speculate for his or her own account. To the extent a dealer is engaging in speculative activities, it will be taxed like a speculator/investor and the §1256 contracts will be taxed using mark to market. As with a speculator/investor, the gain or loss will be capital in nature.

Although dealers may enter into speculative transactions, they more frequently engage in hedging transactions. Hedging transactions are not subject to the mark to market rules under §1256. In general, a petroleum products futures contract that qualifies for hedge accounting under the financial accounting rules may also meet the tax definition of a commercial hedge under §1256. These hedging transactions must be identified before the close of the day they were entered into.

A dealer's hedging transactions are always treated as ordinary income. Realized gains and losses are treated either as adjustments to inventory or recognized as ordinary gains and losses at the time of realization, depending on the dealer's method of accounting.

In most instances, it is advantageous to have a §1256 contract treated as a hedge. Hedging transactions are exempt from the regulated futures contract marked to market rules, straddle loss deferral rules, wash-sale rules, and capital gain or capital loss rules.

INTERNAL CONTROL CONSIDERATIONS

Several corporate organizations have suffered significant losses and even bankruptcy due to rogue trading personnel and a weak internal control infrastructure. A primary risk of any trading organization continues to be the risk of loss from unauthorized trading activity by authorized/unauthorized trading personnel. Often times, trading personnel conducting unauthorized trades will intentionally keep transactions out of a trading portfolio in order to attempt to recover unrealized and unrecognized losses. Internal controls surrounding a trading and marketing infrastructure are extremely important and vital to the success of the organization. The risk characteristics and controls necessary to mitigate those risks are similar whether the trading function centers around foreign currency products, agricultural products, interest rate products, or energy products.

Trading controls differ from one company to another because a company must consider not only the risks involved but also the costs of maintaining the controls. They generally depend on the reasons for trading, the volume of transactions, and the sophistication of the system that covers other investment-related activity. All companies engaged in trading should consider the following basic internal control procedures:

Policy and procedures

As with any system of internal controls, the policies and procedures relating to trading activity should be documented in a corporate trading policy and procedures manual. The board of directors should approve and monitor trading policy and trader compliance by the trading control officer. All traders should sign an acknowledgement of the objectives and content of the policy on a yearly basis. The trading policy should address the following at a minimum:

- Trading objectives

- Products, markets, and commodities authorized to trade

- Duties and responsibilities of the Board of Directors, trading control officer, risk management committee, senior management, and internal audit

- Minimum internal control of elements

- Process controls and responsibilities

- Trading limits and warning signals—value at risk, stop-loss, volumetric limits, portfolio limits, etc.

A trading policy should communicate the overall corporate objectives of the entity's trading activity. Separate policies or manuals for detailed trading procedures, credit, contract administration, or any other specialized trading support operation can be created to provide more insight to the specific functions of the entity.

Management oversight and reporting

The trading organization should be arranged to ensure that there is adequate control and communication between management and the trading function. The management team responsible for the implementation and oversight of internal controls should include the risk management committee, the trading control officer, internal audit, and senior management. The risk management committee is responsible for actively monitoring overall trading strategy and settling all trading limit violations appropriately. The trading control officer performs an independent function from the trading group, and is authorized to monitor trading activities and adherence to the company's approved policies, procedures, and limits on a daily basis.

Management reporting will vary by company depending on the level of trading activity conducted. At a minimum, however, the following should be reported to management and validated daily:

- All open positions segregated in some meaningful way (*e.g.*, on an operation or segment basis) along with the trading transactions and related income effects, both current and historical

- Realized gains/losses and market appreciation/ depreciation on open positions for the period

- A comparison of open positions with authorized position limits

- Credit exposure

- Overall market exposure

- A reconciliation between the roll off of forward transactions and actual results

Trader duties

Only traders knowledgeable in the markets and in related company policies and procedures should be authorized to initiate transactions. Appropriate background investigations should be performed on all trading personnel prior to employment. The company's brokers and counter-parties should be informed that they must deal only with these authorized individuals, and they should be informed immediately when a trader is no longer authorized to trade for the company. In addition, to ensure the proper segregation of duties and control, the traders should not have the authority to unilaterally authorize the disbursement of funds, establish brokerage accounts, invoice or reconcile transactions, or change remittance instructions. Traders must also be prohibited from trading similar commodities for their own personal account.

Position limits

Position limits should be set that cover all physical and financial positions. Limits should cover volumetric exposure, dollar exposure, and concentration exposure time, location, counter-party, and cash flows. Position limits are somewhat ineffective as preventive controls without strong monitoring processes in place.

Deal origination and capture

The overall trading strategies of the company should be discussed and approved by the risk management committee or at least senior management, and communicated to trading personnel. Daily strategy meetings should be conducted to share market intelligence, such as key events that pose significant competitive challenges or signal emergence of important industry trends, and to review the company's position. These meetings ensure that management is kept abreast of trading activity and how that relates to long-term strategies, and keeps traders informed of market conditions and corporate goals.

As traders begin dealing with customers and other market makers, all phone lines should be recorded to ensure the accuracy of the verbal agreements made. These recordings should be retained for a maximum of the tenure of trades and stamped for date and time. Company policy should state that all transactions must be conducted over a recorded phone line. Upon execution, a sequentially numbered deal ticket should be completed with trade date, time, buy/sell, counter-party contact, price, volume, location, delivery period, contract number, and trader's initials. The deal ticket and recorded phone lines initiate the audit trail and provide trading control personnel with appropriate information. In addition to the deal ticket, the transaction should be entered into the risk management system upon execution or, at the latest, by the end of the day, to ensure that the system contains complete and accurate information.

Deal validation

All traders must be responsible for verifying the accuracy of their transactions in the risk management system. Subsequent to trader verification, transactions must be validated by a group that is independent of the trading function. This process includes trade confirmation, price curve validation, portfolio valuation, and broker reconciliation. Contract administration should confirm each deal in writing within 48 hours, regardless of type or term, and follow up on late confirmations on a timely basis. This ensures that all counter-parties have reflected their approval of the terms and conditions of all transactions, thus reducing the risk of later disputes.

The trading control group should validate price curves, net trading positions, and market exposure against independent price quotes on a daily basis to ensure that all transactions are correctly priced and valued. In addition, this group should validate all trades entered into the risk management system for accuracy against confirmations and deal tickets on a daily basis. This ensures that the deals are captured correctly and can be reported to management accurately.

All "brokeraged" deals must be reconciled from the risk management system to the broker statement on a daily basis to ensure that these financial deals are captured correctly. Additionally, a reconciliation of the brokerage margin accounts should be performed daily to accurately reflect changes in margin balances.

Trade settlement and accounting

The records necessary to account for and control futures, forwards, and options transactions should be maintained by accounting personnel who are independent of the trading function. They should contain all the information necessary to verify statements received from the broker or counter-party, support entries to the general ledger, designate appropriate trades as hedges, and generate the internal reports needed to monitor the overall trading position.

At the end of the trading month, all invoices should automatically be generated from the information system(s) and reconciled to the transactions in the risk management system to ensure that invoices reflect the most accurate information available and to resolve any discrepancies on a timely basis. An accounting supervisor should review the invoice batches prior to being sent to counter-parties for reasonableness and to monitor the communication being sent out on behalf of the company.

Separate from the invoice generation and verification function, the accounting and treasury departments are responsible for recording all cash movements and disbursements of funds, respectively. Authorized personnel must approve all fund disbursements with actual disbursements being posted to the sub-ledger on a timely basis. All cash receipts should be posted on the day of receipt, even if they are not applied to an actual invoice in the sub-ledger to facilitate an accurate assessment of cash, total receivables, and credit risk. The receivable and payable sub-ledgers should be reconciled to the general ledger on a monthly basis to ensure that the accounting systems reflect the same account balance information. To enhance the efficiency of the settlement process, companies should make an active effort at resolving and collecting outstanding balances, and monitoring the aged receivables and payables.

Credit establishment and monitoring

The credit department is responsible for establishing individual counter-party credit limits based on an objective scoring system, monitoring credit limits, and tracking credit exposure risk. The scoring system should consider financial history, independent credit ratings, credit references, industry reputation, and payment history. Based on these combined attributes, a credit limit is established and checked by trading personnel prior to deal execution.

The company should establish an active credit exposure monitoring process comprised of the following elements:

- Capture actual credit exposure utilizing mark-to-market valuation of forward transactions, physical flow that has not been invoiced, and net accounts receivable due.

- Analyze portfolio concentration by comparing the percent of a counter-party's value and volume of the portfolio to the total portfolio to ensure that the portfolio is not dominated by one particular counter-party that may pose a significant credit risk to the company.

- Capture potential credit exposure by statistically modeling the impact of volatility on forward positions.

These credit limits and exposures should be reported to the traders and management on a daily basis to ensure that all personnel are aware of credit risk. The override of certain credit limits should be adequately discussed and documented by senior management.

Managing Supply and Trading Organizations

by John Elting Treat & Matthew C. Rogers

Energy supply and trading organizations have grown over the past decade from simple logistics groups to become critical strategic value managers. In many respects, the fundamentals remain unchanged—the best supply and trading organizations bring together advantaged assets, deal streams, and information to generate superior profits. However, as markets have matured, the capabilities required to participate successfully in these markets have increased exponentially.

Early in the decade, even the best supply and trading organizations focused on balancing supply and demand at minimum cost. A few commodities trading firms (*e.g.,* Phibro J. Aron) made substantial sums trading relatively low-risk arbitrage opportunities (*e.g.,* crude contango plays, Rotterdam-Houston VGO plays/ West Coast—as in distillate plays), but the center of gravity was clearly around supply balancing with a little opportunity trading thrown in for fun.

During, the last 10 years, markets have changed significantly. Supply margins have fallen systematically as markets have become more transparent. Asset rationalization and working capital minimization decisions have reduced the cushion in the system, limiting the degrees of freedom available in the market. Lower inventories and increased market fragmentation have increased volatility and forced traders to react more quickly to market discontinuities.

Falling transportation costs have increased global linkages across markets, expanding the scope of any trading decision. Likewise, the development of parallel trading markets across the energy complex in crude oil, refined products, natural gas, and electricity have multiplied the differentials available for trading and brought new players into the game. Sophisticated over-the-counter risk derivative products have reduced the cost, but increased the complexity of managing risk.

Cost pressures across energy markets have limited the resources available to supply and trading organizations. At the same time, increasing market efficiency has created demand for even more sophisticated (and expensive) information systems to identify transient arbitrage opportunities and to manage increasingly complex portfolios. Likewise, it now costs more to find, hire, and keep the top people talent.

As a result, those companies who wish to survive and prosper play the game differently than they did a decade ago. Today, the best organizations have developed sophisticated midstream strategies that leverage supply and trading capabilities to enhance profitability across the entire value chain. They do this by:

- integrating supply and trading market perspectives and optionality analytics into core business strategy decision-making

- creating options by building asset networks in specific markets, creating an advantaged position that the trading organization can systematically exploit

- integrating information across the organization to exploit short-term market discontinuities based on advantaged market positions

- leveraging a company's natural deal streams into wide, deep, and flexible market driving deal streams

- optimizing integrated profitability in niche markets

- managing corporate market and credit risk exposure while translating market volatility into a profit making opportunity

- developing the ability to reach sophisticated end-use customers directly with highly tailored products and services

- utilizing sophisticated process management tools to minimize working capital and maximize asset utilization, while keeping service levels high

- enhancing speed and flexibility to respond to market changes with strong cross-functional teamwork and decision-making processes

- maintaining low unit costs by capturing significant scale and scope economies and by focusing resources on the least efficient markets

These new strategies require new business processes, organizational structures, and capabilities. The processes must integrate across organizational boundaries to optimize the supply chain end to end. The organizational structure must align the strategies with the external markets and capture scale information and transaction processing.

The people who comprise these organizations require sophisticated analytical and commercial skills and experience. The staff and systems support infrastructure must respond to the market more rapidly and with more precision than ever before. The performance measures and reward plans need to capture the full strategic contribution these organizations make. The control models need to reflect the risk of high-volume, high absolute-dollars risk transactions.

The lessons learned about managing supply and trading organizations can be broadly applied across multiple energy commodity groups. Companies that can successfully develop and execute these sophisticated midstream strategies can gain measurable competitive advantage in crude, products, gas, and electricity. Companies that fail to respond adequately to these rapidly changing markets will be forced either to exit the business or to stumble along, trying to hold things together while their overall market positions and profitability deteriorate.

These lessons were first proven true in crude and refined products trading early in the decade. By the middle of the decade, the shakeout in natural gas was underway. Many of the gas marketers and gas trading groups that started operation with such bravado early in the decade fell hard as markets matured. We expect the new millennium will see the consolidation of the electricity supply and trading business among a very few winners.

The last decade provided a wonderful opportunity for companies to learn the game. Those companies that have learned their lessons will have enviable opportunities as we enter the new millennium.

A STRATEGIC ROLE FOR SUPPLY AND TRADING

As market volatility has increased and markets have globalized, the leaders of the best supply and trading (S&T) organizations have guided their organizations to take on broader strategic roles. For example, the S&T organizations provide broad based support to exploration & production (E&P) in many ways:

- Supporting the application of options valuation techniques to reserve acquisition and production decision-making

- Bundling crude placement and risk management services into producing country relationship equations

- Designing innovative and value maximizing solutions to production logistics challenges

- Applying sophisticated refinery modeling capabilities to establish pricing parameters and target placements for new crude

- Highlighting quality segregation and blending opportunities to enhance the value of mature fields

These roles can position S&T as part of the E&P strategic leadership team, creating enormous value above and beyond the traditional trading service that S&T organizations supplied at the beginning of the decade.

Likewise, refining/supply and trading organizations are significantly increasing the knowledge-to-capital ratio in refining strategic decisions. Tosco provides the best example of the potential benefits of applying supply and trading strategic logic to refinery asset decision-making:

- Investing in flexibility to take advantage of market volatility

- De-bottlenecking aggressively with full confidence that S&T can place the barrels

- Optimizing the refinery in response to very short-term market signals and turning the asset into a nimble "demand pull" rather than a laborious supply "push machine"

- Utilizing risk management to lock in the value of incremental production

- Employing project financing and outsourcing to "dollarize the optionality" in the refinery site (*e.g.,* cogen and polypropylene integration)

- Restructuring long-term crude slate decision-making as crude balance shift

- Capturing opportunistic "wounded duck" cargos (buying crude, selling specialty products, buying odd intermediates) for incremental profitability

- Using trading and aggressive product shifts to exploit competitor reliability difficulties

- Optimizing product stream realization as rack market differentials fluctuate

In marketing, the pattern is the same—the best S&T organizations build a strong strategic foundation for marketing decision-making:

- Framing the sources of supply for the market so that marketing understands competitor bulk economics

- Evaluating and maintaining the supply demand balance in micro market to maximize marketing profitability

- Identifying advantaged approaches for supplying new markets and restructuring supply arrangements for existing markets to maximize local advantage

- Developing strategic pricing postures at the racks that reflect underlying supply and demand fundamentals

Electricity provides today's most significant example of the "power" of integrating supply and trading into strategic decision-making. Recent auctions of electricity generating assets have been dominated by trading firms seeking to build advantaged portfolios of peaking, mid-merit, and base load assets. The bids in these auctions have recently begun to reflect the optionality found in these assets that can exploit volatility in ways that the utility industry has never seen before. Decisions on generating asset sizing, location, financing, and configuration—including cogeneration—must now reflect the volatility of trading markets rather than the certainty of fixed price power purchase agreements.

Similarly, electricity commercial marketing now depends heavily on integrated electricity and gas trading services to create value in the deal.

Natural gas provides the model for the importance of the strategic influence of "the midstream." Enron and Natural Gas Clearing House—now Dynegy—redefined the industry with hub trading and gas banking. Others followed, but the fundamental S&T-driven strategic insights heralded a significant shift in the available profit pool of natural gas from producers to midstream traders with the information, assets, and deal-streams to capture—some would say create—large arbitrage opportunities between and among markets as the market integrated.

Today, S&T "thinking" is driving network consolidation among natural gas pipeline companies (e.g., Sempra, KN Energy) and the convergence of midstream gas and electricity. Indeed, these frameworks are at the forefront of the changes coming to the electricity and gas markets in Europe over the next decade.

The message is clear—in volatile, deregulating markets, S&T organizations have a critical role to play in strategic decision-making. Far from being simple service organizations that maintain system balance, S&T organizations drive innovative strategic differentiation across the energy complex.

Distinctive Supply and Trading Operating Processes

With their strategies in place, the leaders of S&T organizations deliver superior operating performance. The challenge is building, maintaining, and exploiting advantaged market positions where the company holds asset networks, deal streams, and information superior to the competition.

Information management

Information presents the largest challenge. Successful S&T organizations must integrate massive amounts of data from disparate sources—external market data, internal market information, financial and accounting information, and logistical and operational information.

This massive amount of information presents a significant systems challenge (discussed elsewhere in this book). The sophistication and scope of these IT networks—from Bloomberg terminals to county-by-county U.S. Weather Service data systems—continues to grow.

Hence, the investment necessary to compete successfully in the midstream continues to increase. As a result, massive scale and careful strategic focus become critical success factors in the midstream. Indeed, only four to six companies may eventually be able to compete successfully in the market given the magnitude of the challenge as markets like gas and electricity integrate.

The most vexing informational challenge, however, is not the systems, but rather creating and nurturing the web of internal, privileged market intelligence that truly creates advantage. Anyone can rent a Bloomberg terminal, but only a few players can build the human infrastructure and management discipline to identify unexpected market information quickly (*e.g.*, in a refinery or a rack "going down") and act on that information profitability before the market responds.

S&T organizations profit from their own adversity—going long if a refinery has a fire and cushioning the blow and profit from competitor adversity by enhancing the game. Success requires disciplined cross-functional market teams who know what to look for, and explicit trading strategies that define how to win. The difficulty of building and nurturing these networks implies either a massive investment in an integrated national or global network or an intense focus on a few niche markets in which even a small player can dominate.

Deal stream management

S&T groups usually begin with a modest natural flow of physicals transactions to manage. However, in order to capture economies of scale in information and to create degrees of freedom in execution (camouflage), S&T organizations capture the market-driving share of a few deal streams.

These deal streams position their owners as market makers. Any company wanting to track that stream—for either the buy side or the sell side—must then deal with the market maker. The market concentration dynamic creates a virtuous cycle: He who owns the deal stream has the best market information and can capture more value from the next deal stream—and so become the natural owner of the next deal—to deepen the stream and extend the advantage.

Hence, S&T organizations command deal streams 10–20 times larger than the natural flow of physicals from their own assets. To some, this sounds like speculation. Indeed, managing trading books for these massive deal streams to ensure they remain largely balanced represents one of the most important managerial processes of S&T organizations. Nevertheless, building market-driving positions through the development of massive deal streams is not an option, but a requirement to participate profitably in S&T markets today.

Assets, then, represent the last—and potentially the least important—part of the equation. S&T organizations maintain a very high information and deal stream-to-asset ratio. A few strategic assets are critical, but a surfeit of assets can under-mine the success of S&T organizations.

Today, the key is to build a network of assets with significant optionality:

- storage at key trading points and behind critical bottlenecks in the system

- transportation networks that support arbitrage across multiple markets

- flexible production assets (*e.g.*, refineries, power generating stations) that can shift the level and mix of output quickly in response to near-term market moves, etc

The best players consistently make assets the last part of the equation. Superior deal streams create advantaged informa-tion that enables a company to build a network comprised of the few assets that matter.

Asset optimization and working capital stewardship

In addition to their basic strategic and operational roles, the best S&T organizations have also taken on a far greater role in asset optimization and working capital stewardship.

Asset optimization stems from the need to respond quickly to market volatility and the challenge of capturing the integrat-ed value of attractive deal streams. S&T organizations take a lead in refining optimization—usually with the refinery opti-mization team sitting just off the trading floor to provide access to the latest market intelligence in real time. Likewise, many of the top S&T organizations have a responsibility for pipeline, marine, terminal, and truck integration to apply sophisticated load leveling and dispatch capabilities to more disciplined development exercises in new businesses. As companies set up multiple independent, stand-alone business units, the importance of having someone standing on the bridge, managing the few shared resources, grows.

These S&T organizations have proven very effective in minimizing working capital and enabling companies to rely on the pooled inventory available in the market instead. Beginning in the early 1990s, S&T organizations began applying sophisticated demand forecasting and stocking the largest software-to-inventing decision-making when downstream returns raised pressure to generate cash. Now these organizations are systematically working each of the assumptions in these forecasting equations to drive a structural decrease in working capital requirements:

- Reducing resupply time by identifying local sources of emerging supply and by shifting pipeline drop volumes at the last minute—making in-transit inventions a pooled safety stock

- Segmenting service levels for commercial customers, rewarding the stability of the reliable, low cost to serve segment

- Restructuring pipeline shipment patterns to reduce drop size and increase drop frequency

- Renegotiating credit terms to prevent financing problems

- Restructuring invoice processing to prevent broken invoices and invoice disputes that often account for a third or more of the working capital opportunity of a large oil company

Taken together, the asset optimization and working capital initiatives for S&T organizations have fundamentally reshaped the supply chain:

- Reducing cycle time

- Increasing market responsiveness

- Decreasing working capital requirement to play

- Enhancing flexibility to capture arbitrage opportunities

- Shortening supply lines

As a result, the asset productivity for the best organization may add two to four points of ROCE vs. the typical player in these markets.

Risk management

As market volatility has increased, S&T organizations have reshaped their approach to risk management. These companies are segmenting the risks the corporation seeks to manage, and they're developing more streamlined, cost-effective approaches to managing net risk. Companies who have failed to adjust as the risk markets have shifted face higher costs for risk management and all too often deliver unpleasant earnings surprises to their shareholders when risk management decisions have gone bad.

These organizations have segmented corporate risk from managerial risk and established separate risk management product development. These approaches both encourage better decision-making about risk and minimize the cost of overall corporate risk management. In an effort to allow business units to focus more on controllable costs than on volatile margins, S&T organizations have established central risk management banks that will hold managers risk neutral for taking appropriate market risks.

For example, an inventory manager can lock in contango inventory carry plays, a refining manager can lock in a set crack spread, and a distillate sales manager can lock in forward sales for the coming winter with appropriate risk pricing—but without requiring these managers to utilize futures or options. This type of risk management encourages appropriate physical flow decision-making—the right inventory builds and draws, the optimal refining optimization and investment decisions, the appropriate long-term sales commitments—in the midst of market volatility. This approach minimizes risk management costs by netting discrete business unit transactions into a common corporate book. Perhaps most importantly, this approach enables the corporation to encourage appropriate managerial risk-taking when the tendency of managers is to be overly risk-adverse.

The most effective S&T organizations have made risk management an integral part of their product development capabilities. Koch and Enron have built considerable upstream business positions by wrapping lease crude purchase commitments in a well- structured financial package. Likewise, the best distillate organizations have developed highly flexible financing packages to support distillate sales across multiple channels. These risk management product development capabilities have proven decisive in the growth of wholesale electricity and gas businesses. The key in each of these cases is developing an ability to offer high-volume risk management service at very low cost, and an ability to package risk management into attractive product bundles. Such organizations have built sophisticated market tracking processes to aggregate these customer risk exposures into the common corporate books.

At the corporate level, the challenge is to develop a precise understanding of the firm's at-risk position and then appropriately hedging this corporate risk in the market. This requires sophisticated information systems to bring together information on the corporation's physical flows and inventories, contractual commitments, and financial positions. The best corporations then utilize the financial markets to hedge the exposure to deliver a consistent risk exposure to the market, even as they seek to maintain stable balance sheet ratios in the capital markets.

As the risk management markets have become more sophisticated, the best organizations have also moved toward utilizing more flexible over-the-counter risk management instruments to minimize the cost of hedging this corporate net risk position. With large complex exposures, the standard futures and options approach becomes both unwieldy and expensive. Derivatives enable the development of tailored, low-cost solutions—as long as the risk management purchaser has a good understanding of how much risk should cost.

INNOVATIVE ORGANIZATIONAL APPROACHES

These new roles and strategic approaches to S&T require new organizational models to be successful. Fundamentally, the organization must align itself with the advantaged market positions the company holds—specific markets with advantaged assets, deal streams, and information. Hence, S&T organizations now align the organization around market-driven asset teams that share commodity resources across teams. S&T organizations staff to meet demand and avoid the temptation toward functional excellence. Finally, these organizations relentlessly focus trading activities on the few advantaged trading positions. Such organizational approaches support speed and flexibility while keeping costs low.

The best trading floors are organized around a series of concentric rings reflecting the economic structure of the markets in which the company trades. The paper traders occupy the center, managing the risk position for the trading floor as a whole. The economies of scale in paper trading remain large—one paper trader can support six to eight wet barrel traders. Moreover, the economies of "scope in information" for paper traders are exceptionally high—the best paper traders work crude and products or electricity and gas together, trading off the same fundamental market insights. All the trading books clear their net at risk position to the center of the floor. All the paper risk management and speculation is held by the small paper trading team at the core.

The physicals traders occupy the first ring—usually with crude on one side of the floor and products and/or electricity on the other side. Most of the physicals traders are organized around specific basis trading opportunities built around a particular deal stream supported by specific asset positions.

For example, on the crude side of the floor, a Gulf Coast refiner could have a West Africa team, a heavy team, a Louisiana team, a West Texas sweet team, and a West Texas sour team. A dedicated trader leads each team and assumes sufficient volume—100–200 MBD. These traders would be integrated into global trading networks to capture market arbitrage opportunities—West Africa with the Brent book, West Texas light with the Middle Eastern light book, etc.

Likewise, on the products side of the floor, a Gulf Coast refiner would likely have a Gulf Coast distillate trader, a Gulf Coast gasoline trader, a Colonial destination trader, a Williams/Group III trader, and a fuel oil/intermediates trader, each reflecting a specific, liquid market. Again, these traders would be linked globally with global distillate, gasoline, and intermediates book to capture global arbitrage opportunities.

The schedulers control the next ring, organizing the logistics to keep the markets in balance. The schedulers keep the supply points "wet" with product. Typically, the schedulers have primary stewardship responsibility for working capital inventories along the supply chain. Importantly, the schedulers at S&T organizations represent integral members of the trading team. In most cases, the schedulers take the lead on in-transit trades (*e.g.*, trading the back to the front of pipeline cycles) and local convenience trades (*e.g.*, picking up from neighboring terminals to handle outages).

Perhaps more importantly, the schedulers serve as a critical conduit of advantaged information from the local market to the physical traders. The best schedulers maintain a comprehensive information network. Moreover, they have the insight to identify and prompt action on tradable information before it becomes widely available in the market.

In S&T organizations, the schedulers are the workhorse heroes, creating opportunities by working in the trenches. Traders may capture the headlines, but the best traders develop exceptional relationships with their scheduling teams to maintain strategic market advantage.

The planners and optimizers control the outer ring, dedicating themselves to providing support to the asset-based trading and scheduling teams they support. These analytical resources are looking ahead, seeking the next major swing in differentials, looking for structural geographic arbitrage opportunities, planning seasonal changeovers, assessing term contract structure, and supporting the strategic planning analyses discussed earlier. S&T organizations have the analytical staff on the trading floor, aligning short- and long-term perspectives and developing the detailed market understandings that can only come from living in the tempest of the trading room.

It is important to note that while the rings are functional, the day-to-day operating team is a radial slice of the trading room. The operating team comprises traders, schedulers, and planners, all of whom are focused on and dedicated to trading a specific deal stream around a specific asset, utilizing the full scope of the company's local market information to capture arbitrage opportunities. Nevertheless, the team also should include asset-based operations managers, local distribution management, and local marketing management. The best teams are cross-functional—extending the reach of the supply and trading organization into the market.

Likewise, while trading rooms tend to be regional—centered around Houston, Rotterdam, and Singapore—the need for global teams and global coordination has increased markedly as the crude and products markets have globalized. Global trading book management, global sourcing planning, and global logistics optimization all have real impact today. Local players will find it difficult to compete against the mature global networks of the major oil companies and the trading houses.

Staffing levels across these organizations are driven by a clear understanding of two issues: the economies of scale available in trading and the market arbitrage opportunities. So traders in deep liquid markets may be trading 200–300 MBD of crude and 100–200 MBD of products on average, with one scheduler supporting two traders and half a planner working the analytics. In contrast, the same company may have a small, advantaged niche position with significant arbitrage opportunities where a trader handles only 50 MBD with two schedulers and a full time planner in support. The goal is to keep reasonably equivalent contribution margin per person from each of the asset teams.

To maintain balance, focus, and alignment, S&T organizations hold these teams accountable for performance against a balanced scorecard:

Operating costs

- S&T organizational costs
- Transportation and demurrage costs

Contribution

- Risk adjusted return on speculative capital
- Regional supply margins

Working capital employed

- Inventory levels
- Trade accounts receivables
- Return on fixed distribution assets under supply's control

Operating performance

- Supply availability
- Quality give-away

Strategic contribution

- Business unit decision making
- Corporate stewardship of integrated assets

In S&T organizations, these performance scorecards are used to support significant incentive compensation. Incentive compensation can comprise 25% (or more) of the total compensation for traders, schedulers, and planners, based on a combination of team and firm performance.

The trading organizations build their teams through disciplined use of career ladders. Career ladders enable S&T organizations to develop talent over time even when a straight path may not exist from the bottom to the top of the S&T organization. Good career ladders enable S&T organizations to attract and retain people from a variety of backgrounds, providing differentiated development programs for technical, commercial, and analytical backgrounds. More importantly, effective career ladders contribute to strong alignment between the other business units and supply by bringing some of the best and brightest from interface roles in the business into supply for a tour of duty, creating a sophisticated interlocutor for supply when the business unit manager returns. So, for example, a major oil company may send a refinery planner to manage scheduling before returning to the refinery as operations manager. Likewise, a marketing organization may have a regional marketing manager trade and schedule the supply source market as an effective commercial training ground before moving out to the field.

Organizationally, then, S&T organizations have restructured significantly over the last decade. They emphasize:

- Stronger cross-functional teamwork

- Significantly increased global linkages

- Enhanced focus on tradable micro-markets

- Leaner staffing levels reflecting economies of scale and available arbitrage opportunities

- Clear delineation of functional roles (*e.g.,* separating flat price "paper" trading from "wet barrel" basis trading)

- Broader measured accountability

As a result, these organizations have significantly increased efficiency and effectiveness over time. Costs are down. Unit contribution margins are up. Speed and flexibility have increased significantly. Perhaps most importantly, however, S&T organizations have had substantial strategic impact across the business.

CONCLUSIONS

S&T organizations have transformed themselves over the last decade from a logistics service group to critical strategic value managers. At the beginning of the 1990s, the aspiration for many was to become Wall Street traders, leveraging information to speculate for profit. Instead, S&T organizations have matured over the last decade to become credible strategic partners with the production and marketing business units across the energy complex. These organizations have made art out of creating strategic constellations of advantaged deal streams, assets, and information. Even as the markets have become more liquid and more efficient, these organizations have used exceptional market strategies, scale operating processes, innovative information networks, and team-oriented organizational designs to squeeze increased contribution margins from the midstream.

Tremendous challenges remain. Across the next decade, margins will likely continue to fall for commodity products as market deregulation and globalization continues to spread across the energy complex. As commodity margins fall, cost pressures will become intense. As consolidation continues, scale requirements will continue to increase rapidly. Perhaps more importantly, the capabilities required for staying in the game will continue to increase—those that fail to keep pace will fall to the way side. A significant shakeout likely lies ahead in electricity and gas trading especially.

Yet, immense opportunities remain. The North American electricity trading market will mature, following the pattern of the gas business, creating significant opportunities in the transition. Europe will see a tremendous integration of refined products, natural gas, and electricity as deregulation spreads, creating unprecedented supply and trading opportunities. Latin America and Asia will begin to take advantage of the market efficiencies that deregulated supply and trading make available, reshaping the supply curve for energy across these regions.

S&T organizations will continue to transform themselves in order to remain at the forefront of strategic thinking for the market leaders across the energy complex. Likewise, the best corporations will nurture their S&T talent to continue to find opportunities for rapid strategic market innovation in these rapidly changing energy markets.

ENERGY INFORMATION: CONTENT, DELIVERY, AND USE BY FUTURES TRADERS

by Richard N. Fletcher

INTRODUCTION

Information is the essence of futures trading. It is also a global market unto itself, worth some $6 billion.[1] Fifteen percent of this market (or about $900 million)[2] is generated by sales to global energy industries. In addition to real-time systems, information content providers, and analytical software vendors, a host of ancillary products and services make up the bulk of the industry.

Tables 13–1 through 13–4 offer a selective list of real-time systems, information content providers, and software vendors. Their appendices provide useful addresses, contact numbers, and web sites. These sources should provide the reader with a starting point for researching energy information systems for trading.

In the 1970s and 1980s, energy information became a commodity that grew in tandem with the evolution of crude oil spot markets and futures trading. The "push" of crude oil price volatility during that time and the "pull" of rapidly evolving computer technology and telecommunications networks helped create real-time

REAL-TIME SYSTEM VENDORS	PRODUCT/ SERVICE(S)	O	G	E	DATA FORMAT	DELIVERY	URL http://www.
Bloomberg	Bloomberg Energy	X	X	X	Electronic, hardcopy	Internet, proprietary system	bloomberg.com
Bridge/Dow Jones Markets (formerly Telerate)	BridgeFeed, BridgeStation Dow Jones Energy Service, Powerhub	X	X	X	Electronic	Proprietary	telerate.com powerhub.telerate.com
Data Broadcasting Corporation	BMI Quotes, Signal	X	X	X	Electronic	Internet, wireless	dbc.com bmiquotes.com
Data Transmission Network Corp.	DTNergy	X	X	X	Electronic	Internet, proprietary	dtnergy.com
Future Source	FS Quotes, FS Expert, FS Advisor, FS Technical, FS Analyst, FS Data	X	X	X	Electronic	Internet	futuresource.com
ICV Datastream	Market Eye, TOPIC3	X	X	X	Electronic	Internet, proprietary	datastream.com
Reuters	Energy 2000	X	X	X	Electronic	Internet, proprietary	commods.reuters.com
Telekurs	FinXS, InvestVision	X	X	X	Electronic	Internet, proprietary	telekurs-financial.com
Track Data Corp.	MarkeTrack 98, Dial Data	X	X	X	Electronic	Internet, proprietary	tdc.com

Table 13–1   *Real-Time System Vendors*

REAL-TIME SYSTEM VENDORS	CONTACT	ADDRESS	PHONE/FAX	URL http://www.
Bloomberg		100 Business Park Dr. P.O. Box 888 Princeton, NJ 08542-0888	P: 800-388-2749 P: 609-279-3000 F: 609-683-7523	bloomberg.com
Bridge/Dow Jones Markets (formerly Telerate)	Cary Drake, Marketing Manager	Two World Trade Center Suite 750 New York, NY 10048	P: 800-334-3813 P: 212-390-6025	telerate.com powerhub.telerate.com
Data Broadcasting Corporation	Chuck Thompson, Sr. VP Marketing	3955 Point Eden Way Hayward, CA 94545-3720	P: 510-723-3581	dbc.com bmiquotes.com
Data Transmission Network Corp.	Darius Lechtenberger, Sales Manager	9110 W. Dodge Rd., #200 Omaha, NE 68114	P: 402-255-3794 F: 402-255-8350	dtnergy.com
Future Source	Chris Mahlmann, Marketing Dir.	955 Parkview Blvd. Lombard, IL 60148	P: 800-621-2628 P: 630-792-2001 F: 630-792-2600	futuresource.com
ICV Datastream	Alan Schwartz	120 Wall Street, 15th Floor New York, NY 10005	P: 212-804-4000 F: 212-804-4001	datastream.com
Reuters America, Inc.	Robert Garfield, Director, Energy & Commodities Markets	199 Water Street New York, NY 10038	P: 212-859-1850 F: 212-859-1872	commods.reuters.com
Telekurs		Hardturmstrasse 201 Postfach 8021 Zürich Switzerland	P: 41-1-279-51-11 F: 41-1-279-51-12	telekurs-financial.com
Track Data Corp.	Alan Schnerwar Sr. Vice President	56 Pine Street New York, NY 10005	P: 212-422-4300	tdc.com

Table 13–1a *Appendix to Table 13–1*

INFORMATION CONTENT PROVIDERS	PRODUCT/ SERVICE(S)	O G E	DATA FORMAT	DELIVERY	URL http://www.
Bloomberg	Bloomberg Energy	X X X	Electronic, hardcopy	Internet, proprietary	bloomberg.com
Energy Intelligence Group	Energy Compass, Petroleum Intelligence Weekly, World Gas Intelligence, Oil Market Intelligence, Oil Daily, Natural Gas Week, among others	X X X	Electronic, hardcopy	Internet, email, hardcopy	energyintelligence.com
Dow Jones Interactive	Dow Jones News Retrieval	X X X	Electronic	Internet, proprietary	djinteractive.com
Futures Magazine	Monthly magazine and annual sourcebook	X X X	Electronic, hardcopy	Internet, hardcopy	futuresmag.com
ICIS-LOR	World Crude Report, World Products Report	X X	Electronic, hardcopy	Internet, hardcopy	icislor.com
Oil & Gas Journal Database	OGJ Online	X X X	Electronic, hardcopy	Internet, hardcopy	ogjonline.com
Oil Price Information Service	Rack Prices, Spot Price History, Futures History, API History, among others	X X	Electronic, hardcopy	Internet, hardcopy	opisnet.com
Pasha Publications	Gas Daily, Megawatt Daily, among others.	X X	Electronic, hardcopy	Internet, email, hardcopy	pasha.com
Petroleum Argus	Weekly Petroleum Argus, Argus Global Markets, among others	X X	Electronic, hardcopy	Internet, hardcopy	petroleumargus.com
Reuters	Reuters Energy	X X X	Electronic	Internet, proprietary	commods.reuters.com
Saladin Information Services	Offers more than 30 sources of data for futures traders from 3rd party data providers	X X X	Electronic	Internet	saladin.com
S&P Platt's	Global Alert, Natural Gas Alert, Electricity Alert, Oilgram News, Oilgram Price Report, among others, including DRI Energy Services	X X X	Electronic, hardcopy	Internet, proprietary, email, hardcopy	platts.com
U.S. Dept of Energy/ Energy Information Administration	Provides a wide range of data covering domestic and international energy information	X X X	Electronic, hardcopy	CD-ROM, Internet e-mail, hardcopy	eia.doe.gov

Table 13-2 *Information Content Providers*

INFORMATION CONTENT PROVIDERS	CONTACT	ADDRESS	PHONE/FAX	URL http://www.
Energy Intelligence Group	A.J. Conley, Associate Publisher	575 Broadway New York, NY 10012	P: 212-941-5500 F: 212-941-5509	energyintel.com
Dow Jones Interactive	Kathleen M. Downey, Manager	P.O. Box 300 Princeton, NJ 08543-0300	P: 609-520-4000 F: 609-520-7133	djinteractive.com
Futures Magazine	Barbara Vogel, Publisher	250 S. Wacker Sr., #1150 Chicago, IL 60606	P: 312-977-0999 F: 312-977-1042	futuresmag.com
ICIS-LOR		Quadrant House The Quadrant Sutton, Surrey SM2 5AS U.K.	P: 44-181-652-3535 F: 44-181-652-3923	icislor.com
Oil & Gas Journal Energy Database	Sandra Meyer, Database Manager	P.O. Box 1260 Tulsa, OK 74101	P: 800-345-4618 P: 918-832-9346	ogjonline.com
Oil Price Information Service	Sherri McCall, Energy Coordinator	11300 Rockville Pike Rockville, MD 20852	P: 301-287-2645 F: 301-816-8945	opisnet.com
Pasha Publications		1600 Wilson Blvd. #600 Arlington, VA 22209	P: 703-528-1244 F: 703-528-7821	pasha.com
Petroleum Argus		93 Shepperton Rd. London N1 3DF U.K.	P: 44-171-359-8792 F: 44-171-359-6661	petroleumargus.com
S&P Platt's	Mike Misner, Product Manager	1221 Avenue of the Americas New York, NY 10020	P: 212-512-4047 F: 212-512-2596	platts.com
U.S. Dept. of Energy/ Energy Information Administration	National Energy Information Center	Energy Information Administration U.S. Dept. of Energy Washington, DC 20585	P: 202-586-8800	eia.doe.gov

Table 13–2a *Appendix to Table 13–2*

ANALYTICAL SOFTWARE VENDORS	PRODUCT/ SERVICE(S)	DESCRIPTION	URL http://www.
Aspen Research Group, Ltd.	Aspen Graphics	Trading software, charting, and technical analysis	aspenres.com
Omega Research	TradeStation, OptionStation	SuperCharts Custom trading systems, analysis	omegaresearch.com
Saladin	Petroleum Analysis Workstation	Integrated historical data and analytical software, charting	saladin.com

Table I3–3 *Analytical Software Vendors*

ANALYTICAL SOFTWARE VENDORS	CONTACT	ADDRESS	PHONE/FAX	URL http://www.
Aspen Research Group, Ltd.	John Prim, Sales Executive	P.O. Box 1320 802 Grand Ave., #120 Glenwood Springs, CO 81601	P: 970-945-2921 F: 970-945-9619	aspenres.com
Omega Research		8700 W. Flagler St. #250 Miami, FL 33174	P: 305-551-9991 F: 305-551-2240	omegaresearch.com
Saladin Walton Court		Station Avenue Walton-on-Thames Surrey KT12 1NT U.K.	P: 44-1932-243233 F: 44-1932-244786	saladin.com

Table I3–3a *Appendix to Table 13–3*

ANCILLARY PRODUCTS & SERVICES	PRODUCT/ SERVICE(S)	DESCRIPTION	URL http://www.
Futures Industry Association and Futures Industry Institute	Industry Association	Provides a range of products and services for the futures industry	fiafii.org
Sagemaker, Inc.	SageBlade (formerly DAR-WIN), SageServer, SageWave	Provides single front-end for internal and external industry data sources	sagemaker.com
Waters Information Services	Market Data Industry, Real-Time Financial Information Index	Provides analysis of trading systems, data vendors, among others	watersinfo.com

Table I3–4 *Ancillary Products and Services*

ANCILLARY PRODUCTS & SERVICES	CONTACT	ADDRESS	PHONE/FAX	URL http://www.
Futures Industry Association	John M. Damgard, President	2001 Pennsylvania Ave NW Suite 600 Washington, DC 20006	P: 202-466-5460 F: 202-296-3184	fiafii.org
Sagemaker, Inc.	Andrew White, VP Marketing	883 Black Rock Turnpike Fairfield, CT 06430	P: 203-368-4888 F: 203-367-6849	sagemaker.com
Waters Information Services	Andrew Delaney	270 Lafayette Street Suite 700 New York, NY 10012	P: 212-925-6990 F: 212-925-7585	watersinfo.com

Table I3–4a *Appendix to Table 13–4*

systems for oil trading. These systems—pioneered by Reuters, Dow Jones Telerate, and S&P's McGraw-Hill subsidiary—offered traders unprecedented access to real-time electronic news and global oil market prices and represent one of the early electronic "links" in the global marketplace.

By June 1993, the New York Mercantile Exchange opened its NYMEX ACCESSsm system for electronic trading to supplement traditional trading floor operations. Electronic trading commences at 4 PM—just after regular trading ends—and stays open until 8 AM the following morning—just before regular trading begins. By September 1998, the International Petroleum Exchange became the first major exchange to publish its real-time prices directly on the World Wide Web with its EnergyLive service.

"Screen-based trading"—as electronic trading is often called—is particularly strong in financial markets. In early 1998, screen-based trading replaced the traditional open outcry pit at Matif, the French futures exchange.[3] Electronic trading has demonstrated liquidity, transparency, and lower costs, and as the technology improves, other exchanges will likely have to decide whether to move wholly or in part to the electronic marketplace. However, the jury is still out concerning its value to energy markets such as NYMEX and the IPE, where local participants generate the majority of trading volume. While energy markets have hundreds of participants, financial markets have tens of thousands of participants, offering greater market depth and liquidity. It is likely that electronic trading and Internet-based services will radically alter the current energy trading landscape. One need only look at the burgeoning electricity markets to discover the impact.

In 1998, U.S. power markets traded about $70 billion worth of electricity, based on first-quarter cash volumes reported to FERC. NYMEX crude oil futures—considered the largest commodity market in the world—registered about $350 billion in annual trading in 1998 based on current oil prices, but it took NYMEX 15 years to reach such a level. Commoditization of wholesale electricity is still in its infancy. The number of independent power trading companies approved by the Federal Energy Regulatory Commission (FERC) has grown to more than 400, and 77 utilities have opened trading subsidiaries.[4]

The Internet changes everything

The emergence of the Internet as a business tool in the early 1990s, combined with advances in telecommunications technology and computers, created a "global" phenomenon. The significance of this remarkable technological revolution is illustrated by a basic fact: microprocessor prices—measured in millions of instructions per second (MIPS)—fell from $230/MIPS in 1990 to $3.42/MIPS in 1997[5] while computational power increased exponentially. What does this mean? Lower costs, advances in productivity and technology, and the emergence of "network economics" are changing industry economics— and it is change measured in months, not years.

Three companies leading the changes in energy trading are Altra Streamline (www.altranet.com), Enermetrix.com (www. enermetrix.com), and QuickTrade (www.quicktrade.com). These companies offer Internet-based systems that facilitate power and natural gas trading in deregulated markets. They provide consumers, brokers, and producers of power and natural gas an on-line forum in which to place competitive bids and consummate sales. Using this method of trading in a deregulated marketplace has resulted in savings by commercial consumers that are conservatively estimated to be 15 to 20%. Producers gain access to new markets with the opportunity of increasing their sales. Transaction costs in this Internet environment are incredibly cheap—on the order of $.0025 (a quarter of a penny) for natural gas[6]—thus creating the need for volume.

The Internet lowers the cost of doing business and allows direct access to consumers. This powerful combination is attracting attention from many of the world's largest companies. Telecommunications, energy, and entertainment companies are in the early stages of major transitions to be able to respond to network economics. If the trend in Internet computing continues—and if energy prices remain trending low, despite recent run-ups—consolidation among power, natural gas, and oil companies is inevitable.

Vivek Ranadive is CEO of TIBCO, a Reuters subsidiary that develops advanced technologies for the Internet. He expects everything that is available to a power trader—as in power user—on Wall Street to be accessible to every human being on the planet in five years. Further, he expects the Internet will have the reliability, scalability, performance, and security to do everything that proprietary networks—such as Reuters—do today.[7]

Customized information delivery, intelligent agents, and a host of other technological innovations are already strengthening the trader's ability to assess disparate information elements. Soon, new software for decision support using neural networks may further the revolution that is already underway.

Ubiquitous information—making the right choices

Saladin (www.saladin.com) provides analytical software and information services to energy traders. In 1997, Saladin conducted a survey of "The Successful Energy Trader" and in 1998, "The Successful Energy Trading Room." Summaries of these two very useful documents can be found on the Saladin website.

In brief, the 1997 survey reported that energy traders spend about half their working day connected with information—spot and futures prices, fundamentals, news, brokers' reports, freight rates, weather data, swaps data, and refinery yields. The greatest proportion of the trader's day (47%) is spent dealing with and using information—around 35% of this time is spent searching for information, 28% sharing it, and 38% analyzing it. Information deemed most important includes daily market prices, futures prices, and fundamentals. Questioned on their main sources of information, traders named 20 different vendors. With regard to industry publications, the most frequently mentioned were *Petroleum Intelligence Weekly, Petroleum Argus,* and *Energy Compass.*

The 1998 survey reported that of the many types of information used in energy trading rooms, real-time prices were considered the most important by 95% of the respondents. News is also considered key by 68% in the oil sector. Historical data are important for 57%, but used less in power and gas, as there is far less historical data available. Weather data were cited by another 13%, particularly electricity traders.

Reuters is the main source of both real time prices (54%) and news (75%), followed by Bridge/Dow Jones and Platt's. For historical data, 49% of respondents named delivery systems such as PAWS (Saladin's petroleum analysis workstation) rather than specific data publishers. The gas sector has seen more growth in analysis than other sectors, and the power sector has seen more information growth than others.

Internet use among energy traders is on the rise, according to the Saladin survey. Power and gas/power traders are the heaviest Internet users, while crude oil and trading companies are the lightest. Today, information is delivered faster and more easily than ever before, but the same caution exists for energy information users—consider the source, the reliability, and the reputation of the information provider and/or data vendor when purchasing data and systems. Typical data problems include units, measurement methods, timeliness, and standardization, according to industry norms.[8]

Discuss your information needs with your colleagues, your corporate librarian, a knowledge manager, or competitive intelligence groups. Learn from their experiences the easiest route to the needed information. The web is a great information resource, but searching can be very time consuming and much of the best data isn't free. Often, a well-placed phone call can be more effective.

Notes

1. Reuters 1996 Survey

2. Author's estimate

3. Remarks by Neal Wolkoff, Executive Vice President, NYMEX, to the Managed Futures Association Forum on Electronic Trading, June 25, 1998, Chicago

4. "Young and Wild, Electricity Trading is Fast Becoming one of the Biggest Commodity Markets in the Country," Mark Golden, Dow Jones Newswires, September 14, 1998

5. Intel

6. Richard Gelber, Gelber & Associates, remarks to Interactive Energy 98 conference, Houston, August 26, 1998

7. Reuters World, March 1998, "TIBCO—Setting the Laws of the New Age of the Internet"

8. For an interesting and enlightening article on this topic, see "Crude Oil Prices: An Empiricist's Guide," by Paul Horsnell, published in *The Journal of Energy Literature*

REGULATION OF ENERGY FUTURES AND OPTIONS TRADING

by David Yeres and Brett Little

Since the last edition of this volume a decade ago, we have seen the continued strong growth of U.S. and U.K. futures and option markets for oil and other energy commodities, including most recently the establishment of electric power trading. This chapter examines the regulatory regimes in these two jurisdictions as well as the ongoing trend of international regulatory cooperation.

Regulation, like the markets, is complex and dynamic. This chapter provides a summary of the regulatory situation at the time of its writing. Readers should consult with knowledgeable advisors for a more complete and current analysis before undertaking regulated activities.

UNITED STATES

Trading of commodity futures and option contracts in the U.S. is regulated by the Commodity Exchange Act of 1936 (CEA), as amended. The CEA establishes a system of federal government regulation and industry self-regulation. The Commodity Futures Trading Commission (the Commission or CFTC), an independent federal regulatory agency, is the hub of the regulatory system.

What is regulated?

CEA jurisdiction and CFTC regulation extend to contracts for the future delivery of a commodity—futures contracts—and option contracts on a commodity or on a futures contract. Regulation is built upon the concept of exchange trading and exchange self-regulation. With few exceptions, it is unlawful to engage in any futures or option contract transaction other than those executed on or subject to the rules of an exchange designated by the CFTC.

Consequently, the definitions of "futures contracts" and "option contracts" are of significance to traders in the growing "off-exchange" (over-the-counter or OTC) energy markets. However, neither the CEA nor the CTFC rules provide definitions of these key jurisdictional terms, and the CFTC maintains substantial flexibility in this area.

The boundaries of regulatory jurisdiction over OTC transactions have not been fully explored by the CFTC or the courts, except to ban commodities investments that are fraudulently sold to the general public. Consequently, it is unclear to what extent non-public, commercial, or financial transactions that share certain characteristics with futures or options are subject to regulation.

The CFTC does from time to time provide guidance as to its jurisdictional reach. The principal means of exemption from CFTC jurisdiction—for "futures-like" as well as certain options instruments—is a 1993 CFTC rule concerning swap transactions. Qualifying swap transactions—including those relating to energy prices—are exempt from all aspects of CFTC regulation, except anti-fraud provisions. Furthermore, certain commercial energy transactions that can be settled by either physical delivery, or net cash payment, have been exempted from CFTC regulation by a special energy order published by the CFTC in 1993.

This has not, however, ended all regulatory uncertainty concerning OTC energy transactions. For example, in 1995 the CFTC brought an enforcement action against various affiliates of Metallgesellshaft (MG), the large German chemical and energy company, for entering into certain privately negotiated OTC heating oil contracts in the U.S. The CFTC alleged that MG's contracts had certain features that rendered them illegal off-exchange futures contracts. MG settled the case and paid a substantial fine.

In another recent showing of interest in regulating OTC markets, the CFTC in May 1998 solicited public comment concerning the operation and regulation of OTC commodity swaps and options (OTC derivatives) trading.

Due to industry concern, and the perception that CFTC was seeking to expand its regulatory reach with respects to OTC derivatives, the CFTC initiative was withdrawn in November 1999.

In June 2000, the CFTC propoesed rules which may enhance regulatory certainty with respect to OTC derivatives by broadening the scope of its swap transactions exemption and permitting exempt transactions to be standardized and cleared. Congressional action is also expected, which will expand the class of OTC derivatives excluded from the CEA beyond those currently exempted under the CFTC swap exemption.

CFTC regulation

The Commission consists of five full-time members, including a chairman, selected by the president and confirmed by the senate. It is headquartered in Washington, D.C. and employs approximately 500 staff members.

The CFTC has exclusive jurisdiction over the regulation of the commodity futures and options-trading complex. Its regulatory objectives can be summarized as protecting customers, ensuring financial soundness, and preserving market integrity. CFTC rules designed to further each of the objectives are backed up by a staff enforcement division, which may investigate and prosecute violators. Penalties may include fines, loss of trading privileges, loss or suspension of registration, and injunction.

Customer protection is achieved through a combination of specific preventative measures and a general prohibition against fraud. Risk disclosure in a form specified by CFTC rule is required prior to opening a customer trading account. Broker guarantees against losses are expressly prohibited. No discretion may be exercised over trading unless the customer gives written authorization, and all trades must be promptly reported to the customer. Furthermore, customers' trades are required to be given priority in execution over proprietary trades. The antifraud provision prohibits any intentional or reckless deception of the customer, and a customer is provided an express right of action in federal court in the event of a violation. Further, the CFTC itself offers a forum where a customer may obtain reparations for injury suffered as a result of a violation of the CEA or CFTC rules.

The nature of trading in the mark-to-market system employed by U.S. exchanges requires initial deposit of margin funds and often requires additional flows of margin to secure contract obligations. In order to safeguard these customer funds, the CFTC requires that segregated custodial accounts be maintained by the futures commission merchant (broker) and the exchange, and that accountings be made regularly. Further, special rules govern the treatment of funds in the event of a futures commission merchant bankruptcy.

Market integrity is protected at various levels beginning with standards for permitting an exchange market to be established and operated. CFTC rules also govern the conduct of trading practices to ensure that prices are arrived at fairly and by open auction. Further, anti-manipulation provisions exist to prohibit purposeful creation of artificial prices.

EXCHANGES

Although not defined by the CEA, an exchange is the organization within which a designated contract market operates. Trading in futures and options contracts is unlawful unless and until contract-market designation occurs. An exchange may be designated by the CFTC as a contract market for several commodities. Conversely, separate contract markets for the same commodity may be designated on more than one exchange.

Perhaps the CFTC's most important function is determining whether to designate an exchange as a contract market for a particular futures or option contract. The CEA lists specific criteria that must be met for a contract-market designation. Among other things, it must be demonstrated that the contract is well designed as to delivery, and that manipulation of prices is provided against. Furthermore, it must be shown that designation will not be contrary to public interest. In order to meet this test, the CEA requires a showing that the contract is likely to be used for commercial price-risk hedging, or will be a mechanism for price discovery and dissemination.

In addition to granting a virtual monopoly—or oligopoly, if more than one exchange is designated—CFTC designation acts as a blessing of the exchange's role as a self-regulatory organization. An exchange whose rules have been reviewed and approved by the CFTC is free of state regulation, and generally immune from civil liability for its self-regulatory actions, absent a showing of bad faith. However, an exchange remains subject to comprehensive oversight by the CFTC.

CEA and CFTC rules provide for CFTC monitoring and supervision of essentially all exchange rules and operations. With the sole exception of rules relating to the levels of margin deposits, all significant exchange rules and rule amendments are subject to CFTC approval before going into effect. The CFTC is particularly interested in rules that relate to the terms and conditions of a futures or option contract, and will publish such rules or amendments for public comment. Once a rule is approved, it must be enforced. Furthermore, an exchange can be required by the CFTC to adopt or amend a rule. The CFTC conducts regular exchange-rule enforcement reviews and publishes reports on each exchange's efforts. The CFTC is also authorized to sue an exchange to compel rule enforcement. In the event of a market emergency, the CFTC may invoke special powers to direct exchange action. Finally, the CFTC may revoke or suspend a contract market designation as a means of disciplining an exchange or protecting the public.

In addition to oversight, the CFTC has authority to directly regulate trade practice. Any exchange member who executes trades for customers is required to be a CFTC-registered floor broker. Floor brokers and other traders are subject to CFTC rules—as well as exchange rules—concerning trade practices as well as price manipulation.

The CFTC recntly proposed sweeping changes to its regulatory framework for futures trading. The rules, if they take effect, would recognize three new categories of futures markets, two of which would be regulated. The CFTC proposed to regulate these markets depending on the nature of the products offered and the sophistication of the users. As presently drafted, energy futures and options would qualify to be traded on either or both of the regulated markets depending upon the participants in the markets.

New York Mercantile Exchange

Energy futures and options are principally traded on the New York Mercantile Exchange (NYMEX). For this reason—and because of the similarity among the rules of most domestic exchanges—NYMEX will serve as the subject of this explanation of exchange self-regulation.

As a designated contract market for several energy (as well as metals) futures and options, NYMEX, its members, and their customers are subject to a panoply of CFTC regulations. In addition, NYMEX is a self-regulatory organization that imposes upon its members a comprehensive scheme of rules.

NYMEX, like most other futures exchanges, is owned by its members and governed by an elected board of governors. Rules adopted by the board and approved by the CFTC are interpreted and enforced by various standing committees assisted by a professional staff. NYMEX rules regulate membership, financial standards, contract terms, and trading practices. NYMEX is an integrated exchange and clearing association, and its rules also govern clearing and settlement of trades.

A number of exchanges, including NYMEX, have recently implemented plans for "demutualizing" or separating the equity ownership component of membership from the trading rights of membership. It is anticipated that demutualized exchanges will be better able to compete with other market places, especially those where trading is conducted electronically. At present, the equity and trading rights remain together and are owned by the same persons or entities who were previously members of the exchange; however, most demutualized plans provide for the safe transfer of these rights to persons who will not have trading privileges.

Membership. Only members are authorized to execute trades on the NYMEX floor and to receive special rates with respect to exchange fees. NYMEX regulation focuses on its members. Members must be natural persons, however, two members may confer *member-firm* status upon a business. A member firm enjoys the benefit of membership, but as such, it also becomes subject to NYMEX rules. Only specially qualified *clearing members* may clear and settle trades, and these firms are subject to special regulations concerning financial requirements.

Admission to membership is a principal means of self-regulation. Candidates are required to provide extensive information about their personal, educational, and professional backgrounds as well as to supply current financial information. A minimum liquid net worth is required, except for employees of member firms. All candidates must undergo interviews before membership is conferred and must complete a training course prior to actual trading. NYMEX has the right to suspend or expel any member for violation of its financial or other rules.

NYMEX requires its members to adhere to just and equitable principles of trade, and has promulgated special ethics guidelines for its members. Although most specific rules relating to customer relations are left to the CFTC or the National Futures Association (NFA), NYMEX regulates its members' financial relationship with customers by requiring that customer margins be promptly posted and by prohibiting any member from lending initial margins.

Trading. Unlike the cash markets, NYMEX energy futures and options are not privately negotiated. NYMEX trades are executed by competitive auction in a designated area on the exchange floor and in electronic form on an exchange electronic trading platform. With the exception of a certain procedure known as an *exchange of futures for physicals* (EFP), private negotiation of a trade is a major rule violation. Indeed, the mere discussion of a proposed trade may taint a subsequent execution and violate rules prohibiting prearranged trading. NYMEX also prohibits cross-trading—with certain exceptions—and otherwise requires trades to be open and competitive.

EFP transactions are a means of establishing or liquidating a NYMEX position without an open auction trade. Two traders may post and be credited with a trade that is equal and opposite to a transaction in the same (or a related) commodity executed in the cash market (*e.g.,* a forward sales transaction in wet barrels of oil will support a corresponding EFP). The cash market transaction must be *bona fide* for oil, and independent as well as properly documented. Furthermore, the firms that clear an EFP trade must certify in writing to NYMEX that the cash-market transaction will result in a change of ownership.

NYMEX imposes a limit on the net long or short position a trader may hold or control with respect to each commodity traded. The rules generally provide for limits for all contract months as well as for any one month. A lower limit is provided for the spot month. Further, the positions of affiliated companies and persons who trade in concert are combined for purposes of determining compliance. Policing is done through the exchange member firm, which who is subject to financial and other penalties for carrying an above-limits position for its own account or the account of a customer. Specified exemptions from these limits may be obtained by qualified traders upon application to NYMEX.

Market-price integrity is regulated by NYMEX rules prohibiting price manipulation or attempted price manipulation. Although one court has said that the means of price manipulation are limited only by human ingenuity, in practice, allegations principally focus on large-trader conduct during the delivery process. Shortages of deliverable supply or congestions in the delivery mechanism may trigger exchange concern that a large trader may take advantage of the situation to extract prices that may not otherwise be achieved.

Each of the energy contracts traded on NYMEX provides for delivery of a physical commodity at expiration. However, it is generally accepted that less than 10% and often less than 2% of futures or options contracts result in delivery. The vast majority of contracts are extinguished by an offsetting trade. The possibility of delivery continues to exist, and NYMEX rules establish elaborate and precise delivery procedures for each commodity. The exchange-clearing organization acts as a middleman between members arranging deliveries—for themselves or for their customers; failure to follow the procedures or to make or take delivery would be a rule violation. NYMEX rules impose particularly strong financial penalties for delivery rule violations. Traders should also be aware that most futures commission merchant-customer agreements provide that penalties paid to an exchange are reimbursable by the customer. Consequently, traders should be well-versed in the rules if making or taking delivery is planned.

Clearance. As a unified exchange and clearing organization, NYMEX is responsible for trade matching and, thereafter, to assure that proper margin payments are made and collected. It is often said that the exchange acts as the buyer to every seller and the seller to every buyer, thus eliminating normal counterparty credit risk. NYMEX rules govern the clearing system and are built upon the foundation of adequately capitalized clearing members and the requirement that all customer funds be segregated and safeguarded. Furthermore, NYMEX imposes capital-based limits on the number of contracts that any clearing member may carry. In the event that a clearing member should fail to make a margin payment, the exchange would pay any shortfall and, pursuant to its rules, assess non-defaulting clearing members for any funds not available from reserves. NYMEX rules provide a formula that ties assessments to the level of each member's clearing activity and caps the amount assessed.

National Futures Association

Although futures and options transactions must be effected through a contract market, not all persons involved in marketing are required to be contract-market (exchange) members. Consequently, exchange self-regulation does not extend to the far reaches of CEA jurisdiction.

In order to provide a mechanism for the self-regulation of the remainder of the industry, the CEA contains a provision for the CFTC to register one or more futures associations to act as self-regulatory organizations. To date, only the National Futures Association (NFA) has been registered. NFA's membership, which is compulsory, includes all futures commission merchants, introducing brokers, commodity trading advisors, and commodity pool operators. NFA does not regulate any activities in connection with order execution or trade practice that remain with the exchanges. NFA regulation focuses on solicitation, promotional material, recordkeeping, and financial integrity. NFA audits its members and has the power to fine, suspend, or expel a member.

Futures commission merchants. Any person who solicits and accepts customer orders for futures or options and accepts money or property as security is required to register as a *futures commission merchant* (FCM) and to be a member of NFA. Registration functions are delegated by the CFTC to the NFA, which passes on each applicant's fitness—and the fitness of its officers, directors, and principals—as well as its finances.

An FCM must have and maintain a specified minimum adjusted net capital. If adjusted net capital drops below 150% of the minimum requirements, an FCM is required to give prompt notice to the CFTC and to each exchange of which he or she is a member. An FCM that ceases to meet minimum capital requirements must immediately stop doing business. In order to monitor the financial health of FCMs, the CFTC requires regular filing of financial reports.

No insurance fund is generally available to customers of FCMs. Consequently, the failure of an FCM would leave its customers unprotected. Fortunately, FCM failures have been exceedingly rare, perhaps partly as a result of rules requiring that customer funds be segregated for the benefit of customers, the close monitoring of FCMs by the exchanges, and NFA. Commingling of customer funds with FCM funds or any other funds not deposited to secure domestic futures or options is prohibited. An FCM must maintain separate accounts for customer funds and may invest them only in obligations of the U.S. or other specified governmental units.

Each natural person employed by an FCM who solicits customers or accepts orders is required to be registered as an *associated person* (AP) of a sponsoring FCM. AP registration has been delegated to the NFA, which reviews applicant fitness and generally polices sales activities.

An FCM is required to provide each customer a wide array of disclosures, acknowledgments, authorizations, and other documents at the time of account opening, and thereafter to promptly provide trade confirmations, purchase and sales reports, and monthly statements. CFTC rules require an FCM to diligently supervise its employees, and an FCM will be liable for any act of customer fraud by its employees.

Introducing brokers. Sales are also made by independent solicitors who are termed *introducing brokers* (IB) under the CEA. An IB is required to register with and be a member of NFA, and is subject to fitness and certain financial standards—unless financially guaranteed by an FCM. An IB may solicit accounts and trades, but may not accept any customer funds to secure trades. An IB, like an FCM, may employ APs. An IB is subject to risk disclosure and antifraud rules.

Commodity trading advisors. Any person who for direct or indirect compensation advises others as to the advisability of trading in futures or options is a *commodity trading advisor* (CTA). The CEA excludes from the definition banks, pension plan fiduciaries, lawyers, teachers, newspapers, and specified others who provide advice solely incident to their principal function. A CTA is required to register with and be a member of the NFA if he or she furnishes advice to 15 or more persons within any 12-month period or holds himself or herself out to the public as a CTA. Exemption is provided for any dealer, processor, broker, or seller in the cash-commodity market (such as an oil refiner), so long as advisory activities are solely incidental to regular business. In addition, a special exclusion from the CTA definition is provided for domestic insurance companies' advice in connection with specified money management activities. The CFTC's authority to require CTA registration of publishers of commodities-related advice is presently being challenged in the courts as violating the guarantee of freedom of speech assured by the U.S. Constitution.

A CTA must, with the exception noted below, file a disclosure document with the CFTC (with a copy to NFA) 21 days before he or she solicits the control of any customer account, and a copy of the document must be provided to the customer not later than the time of the account solicitation. The disclosure document must contain specified information about the CTA and his or her principals, his or her trading performance and that of his or her principals (current to within six months), and certain risk disclosure information as well as other information. An exception to these disclosure requirements exists if the client has the financial resources and/or market knowledge to be classified as a "qualified eligible client" under CFTC rules.

Commodity-pool operators.   Any person who organizes or operates a collective investment vehicle that engages in trading of commodity futures or options is a *commodity-pool operator* (CPO). CFTC regulations exempt from registration and most regulation any CPO operating on a specified *de minimus* basis. The regulations also provide a special limited exclusion from the definition of CPO to investment companies, insurance companies, banks and pension plan trustees, and fiduciaries. A CPO must register and be a member of NFA and is subject to the anti-fraud provisions applicable to other industry professionals.

Like a CTA, a CPO must, with the exception noted below, file a disclosure document with the CFTC (with a copy to NFA) 21 days prior to soliciting customers. The disclosure document must be provided in advance to each customer solicited. A CPO operating a pool is responsible for compliance with CFTC recordkeeping and reporting requirements, including certain periodic reports. CPO disclosure and reporting requirements are waived in respect of any pool for which all investors have the financial resources and/or market knowledge to be classified as "qualified eligible participants" under CFTC rules.

UNITED KINGDOM

The Financial Services Act of 1986 (the Act) was conceived as a system for the regulation of "investments" and "investment business" in the United Kingdom (U.K.). The Act's coverage of "investments" and "investment business" is much wider than that afforded by the Prevention of Fraud (Investments) Act of 1958, which it replaced.

What is regulated?

Fundamentally, the Act provides for the regulation of investments and investment business and requires any person who engages in investment business in the U.K. to be authorized under its provisions unless otherwise exempted. The term "investments" is broadly defined in Schedule 1 to the Act and includes, but is not limited to, shares, government and public securities, options, futures, and contracts for differences. "Investment business" is defined under the Act as including dealing in investments, arranging deals in investments, managing investments, investment advice, and establishing collective investment schemes.

Futures are defined under the Act as rights under a contract for sale of a commodity or property of any other description under which delivery is to be made at a future date and at a price agreed upon when the contract is made. The notes to this definition provide for certain exemptions to the regulatory structure, such as "spot" contracts and contracts made for commercial usage rather than for investment purposes. The notes also provide *indicia* for determination as to the nature of a given contract. Together, the definition and notes imply that a given contract would be considered to be a future whether or not it is traded on a "recognized investment exchange" if it carries sufficient *indicia* of being a future. This greatly broadens the scope of potential regulatory coverage under the Act from contracts traded on organized exchanges only to all futures contracts, an interpretation that is much disputed under the U.S. commodities laws. Also similar to the U.S. regulatory scheme is the notion that an indication of the intended commercial usage of the contract—delivery taken, or intent to do so—will remove the contract from consideration as having been made for investment purposes.

Overall regulatory structure

The Act confers overall regulatory authority upon the secretary of state and authorizes the secretary to transfer the majority of such powers by "delegation order" to a designated agency. On October 28, 1997 the Securities Investment Board (SIB), previously the designated agency under the Act, changed its name to the Financial Services Authority (FSA). The FSA is intended to take over the regulatory functions of and eventually absorb, eight other regulatory organizations, including the Securities and Futures Authority (SFA). The first step in the process of integration occurred on June 1, 1998, when the Bank of England Bill came into effect, transferring responsibility for the supervision of banks and the wholesale money market to the FSA. Following the passage of the regulatory reform bill that will create a new statutory regime superseding the Act, the FSA will (re)acquire all the regulatory and registration functions currently exercised by the FSA in its present guise. The FSA will also formally acquire the functions currently exercised by the eight other regulatory organizations and SROs in the year 2000.

Currently, the FSA recognizes three self-regulating organizations (SROs), nine recognized professional bodies (RPBs), six recognized investment exchanges (RIEs) and two recognized clearinghouses (RCHs). The SROs regulate the approximately 6,250 brokers that carry out the bulk of investment business in the U.K. Each SRO, having been recognized by the FSA, may regulate and authorize firms to conduct investment business within the U.K. as defined under the Act. The Investment Services Directive has further expanded the reach of the SROs to authorize and regulate the activities of U.K. firms engaged in investment business throughout Europe. As an initial step in the integration of the SROs into the FSA, the FSA has started to supply regulatory services under contracts to the SROs. To this end, the staff at the SFA have, for the most part, been transferred to the FSA, although they continued to work in the same functions as before.

Each SRO has a distinct area of regulatory supervision entrusted to it, and must meet the criteria set down by the Act and the FSA for continuing recognition and authorization. Each SRO is responsible for overseeing the compliance of its members with the Act and with the internal rules and regulations set down by each organization. This system of SRO regulation is designed to parallel and supplement the direct regulation by the FSA, but not supersede it, dependent as it is on the ultimate authority and provisions of the Act. Each SRO is also empowered to oversee the enforcement function for violations of the Act or the SRO's own rules and regulations, with sanctions up to and including the revocation of a firm's authorization to engage in investment business.

The SFA is the primary SRO for firms in the securities and futures sectors of the financial services industry, regulating approximately 1,330 firms. SFA registered firms are involved in brokering, dealing, or advising in shares, bonds, traded options, corporate finance, financial futures, and commodity futures. The primary regulatory functions of the SFA can be summarized as:

- authorization

- surveillance, through monitoring of business by inspections, and trade analysis

- enforcement

- business conduct

- risk monitoring involving the assessment of management policies and capital adequacy

The RIEs recognized by the FSA consist of:

- London Stock Exchange

- Tradepoint Stock Exchange

- London International Financial Futures and Options Exchange

- London Securities and Derivatives Exchange Ltd.

- International Petroleum Exchange of London Ltd. (IPE)

- London Metal Exchange

The RIEs are organized markets on which or in which members can trade the instruments listed at that particular exchange. The RIE is required to ensure that business is conducted in "an orderly manner and so as to afford proper protection to investors." This mandate extends to regulation of the market as well as the members of the exchange. Clearing houses used to effect clearing and settlement of transactions on RIEs must be one of the two FSA recognized clearing houses, the London Clearing House and CrestCo.

International Petroleum Exchange

The IPE was established in 1980 and listed its first contract in 1981. As an RIE, the IPE is regulated by the FSA, and its member firms are supervised and regulated by the SFA. The member firms of the IPE consist primarily of energy, financial, and brokerage companies.

Currently the IPE lists:

- Brent Crude futures and options
- Gas oil futures and options
- Natural gas futures

The Brent Crude futures contract is a global benchmark for international oil prices. As part of the Brent Blend complex, the IPE Brent Crude contracts are the basis for pricing approximately two-thirds of internationally traded crude oil. In March 1998, the daily volume figure for the IPE Brent Crude contracts reached more than 100 million barrels, or 1.5 times the total world crude oil production. IPE Brent Crude contracts may result in the delivery of the physical underlying commodity through the EFP facility. Pricing of IPE's gas oil contracts is based on physical delivery in the Benelux area, but less than 1% is delivered through the EFP mechanism. The IPE natural gas contract was launched in 1997 and is Europe's first natural gas futures contract. Trading of this contract is executed through the IPE's automated Energy Trading System. All trades executed on the IPE are cleared through the London Clearing House.

Consistent with its status as an RIE, the IPE maintains a rule book containing regulations for every facet of energy futures trading including, among others, membership, compliance, product specifications, floor trading procedures, product contract rules, and administrative procedures for delivery and arbitration.

GLOBAL REGULATION

As markets that draw large international participation and that trade in a vital global commodity, the organized oil-trading markets challenge effective national regulation. Indeed, the recent trend toward global markets, first by cross-border market links and more recently by computerized trading, only increases the strain on traditional, national regulation.

Futures markets have long been open to foreign traders. From time to time, this has resulted in CFTC efforts to obtain market surveillance or other information from abroad. Often, the CFTC met with resistance from foreign authorities anxious to preserve their notion of business confidentially and to repulse extraterritorial application of U.S. laws. In response, the CFTC in 1980 amended its rules to require that each foreign broker or trader designate a U.S. agent to accept delivery and service of communications from the CFTC, and, failing this, that the domestic FCM who carries the account of a foreign broker or trader be deemed to be its agent for service. A companion rule provides that, if a foreign broker or trader does not respond to a CFTC request for information about a particular contract, the CFTC may prohibit the foreign broker or trader from any trading in that contract, except for liquidation. This approach is geared to monitor ongoing trading rather than to investigate any past rule violations.

The CFTC has also established intergovernmental channels for obtaining information abroad. Through the use of various bilateral "memoranda of understanding" the CFTC has put into place a variety of information sharing arrangements with regulators from various financial centers.

Information sharing alone is not likely to be the last word in global regulation. Perhaps more significantly, the CFTC has permitted foreign brokers who are subject to comparable regulation abroad but who are not FCM registered to broker foreign futures and options domestically. The CFTC conducts a comparable regulation review of each foreign jurisdiction for which this special privilege is sought. As part of the process, the CFTC requires that the foreign jurisdiction provide adequately for information sharing. CFTC is presently determining the restrictions to be applied to foreign market computer terminals in the U.S.

The trend is clearly one toward international cooperation. Yet national regulatory schemes remain diverse. The close ties between futures and options markets and a nation's financial and industrial network make international regulation a delicate subject. However, as markets around the world continue to overlap and become integrated, further encroachment upon national economic sovereignty is to be expected.

REFERENCES

United States

Commodity Exchange Act of 1936, as amended, 7 United States Code § 1 *et seq.*

Rules of the Commodity Futures Trading Commission, 17 Code of Federal Regulations § 1 *et seq.*

Commodity Futures Trading Commission, *A New Regulatory Framework Proposed Rulemaking:* 65 FR 38985 (June 22, 2000), 65 FR 39008 (June 22, 2000), 65 FR 39027 (June 22, 2000), and 65 FR 39033 (June 22, 2000); also available at www.cftc.gov/opa/regulatory.htm

National Futures Association Manual

New York Mercantile Exchange Rule Book, published by Commerce Clearing House

Janvey, R., W.G. Lamont, *Regulation of Securities and Commodities Markets,* 1992

Hazen, T.L., P. McBride Johnson, *Commodities Regulation, 3rd edition,* Aspen Law, 1997

Russo, T.A., T.J. Snider, *Regulation of the Commodities, Futures and Options Markets, 2nd rev. ed.*, West Group, 1995

Markham, J.W., *Commodities Regulation: Fraud, Manipulation and Other Claims*, West Group, 1987

United Kingdom

Financial Services Act of 1986

The Financial Services Authority (ex Securities and Investments Board) Rules and Regulations, 1998

A. Whittaker and G. Morse, *Financial Services Act 1986, A Guide to the New Law*, Butterworths 1987

Financial Services Law & Practice, Butterworths 1998

The Securities and Futures Authority Rule Book, 1997

International Petroleum Exchange Rule Book, 1998

IPE Information Pack, 1997

URL   http://www.ipe.uk.com

URL   http://www.fsa.gov.uk

URL   http://www.sfa.org.uk

URL   http://www.lch.co.uk

ENERGY AND E-COMMERCE

by John Elting Treat

Today, the final act is unfolding. The explosive growth of electronic commerce is rapidly closing the gap between physical trading and futures. Within the first years of the 21st century, the convergence of wet and paper markets will be completed as the old analog/physical markets evolve to web-based exchanges. Indeed, the launch of eNYMEX and a number of other web-based trading portals suggests the process will move very quickly. At some point in the not-too-distant future, risk management tools will simply be a click or a pull-down menu away as companies and traders make their deals and fulfill them on the "Net."

Among energy markets, natural gas and electricity leaped ahead to embrace e-commerce, leaving oil to catch up. Ironically, the early deregulation of most of oil's national markets—and the far-flung nature of global oil markets—brought innovation to those markets in the 1970s and 1980s. However, the relatively quick deregulation of natural gas and electricity markets, the high level of market inefficiency spawned by decades of government economic regulation, and the greater homogeneity of product quality has encouraged those markets to move more quickly into the Internet era. Led by companies like AltraEnergy.com and HoustonStreet.com, electronic exchanges are on a roll. Most observers believe that energy is already one of the largest categories of so-called "business-to-business e-commerce."

Electronic commerce will have a growing impact on the energy industry, including:

- Reducing costs and improving service all along the supply chain

- Enhancing existing businesses, especially in the area of customer service

- Transforming existing business models, especially through the creation of "infomediaries"

- Creating new businesses

By lowering entry costs and facilitating access, web-based exchanges will likely expand the range of energy products traded. The process has already started in the chemical industry as sites like Chemdex, ChemConnect, and e-Chemicals compete for business. There will, however, remain two challenges for these sites. First, markets will remain focused on the liquidity of new products. Traders have notoriously short attention spans and will "tune out" if sites do not offer sufficient volume to move reasonable quantities quickly.

Second, as these sites grow in importance and their impact on pricing grows, they will inevitably come under regulatory scrutiny—at least by the U.S. government and possibly by the European community, and other jurisdictions as well. The regulation (and taxation) of Internet transactions will, I predict, become a major political and economic battle during the first decade of the new millennium.

As these markets grow—and they will grow rapidly—there will be significant pressure to develop new risk management instruments as integral offerings. The growth of electronic trading should lower the hurdles for the introduction of new risk management instruments. However, the launching of new futures and options instruments will always depend on their ability to attract liquidity early—traders are notoriously impatient and will not support illiquid markets. I suspect that the future instruments will therefore include a modest expansion of formal futures and options markets and a continued rapid expansion of off-exchange derivatives, perhaps with more standardized settlement terms, and eventually, common clearing mechanisms.

Ideally, the market would like to have a complete suite of energy markets serving both the Atlantic and Pacific Basins. This would imply the development of additional futures and options markets for crude, products, gas, and electricity markets—especially in Asia. Obviously, the growth in interconnections of gas and power grids would tend to accelerate that trend, as would the continued expansion of international LNG trade.

There seems little risk (or hope?) that volatility will soon depart the energy scene. As long as there is volatility, there will be risk and a desire to manage that risk. However, demand and production shift, trade patterns change, and product specifications evolve, all of which will require changes in contract design. Continuous innovation will be essential.

BIOGRAPHIES

John Elting Treat is Vice President of Booz-Allen & Hamilton Inc. and a leading partner in the firm's worldwide energy practice. As president of the New York Mercantile Exchange (NYMEX) from 1982–1984, he introduced gasoline and crude oil futures trading and led the Exchange to international promi-nence. Prior to joining Booz-Allen, Mr. Treat served as president of Regent International, an international energy trading and marketing company; executive publisher of *Petroleum Intelligence Weekly;* and a partner in the investment-banking firm of Bear, Stearns and Company, where he formed that company's energy group.

Prior to joining NYMEX, Mr. Treat was responsible for international energy policy in the White House as a member of the National Security Council Staff under Presidents Carter and Reagan. He served in a variety of senior posts in the U.S. Department of Energy, including appointment as deputy assistant secretary for International Affairs. His Washington service included positions in the Department of State, a special presidential commission on foreign affairs, and the U.S. Senate. He also served as an officer in the U.S. Navy.

Mr. Treat received his B.A. degree from Princeton University's Woodrow Wilson School and an M.A. degree from Johns Hopkins School of Advanced International Studies. He is the author and editor of several studies and books, including *Energy Futures: Trading Opportunities for the 1980s, Energy Futures: Trading Opportunities for the 1990s,* and *Creating the High Performance International Petroleum Company: Dinosaurs Can Fly.*

Peter C. Beutel is an account executive with Merrill Lynch Futures in Manhattan. He is a frequent contributor to a variety of newspapers and oil industry publications. Trading stocks and commodities since he was 11 years old, Mr. Beutel has been a trader, broker, and both a technical and fundamental analyst in oil.

Robert Boslego is president of The Boslego Corporation, an energy risk management-consulting firm. Since 1980, Boslego has assisted the world's largest producers, sellers, refiners, traders, purchasers, and end-users of petroleum and natural gas in the development and implementation of their risk management programs. Boslego's risk services include hedge program consulting services, risk management models, and real-time market price risk analysis.

Mr. Boslego holds an honors degree in economics from Harvard University (1975) and an M.B.A. from Stanford University (1977). Mr. Boslego has been quoted hundreds of times in leading publications and has authored numerous articles and speeches in his field.

Mr. Boslego can be reached at Boslego.com.

Richard N. Fletcher is founder and principal of Energy Futures Research Associates (EFRA), a consultancy dedicated to helping organizations build strategic intelligence capabilities. EFRA provides consulting services in futures research, competitive intelligence, and "knowledge management" to the energy industry. Mr. Fletcher has worked with public and private sector clients throughout the world in oil and gas, power, chemicals, and petrochemicals. His engagements have covered a wide range of issues from benchmarking and business process reengineering to forecasting, strategic planning, competitive intelligence, and knowledge management.

Mr. Fletcher has 18 years experience in research, consulting, and information technology. Prior to founding EFRA in 1997, Mr. Fletcher directed the research and knowledge management program for Booz-Allen & Hamilton's Energy and Chemicals practice. He has also been affiliated with Gaffney, Cline & Associates, I.P. Sharp Associates (now part of Reuters), Petroconsultants, and Rice University.

Mr. Fletcher attended the U.S. Air Force Academy, Northwestern State University of Louisiana, and the University of Houston. He holds a B.A. in English and is an M.S. degree candidate in the Studies of the Future program at the University of Houston/Clear Lake. Mr. Fletcher is a member of the International Association for Energy Economics, Mensa, the Society of Competitive Intelligence Professionals, the Strategic Leadership Forum, and the World Future Society.

W. Walter Green, III is managing director of the Principal Investor Division of Banc One Capital Markets, Inc. a wholly owned subsidiary of Bank One Corporation. Mr. Green joined Bank One (and its predecessor First Chicago NBD) in 1978 in the Atlanta regional office. He has held a variety of positions, including the head of product development and marketing for the Corporate Bank, and head of the Petroleum and Mining division. In his current position, he is involved in arranging leveraged financing for acquisitions made by private equity firms.

Mr. Green graduated from the University of Georgia with a B.A. and M.B.A. Mr. Green has served as director and chairman of the Chicago Energy Analyst Society, and is a member of the American Petroleum Institute and the Independent Producers Association. He has been a speaker and panel member at various energy conferences, including serving as a member of the Domestic Energy Roundtable of the U.S. Department of Energy.

Mr. Green has been featured in periodicals focused on the energy industry including the *Petroleum Economist,* the *Oil & Gas Journal, Oil Daily,* and *Oil & Gas Investor.* He is also a contributing author to *Energy Futures: Trading Opportunities for the 1990s* published by PennWell.

Art Holland is an account manager at Pace Global Energy Services, a full-service energy consulting and energy management firm in Fairfax, VA. Mr. Holland is primarily responsible for supervising the day-to-day activities of the Power Markets group, which is engaged in client services ranging from power market price forecasting to energy asset valuation. Mr. Holland can be reached at HollandA@PaceGlobal.com.

David M. Johnson is the partner in charge of Arthur Andersen's Financial and Commodity Risk Consulting practice in Houston. His focus is on energy and utility risk. Mr. Johnson has worked extensively with the leading power, natural gas, and crude oil traders in all facets of their operations, and has directed a wide range of energy-related consulting projects, including enterprise-wide risk, risk policy development, process design and implementation, risk systems selection and implementation, book structure design, internal control development, management reporting, fraud investigations, and accounting. He is also a board member of the Energy Risk Management Association in Houston.

Bruce Kamich, senior vice president and co-manager of MoneyWatch, is responsible for the technical commentary and analysis on MoneyWatch. Before joining MoneyWatch, Mr. Kamich was employed as a futures and options hedging specialist at Oppenheimer & Co., as Director of Research at ALCO commodities, and as a technical market analyst at Merrill Lynch. He also covered risk management trading as a regional government securities dealer.

Mr. Kamich is a member of the Market Technicians Association in the U.S. and technical societies in Canada and

France. He has held various positions on the board of the Market Technicians Association (MTA), including two years as president. He holds a B.A. in Economics from the University of Connecticut and M.B.A. credits in Finance from Baruch College. Mr. Kamich has had several articles published in the MTA *Journal on Specialized Bond Market Indicators* and received his Chartered Market Technician title in 1992.

Brett Little is a resident attorney in the London office of Clifford Chance Rogers & Wells (formerly Rogers & Wells LLP) and practices international securities and corporate law. Mr. Little came to Clifford Chance Rogers & Wells from the U.S. Commodity Futures Trading Commission, where he worked as a federal trial attorney. Prior to commencing his legal career, Mr. Little was a senior trader for various U.S. money-center banks.

Maureen Lynch is a vice president in the Commodities Department at Morgan Stanley Dean Witter, and a principal trader in all facets of the various energy markets—oil, natural gas, electricity—including physicals, forwards, swaps, and options. Prior to joining Morgan Stanley Dean Witter, Ms. Lynch was the vice-president of research at NYMEX, where she was responsible for the development of their energy futures and options contracts. Ms. Lynch is an economics graduate of Pitzer College, one of the Claremont Colleges.

Dr. Doug McDonald is a project manager in the Fuels Consulting Practice at Pace Global Energy Services, a Fairfax, Virginia-based energy management and consulting firm. In this capacity, he has played a key role in projects involving energy infrastructure development, fuel contracting, price risk management, fuel plan due diligence, and strategic energy planning. Prior to joining Pace, Mr. McDonald held positions at The Washington Consulting Group, The Energy Futures Group, the U.S. Department of the Interior, and Resources for the Future. He holds a Ph.D. in economics from Johns Hopkins University.

Ted E. McElroy is a partner in the Tax and Business Advisory Practice with 19 years of experience serving clients in the energy industry. He became affiliated with the firm in 1980 and was promoted to partner in 1990. Mr. McElroy has extensive experience within the areas of oil and gas exploration and development, natural gas, power marketing, and energy price risk management activities.

Mr. McElroy heads the Gulf Coast Market Federal Business Tax and International Tax Practice as well as the Gulf Coast Market Circle Energy Industry Practice. He received his B.B.A. and M.S. in Taxation from Texas A & M University. He is a Certified Public Accountant, and is a member of the Texas Society of Certified Public Accountants and the American Institute of Certified Public Accountants.

Rutherford S. (Bo) Poats is vice president for Financial Services and Risk Management at Pace Global Energy Services. The Fairfax, Virginia-based energy management and project consulting firm has extensive experience in the fuels, power, and financial markets.

Dan Pocius came to energy risk management from engineering. After receiving his B.S. degree in chemical engineering from the University of Illinois in 1980, he attended Purdue University, where he obtained a M.S. in chemical engineering in 1982. He began his career in petroleum refining with Unocal, where he served in a variety of positions until leaving in 1990 to complete his M.B.A. at the University of Chicago.

In 1990, Mr. Pocius accepted a position with the First National Bank of Chicago in the newly formed Commodity Derivatives Group. Rising to the position of head trader, he accumulated substantial experience in energy price risk management and the issues particular to the petroleum, gas, and utility industries. Mr. Pocius is currently a managing director in Global Derivative Products at Bank One.

Matthew C. Rogers was a partner with Booz-Allen & Hamilton in San Francisco. He led multiple crude oil and refined products trading and supply chain optimization engagements for major oil companies. He also was an expert in downstream strategy, shaping competitive positions for several of the majors on a global basis. He holds an M.B.A. from the Yale School of Management, a B.A. from Princeton University, and is a partner with McKinsey & Company in San Francisco.

Dr. Benjamin Schlesinger, founding president of Ben Schlesinger Associates, is one of North America's leading energy and natural gas consultants, specializing in gas marketing, pricing, trading practices, transportation, strategic planning, and power plant development worldwide. He has 30 years of experience in managing and carrying out engineering/economic analyses of complex energy issues, with particular focus on North American natural gas and energy commodity movements and pricing, policies, and programs.

Dr. Schlesinger has advised more than 300 clients in the U.S., Canada, and 15 other countries, including the top utility, energy trading and producing, manufacturing, regulatory, educational, private power, and financial services companies. A former vice-president of the American Gas Association, Dr. Schlesinger has testified before the U.S. Congress and in 14 states and provinces on the direction of the gas industry, gas contracting matters, purchase and sales prices, royalty valuations, market value, hedging and risk management, and related industry practices.

James E. Toups, Jr. is a manager in the Energy Division of the Federal Business Tax Practice in the Houston office with experience serving clients in the energy industry. He became affiliated with the firm in 1995 and was promoted to manager in 1999. He has experience within the areas of oil and gas exploration and development, natural gas, oilfield services, cogeneration, power marketing, and energy price risk management activities.

Mr. Toups received his B.B.A. and M.S. in accounting, specializing in taxation, from Texas A&M University. He is a

Certified Public Accountant, and is a member of the Texas Society of Certified Public Accountants and the American Institute of Certified Public Accountants.

J. Clinton Walden is a senior manager in the Financial and Commodity Risk Consulting practice of Arthur Andersen. His work has primarily involved energy trading, but he also has experience in the petroleum exploration and production, gas processing, gas transmission, and coal industries. He serves as internal and external auditor to several major energy companies.

Mr. Walden received his B.P.A. in Accounting from Mississippi State University. He is a Certified Public Accountant, and is a member of the Texas Society of Certified Public Accountants and the American Institute of Certified Public Accountants.

David Yeres is a partner in the international law firm of Clifford Chance Rogers & Wells (Rogers & Wells LLP). He is a resident in the New York office and heads the firm's global exchange traded derivatives practice. Mr. Yeres has for more than 20 years specialized in trading related matters and has held senior legal posts in the U.S. Department of Justice and the Commodity Futures Trading Commission.

INDEX